LANGUAGE AND LANGUAGE LEARNING

The Edinburgh Course in
Applied Linguistics

Volume 4

LANGUAGE AND LANGUAGE LEARNING

General Editors: RONALD MACKIN *and* PETER STREVENS

Henry Sweet *The Practical Study of Languages*
J. R. Firth *The Tongues of Men* and *Speech*
Randolph Quirk and A. H. Smith *The Teaching of English*
Neile Osman *Modern English*
H. E. Palmer *The Principles of Language-Study*
N. E. Enkvist, J. Spencer and M. Gregory *Linguistics and Style*
H. E. Palmer *Curso Internacional de Inglés*
J. C. Catford *A Linguistic Theory of Translation*
David Abercrombie *Studies on Phonetics and Linguistics*
Five Inaugural Lectures edited by Peter Strevens
Axel Wijk *Rules of Pronunciation for the English Language*
L. A. Hill *Selected Articles on the Teaching of English as a Foreign Language*
H. H. Stern *Foreign Languages in Primary Education*
Peter Ladefoged *Three Areas of Experimental Phonetics*
A. S. Hayes *Language Laboratory Facilities*
H. E. Palmer *The Scientific Study and Teaching of Languages*
Language Testing Symposium edited by Alan Davies
H. E. Palmer and Sir Vere Redman *This Language-Learning Business*
An Annotated Bibliography of Modern Language Teaching: Books and Articles 1945–1967
    Compiled by Janet Robinson
Languages and the Young School Child edited by H. H. Stern
Prosodic Analysis edited by F. R. Palmer
Edward M. Stack *The Language Laboratory and Modern Language Teaching* Third Edition
The Prague School of Linguistics and Language Teaching edited by V. Fried
The Indispensable Foundation: a selection from the writings of Henry Sweet edited by
    E. J. A. Henderson
J. B. Pride *The Social Meaning of Language*
W. H. Mittins et al. *Attitudes to English Usage*
Chomsky: Selected Readings edited by J. P. B. Allen and P. van Buren
Active Methods and Modern Aids in the Teaching of Foreign Languages: Papers from the
    10th FIPLV Congress edited by R. Filipovic
Peter MacCarthy *Talking of Speaking: Papers in Applied Phonetics*
Randolph Quirk *The English Language and Images of Matter*
The Edinburgh Course in Applied Linguistics. Vols. 1–3 edited by J. P. B. Allen and
    S. Pit Corder. *Vol. 4* edited by J. P. B. Allen and Alan Davies

The Edinburgh Course in Applied Linguistics

VOLUME FOUR

Testing and Experimental Methods

Edited by J. P. B. ALLEN *and* ALAN DAVIES

LONDON

OXFORD UNIVERSITY PRESS

1977

Oxford University Press, Walton Street, Oxford OX2 6DP
OXFORD LONDON GLASGOW NEW YORK TORONTO MELBOURNE
WELLINGTON CAPE TOWN IBADAN NAIROBI DAR ES SALAAM
LUSAKA ADDIS ABABA KUALA LUMPUR SINGAPORE HONG KONG
TOKYO DELHI BOMBAY CALCUTTA MADRAS KARACHI

Library Edition ISBN 0 19 437125 5

Paperbound Edition ISBN 0 19 437060 7

© Oxford University Press 1977

This book is sold subject to the condition that it shall not, by way of trade or otherwise, be lent, re-sold, hired out, or otherwise circulated without the publisher's prior consent in any form of binding or cover other than that in which it is published and without a similar condition including this condition being imposed on the subsequent purchaser.

*Printed in Great Britain at
Western Printing Services Ltd, Bristol*

Contents

EDITORS' PREFACE — ix

1 **Introduction** ALAN DAVIES — 1

2 **Basic Concepts in Testing** ELISABETH INGRAM — 11
  1 Testing and language learning — 11
  2 Measurement — 12
  3 Test requirements — 15
    3.1 Reliability — 15
      3.1.1 Stability reliability — 16
      3.1.2 Equivalence reliability — 16
    3.2 Validity — 18
    3.3 Correlations — 22
  4 Norm-referenced versus criterion-referenced testing — 26
  5 Tests and experiments — 32
  6 Practical work — 35

3 **The Construction of Language Tests** ALAN DAVIES — 38
  1 Introduction — 38
  2 Aims and purposes of testing — 41
    2.1 Research — 41
    2.2 Progress — 42
    2.3 Guide to curriculum — 42
    2.4 Representing terminal behaviour — 43
  3 The influence of programmed instruction — 43
  4 Types of test — 44
    4.1 Uses of tests — 44
      4.1.1 The four uses — 45
      4.1.2 Summary — 48

4.2 Examinations and tests	49
4.2.1 Examination/test levels	49
4.2.2 Standardized tests	50
4.2.3 Ad hoc tests	51
4.2.4 Traditional examinations	52
4.2.5 New types of examination	52
4.3 Types of test levels and skills	54
5 Demands on language tests	55
5.1 Test criteria	55
5.2 Test virtues	57
5.2.1 Reliability	57
5.2.2 Validity	58
5.2.3 Types of validity	58
5.2.4 Schema for education	63
6 Language test analysis	65
7 Teacher made tests	69
7.1 Proficiency and achievement tests	69
7.2 Selection of language areas for testing	70
7.3 Language analysis	71
7.4 Work sample analysis	71
8 Item writing	76
8.1 The framework of a test	76
8.2 Examples of items	78
8.3 Conclusion	100
9 Practical work	100
10 Further reading	104

4 The Design and Interpretation of Experiments
Ruth Clark

	105
1 Introduction	105
2 Measurement	107
2.1 The choice of an adequate measure	107
2.2 Measurement: further sources of bias	109
3 Control	112
3.1 The natural experiment	112
3.2 The controlled experiment	113
4 Interpretation of results	116
4.1 Spanish-teaching experiment: nominal data	117
4.2 Training in the use of pronouns: ordinal data from independent groups	118

4.3 Understanding of logical connectives: ordinal data from related groups	122
4.4 Birth weight of normal and speech-retarded children: interval data from independent groups—subject variable	126
4.5 Summary of the four studies	130
4.6 Dispersion	131
5 The advantages and limitations of certain research designs	133
5.1 Related subject designs and the restriction of variation	133
5.2 Designs with a subject variable	137
6 Sampling	138
7 Randomization	138
8 Conclusion	139
9 Practical work	141
10 Acknowledgements	144

5 Procedures and Computations in the Analysis of Experiments   RUTH CLARK   146

1 Introduction	146
2 Analysing the contingency table	147
2.1 Calculating expected frequencies	147
2.2 The chi-squared test—calculating χ^2	148
3 Frequencies, the median and ranking procedures	149
3.1 Frequency tables	149
3.2 Cumulative frequency distributions and the median	150
3.3 Assigning a rank to each score	151
3.4 Sums of ranks and sums of ranks of differences	152
3.5 The calculation of U	155
4 Conclusion	156
5 Practical work	156

6 Statistical Inference   RUTH CLARK   158

1 Introduction	158
2 The binomial distribution—probability and significance	159
3 The normal distribution and standard scores	167
4 The final steps in the analysis	172
4.1 Mann-Whitney U test—for comparing independent groups by means of the sum of ranks	173
4.2 Sign test—for comparing related groups using number of positive and negative differences	173
4.3 Wilcoxon matched pairs signed ranks—for comparing related groups using the sum of ranks of differences	174

    4.4 Test of difference between means—for independent samples where the variable is on an interval scale and normally distributed in the population   175
    4.5 Chi squared and median tests for analysing contingency tables   176
    4.6 Summary   179
5 Increasing the sensitivity of an experiment   179
    5.1 Sample size   180
    5.2 The control of variability   180
6 One-tailed and two-tailed hypotheses   181
7 Factors affecting the choice of tests   182
    7.1 Level of measurement   182
    7.2 Parametric tests   184
    7.3 Power   184
    7.4 Normalization of scales   184
8 Conclusion   185
9 Practical work   185
10 Further reading   186

Appendix I: Some Statistics used in Language Tests   187

1 Method for working item analysis E_{1-3} 187
2 Method for working rank order (Spearman) correlations   189
3 Formula and method for working product moment correlations   190
4 Formula and method for establishing equivalence reliability Kuder-Richardson (21)   194
5 Method for finding square roots by using logarithms   198

Appendix II: Statistical Tables   200

A Table of probabilities associated with values as extreme as observed values of z in the normal distribution   200
B Table of critical values of chi square   202
C Table of probabilities associated with values as small as observed values of x in the binomial test   203

ANSWERS TO PRACTICAL WORK   204
GLOSSARY OF SYMBOLS   222
REFERENCES   224
INDEX OF NAMES   227
SUBJECT INDEX   229

Editors' Preface

The fourth volume in the Edinburgh Course in Applied Linguistics is concerned with the mechanics of proof which any discipline with a claim to being scientific, or even semi-scientific, must possess. If applied linguistics is more than a set of anecdotes and subjective impressions then it needs the strengthening of the scientific method. This is not to say, of course, that the whole of applied linguistics is scientific; far from it. But applied linguistics does at least permit its claims and procedures to be challenged by making them falsifiable. This is the role in applied linguistics of testing and experimental methods.

Volume 1 was concerned with the background to applied linguistics. In Volumes 2 and 3 the content and methods of the subject are considered. Volume 4 is in part an extension of Volumes 2 and 3 since both testing and experimental methods are part of the techniques of applied linguistics. It would be curious to find an applied linguistics course in which testing and experimental methods were not taught. It will be part of the argument of chapter 1 that the role of tests and experiments in such a course is an important, indeed a central one. But as well as being an extension of Volumes 2 and 3, Volume 4 exists in its own right as a proper and separate element in applied linguistics. The purpose of this book is to present a selection of statistical procedures useful to students of applied linguistics; it is not our aim to attempt a definitive statement of statistical theory.

The present volume contains an Introduction and four other chapters. In the Introduction the need for testing and experimental methods in the field of applied linguistics, mentioned above, is further examined and discussed. The Introduction also discusses the relation between tests and experiments, proposing that each is necessary to the other and that they are related to one another, as it were, at either end of a large telescope. A test can be thought of as an experiment in miniature, and an experiment as testing writ large. All experiments need tests, and this is true of experiments in applied linguistics as much as any. From this point of view, tests are part of experiments, and instruments of research. But from the other point of view, looking at the relationship from the opposite end of the telescope, the construction of a test is an experiment in which the relevant experimental methods are used, and the appropriate statistical techniques applied. The language test, then, is both an experiment in itself, and a tool to be used in experiments.

The following chapters discuss these two related aspects of research in more detail. Chapters 2 and 3 consider the test, chapters 4, 5 and 6 the experiment. In chapter 2 Ingram discusses the concepts of reliability and validity in relation to language testing, norm-referenced and criterion-referenced tests and the role of language testing in educational research. In chapter 3 Davies looks again at the same area as Ingram, but from the point of view of the uses of language tests. The last three chapters are concerned with experimental methods from the broader point of view. In chapter 4, 'The Design and Interpretation of Experiments', Clark shows how we can realize a hypothesis and give it body in the shape of an experiment. She discusses the necessary computations in chapter 5. In chapter 6, 'Statistical Inference', Clark is concerned with the testing of the hypothesis, that is, with the judgement of the results after the experiment has been carried out. The last three chapters on experimental methods provide a parallel to the main themes of chapters 1 and 2, namely, the *experimental* aspect of test construction, and the *instrumental* aspect of test use.

As in the other volumes, the authors and editors owe a considerable debt to their immediate colleagues and to several generations of students who have helped to clarify the concepts set out here, and who have carried out many experiments and tests in applied linguistics over the years. While psychological and educational measurement in general are well-established disciplines, the use of these concepts and techniques in applied linguistics is relatively new, and it is the purpose of this volume to give them their rightful place at the centre of the discipline.

We wish to acknowledge our debt to all those who have contributed to this book, either directly or indirectly. In particular we would like to thank Tony Fielding, Ted Harding, Albert Pilliner, Mike Prentice, Gillian Raab and Jessie Reid, who made many suggestions for the improvement of the text. Although these colleagues have given generously of their help and advice they are, of course, in no way responsible for any errors that may remain. Our thanks are also due to several generations of students taking the Diploma (now M.Sc.) in Applied Linguistics, who worked through the original version of the six chapters and who, by their constant demands for clarification, caused us to seek better ways of presenting the material. Most of the book was typed by Ethel Bacon, Anne MacDonald and Pat Williams. Mary Bratt spent a year as editorial assistant, and the index was compiled by Caroline Clapham. To all of these we express our appreciation of their very valuable assistance.

Department of Linguistics, Edinburgh J. P. B. Allen
January 1976 Alan Davies

1 ALAN DAVIES
Introduction

It is a common criticism of applied linguistics—a criticism made by its practitioners as much as anyone—that there is no objectivity about it, that its views and hypotheses and conclusions are determined by fashion rather than by rigorous scientific procedure, that in fact there are no hard data because there is no way of establishing whether something is a result or a finding. This is a two-fold criticism. It is a theoretical criticism, denying that applied linguistics has any organized body of theory, and it is an experimental criticism, arguing that even if there is any body of theory there is no link between that and arguments as to how to proceed, i.e. how to teach and learn languages. As a result, in language teaching as in education generally, what determines change is the roundabout of fashion which seems recently to be moving back towards a modified grammar-translation method after a number of years in which such an approach to language teaching was anathema to many people. It may be that we shall always have to take account of changing fashion, simply because we have no way of finally establishing 'the best way' to learn or teach a language. Within such changes in fashion, however, there are smaller scale research operations which can be and need to be carried out and which will establish not the best way to teach language but a satisfactory set of procedures within an over-all theoretical approach. Since there is no easy way of evaluating the internal logic of a theoretical model of language, the question of what constitutes the best language-learning theory may not be a matter for experimental research at all, but a matter for philosophical argument about what kinds of aims we are interested in at any one time. Doubtless these will be influenced by the kind of within-theory experimentation we have been discussing. Certainly, our only hope of escaping from the tyranny of fashion is through submitting our guess-work to the rigour of hypothesis and experimentation.

Experimental methods are typically the procedures by which scientific enquiry is carried out. One way of expressing this is to say that within what Kuhn has called a paradigm (Kuhn 1962) various theories are developed, expanded and tested by means of hypotheses. The purpose of a hypothesis is explanatory; but there are different kinds of explanation. Foss (1966) mentions seven of these:

causal, referring to some immediate cause
historical, referring to experiences or events in the past
purposive, referring to some purpose or goal
rule following, referring to some external rules of, for example, society
structural, referring to the components of the organism involved in the events
functional, referring to general rather than immediate causes
contingency, referring to some parallel, relatable event, hence correlational.

What all kinds of useful explanation have in common is that they demand generalization, i.e. they must be applicable to similar events and cases. Hence the need to say precisely how events and cases are judged to be similar, and what is meant by applicability.

The first of these needs is often discussed under the heading of validity, and the second under reliability. These concepts are usually discussed in connection with tests but they also have a relevance to experiments. In order to be accepted as a proper test of a hypothesis an experiment is set up in a highly formalized way by means of an experimental design which ensures that the events or subjects exposed to experiment are sufficiently like others of a similar kind for their results not to be treated as special cases. This area of experimental methods is discussed under sampling and under descriptive statistics; sampling attempts to make sure that the subjects chosen are randomly chosen, i.e., that others who are similar have an equal chance of being selected for the experiment. Descriptive statistics organizes the results, and describes the sample in such a way as to make clear its relation to the population from which it is drawn. Descriptive statistics then helps guarantee an experiment's validity.

The second area of experimental methods determines the applicability of the results to a more general situation, and to other cases; this is done under the heading of inferential statistics. Here the intention is to distinguish a particular finding from chance; to distinguish, in other words, the accidental from the experimental or the significant. This is the purpose of all tests of significance discussed under the heading of inferential statistics. Have we got a bizarre or accidental finding or have we got one that we can rely on? One way of finding out is to repeat the experiment; another way, and one frequently used in the social sciences because of the sheer difficulty of repeating exactly all experimental conditions, is to make use of inferential statistics, which tell the experimenter how likely it is that he would get the same result again and again, ad infinitum. Not even a replicated experiment can tell us this, since replication can only be done a finite number of times. Inferential statistics, then, are concerned with the consistency of results, with reliability.

Experiment in the social sciences is very much more difficult than in the physical sciences. Sampling is more difficult; people do not repeat themselves, and consequently do not lend themselves to random sampling as do beans out of a bag. Laboratory conditions cannot be maintained for people. Often there is no laboratory except the real world, and experiments cannot even be set up with conditions held constant, let alone replicated. It is generally agreed, therefore, that experiment in the social sciences is weaker in scope than in the physical sciences. The question then arises of how weak is 'weaker'. Is teaching a class an experiment, or reading a book or interviewing an applicant for a job? (All these, of course, may be language learning situations.) The answer can only lie in the potential *use* made of the situations. From one point of view every task or experience is experimental. But this is not the viewpoint we wish to present at the moment. An experiment into singing differs from the event of singing a song in that the experiment produces results that are meaningful in other situations and on other occasions. The event, on the other hand, is not generalizable in the scientific sense we are discussing here. Hence the buttressing provided by both descriptive and inferential statistics which are used to distinguish experiments from unique events, to make sure that the results that have been obtained have not occurred by chance, and that what has happened is an experiment and not an event. We are not, of course, making any exaggerated claims for experiment. We recognize that it is never possible to be completely objective, that all experiment is contaminated by the presence of the observer, not so much because he is there but because his results depend on his view of what he thinks he sees. Further, his discussion of his results, like his original conception of what he was trying to do, has a bias reflecting the experimenter's view of the world. So much is granted, but even so it still seems that some worthwhile experimentation *is* possible, and that there is no need to accept the infinite regression dilemma.

An experiment, then, is a series of controlled observations which will inevitably need the use of one or more tests. For example, an experiment into the effects of acceleration on the human body might consist of a series of observations of bodies, human and non-human, in a state of rest, or in a state of acceleration or deceleration. Each observation will be carefully arranged so as to ensure, as far as possible, that it is the right kind of body that is being observed, that it really is at rest, in a state of acceleration, etc., i.e., that the observations are valid. Furthermore, the observations will be designed in such a way that useful comparisons may be made, as between different bodies, different states (rest or acceleration), and so on. The actual making of such comparisons demands a test, or a series of tests.

A test, then, typically is the measurement of a comparison between effects or treatments. In the acceleration experiment the comparison might be between the effect of acceleration, deceleration, etc., on the heart. So, taking the pulse or the blood pressure, however elaborately that is done, constitutes the test. In such cases the test instrument, the blood pressure machine, is already calibrated; hence the test is already in existence, and is widely accepted. It would be possible, though unlikely, for objections to be made to the machine, objections as to whether or not it really does measure blood pressure, objections also as to whether the markings on the scale are accurate. These would be objections to the validity of the machine, on the one hand, and to the reliability of the machine on the other. In applied linguistics such test instruments do not exist. The test therefore not only has to be used during the experiment, often it also has to be made. Hence the extra burden on the experimenter in applied linguistics, as in the social sciences generally, of constructing his own tests as well as conducting his experiments. Inevitably in these circumstances test construction is controversial in the sense that it exposes the experimenter to the criticism of non-validity. Normally speaking we do not question the validity of the blood pressure machine for measuring the reactions of the heart, just as we do not question the validity of litmus paper for testing for acid; but we certainly do question the validity of a language test for testing for control of language and we do this because there is so little agreement as to what it means to 'know' a language. This is another way of saying what we have discussed above, that applied linguistics is not a theoretical discipline.

What most language tests do is to place one student in relation to a group of students—in terms of some particular language ability. The comparison for the test is therefore between students. The comparison for the experiment, on the other hand, is between effects, or treatments, or methods. Most tests compare students by establishing a rank order. A common assumption made in the construction of language tests is that language ability is normally distributed in the population, i.e. that the distribution of the ability among the population—all those who would properly take the test—is in accordance with the normal or bell-shaped curve. Whether or not this assumption about normality is made, it is customary to use the descriptive statistics of *mean* and *standard deviation* as a simple way of summarizing the statistics for any sample who have taken the test.

What has just been said about the establishing of a rank order on the basis of an assumed ability distribution is fundamental to what Ingram calls norm-referenced tests. At the moment it is unclear whether a similar claim could be made for criterion-referenced tests (see p. 8). It is useful to distinguish four kinds of language test according to the use that is being made of the test. These four kinds are: achievement (or attainment) tests, proficiency, aptitude and diagnostic tests. The achievement test is the typical end-of-course assessment which is intended to establish whether a student has learned what he is supposed to have learned. An achievement test, therefore, samples its items from the content of the syllabus on which the course is based. A proficiency test has no known syllabus to sample; the syllabus for the proficiency test has to come from within the mind of the tester. Since the use of the proficiency test is to establish some kind of standard of, for example, English for foreign students wishing to enter British universities, it must be available to all comers. Sampling of a known syllabus is therefore not possible. If the achievement test serves to answer the question: 'How much English have you learned in this course?', the proficiency test seeks to answer the question: 'Do you know enough English to study or work in the medium of English?'

An aptitude test has even less of a known syllabus than a proficiency test since it cannot even be based on some notional 'knowledge of English'. Instead the tester has to make a construct of language aptitude which serves as a guide to the kinds of abilities to test for. The problem still remains, of course, of actually relating these abilities to real language test items.

Finally the diagnostic test is best seen as a species of non-achievement test since it is usually based on a list of errors made by students. Thus its most obvious use is after an achievement or proficiency test when it is constructed from items that cause many errors. The diagnostic test, then, multiplies items of a similar kind in order to check on patterns of error among students.

Different kinds of tests relate to different types of validity. For example, achievement and diagnostic tests make use first of content validity (Cronbach 1960), proficiency tests establish predictive or concurrent validity, aptitude tests claim construct validity. If possible a second validity type will also be established, e.g. content validity for proficiency tests and predictive validity for aptitude tests.

Language tests are often spoken of as though there were an abundant supply available. The number of published tests, however, is limited. The reason for this is that there is little point in publishing a test that is not standardized, i.e. provided with population statistics, or, more correctly, parameters. From one point of view, a test only really becomes a test when it is standardized, when it has been tried out on a random sample and thus shown to produce a normal distribution relevant to language ability. Most so-called tests which are not yet standardized are really trial tests, based on various unsubstantiated ideas and guesses. Useful lists of tests available are given in Buros (1972), CILT (1973) and Davies (1968).

Use of a standardized test in a particular situation does not necessarily provide the rank order we have spoken of, nor does it often do so. It is quite possible to get no spread or very little spread of scores. The reason for this is quite simple, namely that the sample being tested is not a random one. Ad hoc classroom tests devised by teachers during the course of their work often illustrate this lack of spread of scores. It is probably best to regard ad hoc tests as trial tests rather than as finished products. Only standardized tests can properly be called tests. Ad hoc tests rarely achieve this finish because by their nature they are made for a specific and temporary need. They can be more objective than the usual subjective examinations but they must not be taken as final judgements because they do not describe a population.

As we have pointed out above, language experiments need language tests as a means of checking the success or failure of the experiment. An experiment remains indeterminate unless it is put to the test. This is not to say that the test is the experiment. Indeed, as we have seen, in normal science the test often exists already and can be used for different kinds of experiment. In this case the originality goes into the design and creation of the experiment itself. We have also seen that in applied linguistics it is often necessary to construct a test as well as to design the experiment. However from the point of view of the experiment the test remains an adjunct, a necessary one but subordinate to the experiment. Reports on applied linguistics experiments will refer to the tests used during the course of the experiment, and will state whether or not they have been specially created for the experiment. Looking at the experiment-test relation from the point of view of the test, it is possible to see a test under construction as in itself a mini-experiment. The tester's experimental hypothesis then is that the tasks he presents as test items will produce the rank order we have mentioned. Testing, retesting and analysing of the test results become the carrying out of the experiment and the final validation of the test becomes, as it were, the test of the test-experiment. Experiments then need and use tests, while test construction is a form of experiment. In some experiments tests need to be constructed (e.g. Smith and Berger 1968), while in some test construction, further tests need to be written in order to validate the main test under construction (e.g. Pimsleur 1963).

Test construction and test use are, therefore, quite distinct. The first relates to the experimental aspect of testing, the second to the instrumental aspect. One of the abuses of tests under construction—the ideas, guesses, trials we have referred to—is that they are often used as if they were already tests in use and employed in order to validate or assess experiments. The misuse often goes like this. A test is written and trials made. At this stage there are certain results available, though quite simple and yet fundamental things may be wrong, such as no random sampling; these results are then used to describe certain effects as if the test were already reliable. For example, a test might be written to assess primary school French in Britain, a sort of spoken proficiency test. While only the first trials are available the tester draws conclusions about the extent of French known, about the comparative values of different kinds of French teaching (e.g., oral or other methods) and about the general value of teaching French in the primary school. What this means, and what we would wish to underline, once again, is the difficulty of experiment and testing in applied linguistics. No test should be used in an experiment unless it has been properly tried out. It need not be fully standardized—though it is much better if it is—but it must have at least statistics—statistics, that is, for the sample on whom the test has been tried, with a clear description of just who were in that sample. Further, tests under construction should not be ransacked for experimental results before they have reached the validation stage. Anything else is to make available results that are certainly non-valid and possibly unreliable also. Validity, as we have pointed out, means being true to the intention of the test so that an achievement test, for example, must show by content validity that it really does represent a measure of the syllabus; or a proficiency test must show by predictive validity that it really does measure in a similar way, by equating rank orders, some future measure of the population, for example end-of-course exam results. Reliability or consistency of the test is an easier property to establish since it can be calculated statistically. The purpose of evaluating reliability is to establish whether the same results, i.e. the same rank order, would be achieved on every other occasion. Various procedures are available for the assessment of reliability, and these are discussed fully in chapter 2.

We now turn to a consideration of the testing chapters in this volume. In chapter 2, Ingram considers the concept of measurement and the subsequent demands imposed on a language test. Measurement implies rigorous statistical treatment which can also be approached, as Ingram shows, from the point of view of the requirements of reliability and validity. A test measures something; the predicate of this sentence pinpoints these two requirements. *Measures* is the concern of reliability since the process of measurement involves accuracy and consistency. *Something* is the concern of validity since it is obviously crucial that what the test measures must be relevant. Further, the linking of the two requirements in a single predication will indicate that unless the test is measuring there can be no something that is being measured. This clarifies the frequently made comment that a test which is unreliable cannot be valid. This is of course true and explains why, whenever we are constructing a test, we need to demonstrate reliability before going on to calculate one of the statistical validities. At the same time it is possible to look at this relationship the other way round. No test constructor thinks first of reliability, or aims at a highly reliable test without first considering its likely validity. He must first think of constructing a valid test and determine what sort of validity he will appeal to. Then he sets about constructing a set of items which will reliably reflect that validity. From this point of view reliability can be seen as a part, essential but only a part, of validity. Many testers find that neither perfect validity nor perfect reliability is achievable and that above a certain point an increase in validity causes a decrease in reliability, and vice versa.

Ingram's discussion of reliability and validity makes it clear that neither is a unitary concept. The tester, knowing that he must demonstrate satisfactory reliability for his test, can find himself in a dilemma over apparently contradictory results on his test for the different kinds of reliability. What he should do is to quote all the results, thus giving the complete picture of his test; what he often does is to quote only the highest figures. But since all reliabilities are essentially a function of the length of the test—hence of the distribution of the scores—this further argues for reliability as a kind of validity. Ingram's own strategy here is to establish pragmatic validity and to do so, if possible, through the experimental device of the observational sample. The advantage of this approach is that it permits the criterion both to influence the construction of the test and to be used for correlational purposes afterwards, thus combining the virtues of content and of predictive validity. Ingram provides a discussion of the concept of correlation so as to indicate the arguments used in establishing pragmatic validity.

Ingram then goes on to discuss norm-referenced and criterion-referenced tests. For various reasons, some of which have to do with the uncertainty of testers as to what the purposes of testing are, and perhaps some guilt feeling about the use of testing in selection, attempts have been made recently to develop the criterion-referenced test as a more satisfactory general purpose test than the traditional norm-referenced test. Now norm referencing is a kind of idealization of the data, according to which the test constructor acts as if a population exists in which the ability under test is normally distributed, i.e. it has a Gaussian or bell-shaped curve. Reality is often in conflict with this assumption as far as language is concerned, since it is only an assumption that language abilities are normally distributed. But it is a useful assumption when it comes to data handling and statistical operations with the raw scores, e.g. in converting to standard scores. Norm referencing as a test construction technique seems essential, as essential as the idealization imposed on his data by any scientist. The linguist, for example, cannot analyse his data until he has idealized it through the processes of regularization (ignoring errors of performance, e.g. slips of the tongue), standardization (ignoring dialectal variation) and decontextualization (removing all references and appeals to context).

Criterion referencing, on the other hand, seems to be a method of constructing within course tests, tests that possess content validity. Norm referencing insists on selecting those items which discriminate most widely; criterion referencing, attempting to build a homogeneous profile of course ability, seems less concerned with massive item discrimination and more concerned with item relationship to context, whatever figures the item analysis produces. It seems that both from the logical and the practical point of view, criterion referencing, if it has a rightful place in test construction, can only be done *after* norm referencing. After a test has been shown to discriminate on a population then criterion referencing may be used on the same items in order to provide an appropriate achievement test for a particular sample.

Ingram concludes with a critical appraisal of some recent educational experiments involving language tests, and stresses the importance of paying due attention to the process of test construction. Tests are crucial in language experiments and no experiment can succeed unless proper care and enough time is given to constructing and administering the tests. Ingram also provides an appendix of useful language test statistics.

In chapter 3, Davies looks again at the same area as Ingram, but from a more practical point of view. He considers the uses of language tests and suggests that what distinguishes the different kinds of language test may be not so much the content as the purpose for which the test is given or the use to which it is being put. At the same time, purpose and use are likely to influence content, above all in the demand for objective type items. This, Davies suggests, is more critical to a language test than the selection of discrete language skills as against integrative ones for testing. This question is sometimes presented as a choice between testing single skills that do not look like actual language use, and over-all work on job samples that do. The first is said to be reliable and to possess content or predictive validity; the second to have doubtful reliability perhaps and only face validity. In fact the recent popularity of cloze testing has given the lie to this assumption, since the users of cloze tests frequently report high reliability and satisfactory validity (usually predictive). To criticize cloze testing because it is unclear what is being tested makes sense only if it is clear exactly what phoneme discrimination tests, for example, are testing. Can we be sure that what we think are discrete skills are indeed language skills in any meaningful sense? Davies' chapter is based on the central question: What should I test? His chapter concludes with a discussion and set of illustrations of test item construction.

We now turn to a description of the contents of the experimental chapters in this volume. In chapter 4 'The Design and Interpretation of Experiments', Clark is concerned with the realizing of a hypothesis, giving it body in the form of an experiment. A hypothesis is a semi-technical term for an idea that is submitted to trial. The arrangement of that trial is the experiment, the final instrument of judgement is the test. Chapter 5 provides a step by step account of the computation that follows from the experiments presented in chapter 4. In chapter 6, 'Statistical Inference', Clark is concerned with the testing of the hypothesis, that is with the judgement of the results after the experiment has been carried out. Here is an important difference between testing within an experimental situation and testing for one of the test-specific reasons (one of the four test uses described above). We have argued that tests which are used for test-specific purposes should have been put through the experimental trials and come out as respectable instruments complete with all their descriptive statistics. Tests used for experimental purposes, within-experiment tests, on the other hand, do not necessarily need to be standardized, i.e. they may quite properly be constructed in an ad hoc way. For example, a common applied linguistics experiment consists of a comparison between two teaching methods. To test the experiment a simple achievement test could be designed to assess whether the terminal behaviour has been achieved better by one method than by the other. There is no need here for statistics that reach out beyond the limits of the test since it is the experiment rather than the test that carries the burden of the validity.

Rather differently, an experiment might examine children's attitudes to various accents of English. Here texts are recorded representing various accents and played to a sample of children. Their judgements calibrated on a scale of, for example, social class are then compared. There is no need for a further test since the scale itself forms the test for this experiment. Attitude and interest surveys are not our concern here, although they too need care in construction. However, mention of them in the case of the example experiment illustrates a further difference between experiment-tests and test-specific tests, which is in the kinds of statistics needed. Test-specific tests make use of descriptive statistics, quoting means, standard deviations, percentiles, reliabilities and correlations with other tests, i.e. relating any one individual's score to his position in the population. Experiment-tests use inferential statistics, quoting levels of significance in order to determine whether a particular 'score' or a particular 'difference' could have occurred by chance alone—whether, in fact, it is a reliable difference. The link between test-specific language tests and experiment-tests is that both are experimental (and therefore make use of inferential statistics to establish reliability) and that both are tests (and therefore make use of descriptive statistics to establish validity). This book is an attempt to demonstrate our belief in the importance of this link.

2 ELISABETH INGRAM
Basic Concepts in Testing

1 Testing and language learning

Educational assessment is as old as education itself. As long as there have been teachers they have wanted to know how much their students have learned. So have those who pay the teachers to teach, and those who employ the students afterwards. The central concept in all assessment is that of validity: Is the assessment right? Does a given mark or qualification guarantee a certain standard of knowledge and skill in all relevant situations?

The oldest form of assessment in academic subjects was the public disputation. If a student could by common agreement acquit himself honourably in a discussion with his seniors, he ceased to be a student and became a master himself. In many countries the public disputation is still an essential part of the ordeal of a doctoral candidate.

Oral examinations are a simpler, but a more authoritarian form of the public disputation, and this method of assessment also continues to be a part of many examination systems. But it lacks accountability—nobody except the two or three people present at the interview can know what happened and the professorial decision can be neither confirmed or disconfirmed. For this reason the written examination became more and more common. The advantage of the written as against the oral examination is that there exists a record of the student's performance, so the judgement of any one examiner can be checked against that of another. When this is done there is usually a fair amount of agreement between examiners, but not invariably. And so another concept in assessment became more clearly distinguished: the concept of reliability. There are many sources of unreliability in an examination, but the one seized on because it seemed to have a possible solution was marker unreliability. The traditional essay type examination may have its inherent validity reduced by being lacking in marker reliability; since two different examiners may arrive at different marks for the same essay, and one examiner may even disagree with himself when marking the same essay after a delay of several weeks. And no assessment can be valid if it is not reliable.

About the turn of the century a new form of assessment was developed—

the objective test. One of the reasons for this was to avoid marker unreliability, that is, disagreement between examiners. Instead of having to write shorter or longer essays, the learners were asked a series of quick questions, each having only one correct answer, or a set of previously agreed acceptable answers:

a What are the days of the week?
b What is an envelope?

(Acceptable answers to *b* would include 'for putting letters in' or 'you put a stamp on and post it'.) This method of marking was termed *objective*, in distinction to the subjective or individually variable nature of the marking of essays.

One of the major differences between essays and objective tests is that essays are typically awarded one all-over mark or grade, whereas the total score on a test is arrived at by adding up each point scored for a correct answer to a question. This brought with it the need to consider explicitly the theoretical models underlying quantification and quantitative measurement.

2 Measurement

The common definition of measurement is that it consists in assigning numerals to objects or events. When we use numbers to indicate frequencies or amounts of observable phenomena, we are engaged in the practice of applying theoretical mathematical models to the empirical world. We do this in order to find out more about the things we are interested in, or to find it out earlier or more easily. For instance if we know that a whole Edam cheese weighs four pounds, we do not have to cut it down the middle and weigh the parts again to find out what half an Edam cheese might weigh: we simply divide by two.

Mathematical models are formal systems: they include a set of symbols, and a set of agreed rules for manipulating these symbols. The metaphor of *game* is sometimes used: a formal game is played according to formal rules, and if the correct rules have been followed correctly, the outcome is bound to be correct. But in itself the formal game tells us nothing about the empirical world. It is only informative about the world when it is applied appropriately. The game has certain concepts built into it, or rather, different versions of the game have a number of partially different underlying concepts. Unless there is congruence between the underlying concepts of the particular model we choose to apply, and the nature of the phenomena under investigation, the information which we derive from applying the model can be seriously misleading. For instance, one of the properties built into the basic number system is that the difference between any pair of numbers which are next to each other is the same as the difference between any other pair of adjacent numbers. It is this property of equal interval that makes these subtraction statements comparable: $2 - 1 = 1$; $3 - 2 = 1$; etc.

When numbers are assigned to objects, the assumption of equal interval may or may not fit. When we say of three pieces of cheese that they weigh 3, 2 and 1 pounds respectively, the logic of the model and the nature of that property of objects which we call weight is in agreement. The heaviest piece of cheese differs from the middle piece of cheese by the same amount as the middle piece differs from the smallest piece. But when we use the same numbers, 1, 2 and 3, to designate the first three athletes home in a 100 metre sprint, it is highly unlikely that the winner is exactly as far ahead of the runner-up as the runner-up is ahead of the third man. So in order not to mislead we employ a different model, a number series in which there is no assumption of equal intervals between adjacent digits, that is, we use the ordinal number system: 1st, 2nd, 3rd. The ordinal scale is often more appropriate than the equal interval scale for judging the comparative standing of students learning a given subject.

We apply mathematical models to empirical observations in order to discover more about the world to which the observations belong. This process can be informative only if (a) the choice of the mathematical model is appropriate; (b) the observations are accurate. It is because of the importance of selecting the appropriate mathematical model that writers of textbooks on statistics usually refuse to provide what they contemptuously refer to as cook-books, i.e., a compilation of directions of how actually to calculate this, that and the next statistic.

In the search for appropriate matchings between theory and data, four scales of measurement have been established, the nominal, the ordinal, the equal interval and the ratio scale. For each scale a set of permitted statistics has been specified. In educational testing all four scales are used. The nominal scale is used for establishing differences between categories, e.g., boys and girls or art students and science students. When our observations permit us to judge that out of a class of 25 students, in respect of command of English sentence structure, Lucie is first, Andrew is second, Alison is third and so on until we come to Edward who is 25th, this is very valuable. But if we are unable to state by how much Lucie is better than Andrew, and relate it to how much better Andrew is than Alison, then these observations are such that they should be processed by those statistics which are appropriate to measurement on the ordinal scale. Such statistics are called non-parametric statistics.

If, on the other hand, we could say with some degree of confidence that when Lucie gets a score of 70 on a test of English grammar, and Andrew gets 60 and Alison 55, this means that the difference between Lucie and Andrew is twice the difference between Andrew and Alison, then we would be making observations on an equal interval scale, and the statistics appropriate to that scale could be used. These statistics are called parametric statistics. It has been repeatedly stated by testing experts that most educational tests are somewhere between the ordinal and the equal interval scales. How close a test can get to measuring on the equal interval scale, even after repeated administrations to hundreds of students, with intervening item analyses, correlations and other adjustments remains partly a matter of faith.

It would be natural to react to all this doubt with the query: why bother? If the test constructor is not sure that he is justified in using the parametric statistics, why not use the ordinal scale statistics and leave it at that. The reason is that the parametric statistics appropriate to the equal interval scale are more efficient than those appropriate to the ordinal scale. When one statistic is said to be more efficient than another, it means that it brings out more of the information which is potentially available in the data.

Consider the well-known statistic, the arithmetic mean, which is appropriate to the equal interval scale, in relation to the less familiar but comparable statistic appropriate on the ordinal scale, the median. Both express the central tendency of a set of observations. The arithmetical mean of 9, 7, 5, 3, 1, is $\frac{25}{5} = 5$. Means take account of how far each observation is removed from the middle value. So, if we change for instance the two top values, the mean changes also: 12, 9, 5, 3, 1 is $\frac{30}{5} = 6$. The median, on the other hand, is the average which is appropriate to measurements on the ordinal scale. The median of 9, 7, 5, 3, 1, is 5, because the median is that value which is the middle of an ordered series. To put it in another way the median is that value which has as many observations larger than itself as it has observations which are smaller when the set of observations is uneven. But while the mean is sensitive to changes in the outlying observations, the median is not, as long as its middlemost position is preserved. The median of the series 12, 9, 5, 3, 1, is still 5.

So we are faced with a dilemma: either we can use the statistics appropriate to the ordinal scale, which is not so efficient in extracting the potential information of the observations, or we can use the statistics appropriate to the equal interval scale, which, though potentially more powerful, may be misleading, because of the misfit between theoretical assumptions and the characteristics of the observations. Some statisticians are very insistent on not using the parametric statistics unless one is very certain that they are appropriate. Others are more relaxed, and point out that certain of these statistics are *robust*, that is, the information one gets from using them is reasonably accurate, even if some of the conditions for their use are not entirely met. And when numbers are very large, in hundreds and thousands, as in many testing programmes, parametric statistics are nearly always used.

Whatever the mathematical treatment, the value of the information obviously depends fundamentally on the quality of the observations. No amount of high-powered statistics can compensate for poor or inaccurate observations. The sort of observations we are considering are normally made through some measuring device. Scientists spend vast sums of money and take endless trouble to build instruments which register accurately and sensitively that which they are supposed to measure. What is required is that the differences in the readings from the instrument should reflect the true differences in the characteristic which is being investigated—whether it is the expansion of metal in various temperatures, or different degrees of skill in distinguishing the speech sounds of a foreign language in a group of learners. Testers discuss the accuracy requirement under the heading of *reliability*, and the truth requirement under the heading of *validity*.

3 Test requirements

In testing we give the student a set of items to be answered, i.e. we set him a series of tasks. We observe his performance on these items, and from that we generalize to the level of performance which can be expected from the student when he is called upon to exercise outside the test situation the skill or characteristic which we are trying to assess. From a small sample of his behaviour, we make inferences about how he would behave in all other situations demanding the same skills. This generalization cannot be correct unless the items are valid; that is, success in answering the items correctly must depend on possession of the characteristic or bundles of characteristics we wish to measure. Items must also be reliable, that is, in addition to measuring what they are supposed to measure, they must do so accurately and consistently.

3.1 Reliability

The reliability of a measuring device is high when any variations in the readings taken represent true differences between the individuals who are being tested. Any other variation represents error.

A great deal of the effort which goes into test construction is devoted to reducing error. What might be called extrinsic sources of error are examiner variability and variability of testing conditions. These can be greatly reduced by common sense precautions. Examiner variability is virtually eliminated by objective formats, used properly, and variability of testing conditions are reduced by meticulous care in providing instructions to the test administrator and in formulating the explanations to the candidates, and if necessary by giving some preliminary practice, so that people who have not taken an objective test before are not unduly handicapped.

By contrast the intrinsic sources of error are more intractable. They are primarily of two kinds: errors due to lack of stability and those due to lack of equivalence.

3.1.1 STABILITY RELIABILITY

A measuring device is stable if it gives the same result when used twice on the same object. In testing terms, if the same items were given to a group of people twice within, say, ten days and if each individual passed the same items and failed the same items both times, then all the items would possess perfect stability reliability. But this is extremely unlikely to happen. What we are looking for is stability in general. If a test or a subtest produces the same or very nearly the same relative ordering and distance between the individuals in the group on both occasions, the test would be judged to have high stability reliability. Stability reliability is often referred to as test-retest reliability because it is estimated by testing, and then some time later retesting the same individuals, and then correlating their scores.

Some people are more erratic than others—their performance varies appreciably according to mood and circumstances. There is nothing a tester can do about that, except be philosophical. If in the try-out group there happens to be a number of individuals who underperform or overperform on either day, the reliability correlations will be reduced.

Further, some tasks are more vulnerable to variable behaviour than others. For instance, ability to discriminate correctly between speech sounds presented with a minimum of context depends not only on knowing the sound system of a language, but also on attention factors, which are notoriously inconsistent. Reliability values for listening discrimination tests are nearly always lower than those for listening comprehension tests, and all tests which depend on listening are likely to have lower stability values than tests which involve reading. This is not a reason for avoiding listening tests. The main thing about testing is the purpose; if there are good reasons for having listening discrimination tests, one simply makes them as good as one can.

3.1.2 EQUIVALENCE RELIABILITY

A measuring device is equivalent to another measuring device if both devices give the same result when applied to the same objects. In testing terms this can come about in two ways. One way is to construct two parallel tests: for each item with a given content in one series, we write another item testing the same point for the other series, taking care that both items are equally difficult. If twenty individuals take both tests, and if each individual either fails both, or passes both, then the pairs of items possess perfect equivalence reliability. While equivalence reliability for items is hard to come by, what is required is equivalence reliability for whole tests or subtests. If two tests produce the same or very nearly the same relative ordering and distance between the individuals in a group, then the test is said to have high equivalence reliability. The underlying notion is that there is a hypothetical pool of items consisting of all those items which measure the characteristic under investigation, and none that do not, and further, that the items which make up an actual test are drawn from that pool. If the items that go to make up Test A have been drawn from the right pool, and the items that go to make up Test B have also been drawn from the same pool, then the results from test A must be equivalent to the results from Test B, and indeed to any other test similarly made up. Estimates of equivalence reliability can be obtained in the following three ways.

(i) Parallel forms

The test constructor may provide two parallel versions of his test in which every item in one form is matched by a similar item in the other form. Reliability is calculated by administering both versions to the same group of individuals, and correlating the two sets of scores. Correlations estimate the extent to which two sets of scores show the same trend.

(ii) Split half

If a test consists of 100 items, the scores are calculated separately for two sets of 50 items, and the results correlated. The usual method is to take all even-numbered items together, and all odd numbered items together. This is obviously similar to the parallel form method, except that there will normally be fewer items to correlate in the split half technique, and the parallelism of content between pairs of items will not necessarily be observed.

(iii) Variance estimates

This is the usual sense in which equivalence reliability is taken. Simply put, a calculation is made which estimates the mean of all possible split halves on the test. Such a method takes into account the consistency of performance by each individual on each item, and compares that to over-all consistency on the test as a whole. The measure of consistency is the variance. To the extent that items draw differentially upon the collection of factors that make up a given characteristic, consistency in answering is obviously going to be reduced, and this will tend to lower the reliability values somewhat. This should not necessarily lead one to try to make all items as alike as possible—validity is usually greater with tests which contain impure or heterogeneous items, and, as before, it is the purpose of the testing which is the overriding consideration.

The most usual technique for estimating equivalence reliability by taking into account item and test variance is known as the Kuder Richardson. It yields correlation coefficients which are interpreted in the same way as correlation coefficients obtained by other methods. Details of the computation of one version are given in Appendix I on p. 194.

We cannot say that one kind of reliability is better or worse than the other—they are simply different. It is however true that the methods used to assess either kind suffer from different kinds of defects. The test-retest method has one great practical disadvantage: it is often quite impossible to get permission to test a group of students twice. On the other hand it does not matter at all if the students do somewhat better the second time: high correlation values depend on preserving relative ranking and distances, not on obtaining identical scores each time. What does detract from stability reliability values is when some individuals remember more, or learn more from the first occasion than others do, or are coached more in the interval. With the parallel form method, it is sensible to administer the second form after some days' interval. Then both stability and equivalence contribute to the reliability estimate. But in practice this can be difficult to arrange. If both forms have to be administered at the same time, the parallel forms procedure becomes rather like the split half procedure, except that there are twice as many items. While this is likely to be a theoretical advantage, in practice it may take so much time to administer both forms that again permission can be difficult to secure. It is of obvious practical advantage for the parallel forms method, the split half method and the Kuder Richardson method that they do not involve retesting.

3.2 Validity

When a test measures that which it is supposed to measure, and nothing else, it is valid. To the extent that the readings on the measuring device reflect other characteristics—for instance familiarity with the topic when we are looking for general comprehension—or are subject to the kinds of error discussed above under reliability, the validity will be reduced.

The difficulty is that the characteristic or attribute which we wish to measure in education is usually something which is not very obvious, or easy to define. In second language learning, the attribute labelled 'fluency' is conceivably the most elusive of the lot, but 'command of the basic grammatical structures' or 'ability to function at the tourist level', while sounding more concrete, are still in need of a series of operational definitions.

We provoke certain kinds of behaviour in the candidate, in the hope and belief that we can generalize from the way that he behaves on a given occasion on a limited number of tasks, to the way that he will perform on all other relevant occasions. But obviously hoping is not enough. We must have some expression of validity, some way of estimating even approximately that the test is doing the job it is supposed to do. There are three commonly recognized kinds of validity. These are pragmatic validity, content validity, and construct validity. Some writers divide pragmatic validity into two parts, predictive and concurrent (see chapter 3). There is a fourth kind known as face validity. This has to do with the surface credibility or public acceptability of a test, and while it is sometimes important, it can be regarded as a public relations problem rather than a technical one. In this section I shall deal mainly with pragmatic validity.

Estimates of pragmatic validity are obtained by correlating test scores with the scores or ratings obtained from a *criterion* measure. Criterion measures can be standard examinations, established tests, the ratings obtained from experienced judges on observational samples. By definition, anything which serves as a criterion is taken to possess validity. There are obvious problems here, and it is usual to distinguish between immediate and ultimate validity. If a test correlates highly with the chosen criterion, then the test has immediate or first order validity. For instance if a test accurately predicts success and failure in a set of examinations, then the test possesses immediate validity. But the criterion here, the examinations, is supposed to be validly related to some kind of scholastic or professional ability. If the examinations are indeed valid predictors of vocational success, and *if* that is what we wish to predict, then the examinations, and hence the test, possess ultimate validity. In the field of language teaching however, teachers are usually only too aware that the ultimate criterion—ability to use the language—is what matters. The problem is how to arrange the instruction so that the aim is achieved, and how to make sure that the examinations and tests which the learner has to take are good indications of ability to use the target language in real situations.

Not all situations require ultimate validation. One might want to compare the efficiency of two methods of teaching specific grammar points, for instance the use of *some* and *any*. The validation for a set of items testing this could be an ongoing count of the number of errors the learners make in their classroom work for a specific period of time, i.e. in this way we would be establishing the criterion by observational samples. Obviously this is not the sort of activity a teacher can routinely engage in, but the point is that for this purpose immediate validity is what is required. If the purpose was to establish how much the ability to distribute *some* and *any* contributes to skill in performing in a real communication situation, then of course the ultimate criterion would have to be brought back in.

When a test is essentially a job sample, a particular slice of the kind of activity we wish to assess, we are obviously dealing with a special kind of immediate validity—sometimes referred to as inherent validity. Essay writing is often given as an example: if you want to assess how good a person is at writing essays, you get him to write an essay or two. Similarly, if you want to know how good a person is at talking in a foreign language you set up a situation in which he does just that—you give him an oral. Further, if essay writing really is what the teaching process is designed to produce, then essay writing is obviously its own criterion. But it could be that essay writing is simply a convenient subskill to test, out of the whole range of skills which goes into writing. In that case the validity of essay writing should in turn be established against an ultimate and composite criterion consisting of writing in all registers judged to be relevant.

However, let us take the situation where the tests really do constitute a job sample. It is usually true that the activity called for is rather complex and therefore the task of judging it is also complex. As has often been pointed out, the judgements of different examiners of the quality of the same essay can vary considerably. In other words the reliability of the assessment of complex, realistic job samples tends to be somewhat low, and this lowers the effective validity. Reliability of essay marking can be improved by using several judges, each assessing independently. And validity can be improved by requiring the student to write two or three shorter essays, rather than one single long one. Job sample reliability and validity can be improved in the same way.

Obviously, if a test requires a candidate to produce behaviour which is very similar to the behaviour one wishes to assess, this represents the best chance that the test will be valid. But what is not so obvious is which of the many similarity relations are the most important. For instance it is natural to suppose that ability to spell is best tested by the traditional dictation method. The teacher pronounces a word, and the pupils write it down. In a more sophisticated version the teacher pronounces a word and repeats it in context to make sure everybody hears and understands:

a SEARCH Search for the ball until you find it.

Various objective formats have been shown to produce much the same results as traditional dictation. In *b* the pupil has to select the correctly spelt word from a number of alternatives; in *c* he has to complete the word by filling in the blank:

b LOOK FOR serch scearch sarsh search
c LOOK FOR s. . .ch

But the most valid format of all turns out to be giving the pupil a whole sentence with one word misspelt, which they then have to find and correct:

d Serch for the purse in the field.

The criterion for all formats was the spelling which the children produced over a period of time in their own compositions. What format *d* has in common with the criterion behaviour, is that it does not draw the child's attention to a particular word, so in order to do well he has to monitor his performance on all the words. Afterwards it seems only too obvious that this is an essential part of the behaviour of a person who can spell, but that is with the benefit of hindsight.

It appears then that it can be very difficult to establish pragmatic validity. In my view this is not a good reason for giving it up. However imperfect the criterion of validity, some kind of attempt should be made to compare a new test with an external measure, which might take the form of established tests, teachers' ratings or observational samples.

Established tests

When new tests are correlated with older established tests it looks as if one is just shifting the burden of proof one stage further back. In a sense this is true, but there are two reasons why testers find it rewarding to do so.

Firstly, an established test has known characteristics. Its internal consistency and discrimination power is known, its reliability has been computed and some sort of validity estimate is available. However imperfect it may be, the test is as good as its constructors could make it. A new test usually needs extensive revision to achieve the same state.

Secondly, the technical validity estimates we have for a test may not inspire a great deal of confidence, but when a test has been used by a number of people in a number of different contexts and when it has been found to be useful and practical and informative, then it can be said to have the kind of validity which matters: it works for the purposes it is intended for, according to the people who use it. If a new test correlates highly with an established test in the same field, one is entitled to be optimistic about the new test.

Teachers' ratings

When experienced teachers rank the members of a class in order of merit in respect of their relative achievement in a school subject, this appears to be one of the best criterion measures of immediate validity, as long as it is limited to one class and one teacher at a time. When a series of small scale comparisons between test scores and teachers' ratings show sufficient agreement, there is good reason to be satisfied at least about immediate validity.

Observational samples

When the criterion consists of repeated observational samples of accessible behaviour, the difficulties are mainly practical ones. The greatest difficulty in comparing different formats of spelling tests with counts of spelling errors in compositions consists in finding time to do it. Language testers are always planning to assess the validity of tests which involve listening as estimates of actual pronunciation, because assessing pronunciation directly is so troublesome and time-consuming. In the test of proficiency of English as a foreign language which I am responsible for, the correlations lead me to conclude that the listening discrimination subtests should remain part of the total test, but we do not have the evidence which would allow us to predict from listening scores specifically to standards of adequacy in pronunciation. Nor does any one else, as far as I know.

The two other forms of validity, content validity and construct validity, are not established by comparing the candidates' scores with anything, but by examining what goes into the test items. If a test adequately samples the 'content' of a subject, for instance as defined by a textbook or a syllabus then it has content validity. If a test is constructed according to a theory which adequately analyses the components of the behaviour we are interested in assessing it has construct validity.

I shall discuss content and construct validity further in section 4. But first, in order to give some meaning to the notion of pragmatic validity, I shall discuss the concept of correlation.

3.3 Correlations

A correlation coefficient is a single figure which expresses how much two series of numerical observations have in common. There is for instance quite a high correlation between the height and the weight of individuals. Tall people tend to weigh more than those who are not so tall, small people tend to weigh less than others, and so on. Correlations are appropriate when the observations come in pairs—the height and the weight of an individual form a pair because they relate to the same person. Similarly when a group of people have taken two tests, the scores for each individual form a pair, and the two sets of scores for a group of individuals can be correlated, to see how much agreement there is between them.

In testing, correlations are used to assess reliability and validity and also to assess the degree of correspondence which exists among subtests and between subtests and total scores. There are a number of formulae for calculating correlations. Two of the most common, the product-moment method and the rank order method are given in Appendix I. All the formulae are so made that the correlation coefficient—the single figure obtained—cannot be larger than $+1$ or smaller than -1. The symbol denoting the product moment correlation coefficient is r, and r is also often used to designate other correlation coefficients, regardless of the method of computation, in general discussion.

To illustrate how the values of r vary with the amount of agreement between two sets of scores, let us consider some examples, in which x_1 labels one set of scores, x_2 labels the other, and the scores are paired by individuals.

(a) x_1: 0 4 6 8 10 12 14 16 22 26
     x_2: 0 2 3 4 5 6 7 8 11 13

The correlation coefficient here is $+1\cdot0$; the two sets of scores correlate perfectly. This example, and those following, are from Snedecor (1956), and it demonstrates the important point that two sets of scores do not have to be identical in order to correlate perfectly. As long as the relative position of each individual is the same for both sets, and the relative distances between individuals is comparable, there is perfect correlation.

Now consider some further examples. Note that the x_1 series is the same in all the examples, and in the x_2 series the actual numbers are the same as in the first example. It is only the ordering, and therefore the pairing, that is altered.

(b) x_1 0 4 6 8 12 14 16 22 26
    x_2 0 2 4 3 7 6 8 11 13
    $r = 0.986$

(c) x_1 0 4 6 8 12 14 16 22 26
    x_2 2 8 0 6 4 3 13 7 11
    $r = 0.597$

(d) x_1 0 4 6 8 12 14 16 22 26
    x_2 4 3 8 6 7 13 2 11 0
    $r = 0.00$

(e) x_1 0 4 6 8 12 14 16 22 26
    x_2 8 7 6 13 0 2 11 3 4
    $r = -0.368$

(f) x_1 0 4 6 8 12 14 16 22 26
    x_2 11 13 8 4 7 6 3 2 0
    $r = -0.889$

In practice one hardly ever gets perfect correlations, as illustrated in example (a) but very high correlations are not uncommon. For instance, properly constructed large-scale tests should have reliability coefficients of at least 0.95.

Looking at the examples again, one can see that it is the extreme or outlying values which count. In (b) the two upper pairs and the two lower pairs correspond nearly perfectly ($r = 0.99$).

$$0 \quad 4 \ldots 22 \quad 26$$
$$0 \quad 2 \ldots 11 \quad 13$$

In (c) there is still a measure of agreement ($r = 0.60$)

$$0 \quad 4 \ldots 22 \quad 26$$
$$2 \quad 8 \ldots 7 \quad 11$$

In (d) there is no trend at all either in extreme or in central pairs and $r = 0$. But as Snedecor points out, if one changed just one pair, the extreme right one, from 26/0 to 26/9 the value of r changes from 0 to 0.505. This demonstrates two things. One, the importance of outlying pairs, and two, how vulnerable those correlations are which consist only of a small number of pairs.

In order to guard against wrong interpretations of correlation values, statisticians have compiled tables showing the values that r must have, in order to be significantly different from zero. The thinking behind such tables

24 Testing and Experimental Methods

is this: supposing one drew pairs of numbers from a pool, such that any number had the same chance of being drawn as any other number in each draw. The 'real' correlation between series of such pairs of numbers from this pool is zero. But by random variation one might, especially with only a few draws, come up with pairs expressing some degree of common tendency. The table gives the correlation values which could be expected to occur by chance alone no oftener than five per cent of the draws in the long run (the 5% level of significance), and no oftener than once in a hundred draws (the 1% level of significance) for series consisting of varying numbers of pairs. The degrees of freedom equals the number of pairs minus one.

Correlation coefficients at the 5% and 1% levels of significance

Degrees of Freedom	5%	1%	Degrees of Freedom	5%	1%
1	0·997	1·000	24	0·388	0·496
2	0·950	0·990	25	0·381	0·487
3	0·878	0·959	26	0·374	0·478
4	0·811	0·917	27	0·367	0·470
5	0·754	0·874	28	0·361	0·463
6	0·707	0·834	29	0·355	0·456
7	0·666	0·798	30	0·349	0·449
8	0·632	0·765	35	0·325	0·418
9	0·602	0·735	40	0·304	0·393
10	0·576	0·708	45	0·288	0·372
11	0·553	0·684	50	0·273	0·354
12	0·532	0·661	60	0·250	0·325
13	0·514	0·641	70	0·232	0·302
14	0·497	0·623	80	0·217	0·283
15	0·482	0·606	90	0·205	0·267
16	0·468	0·590	100	0·195	0·254
17	0·456	0·575	125	0·174	0·228
18	0·444	0·561	150	0·159	0·208
19	0·433	0·549	200	0·138	0·181
20	0·423	0·537	300	0·113	0·148
21	0·413	0·526	400	0·098	0·128
22	0·404	0·515	500	0·088	0·115
23	0·396	0·505	1,000	0·062	0·081

Portions of this table were taken from Table VA in 'Statistical Methods for Research Workers' by permission of Professor R. A. Fisher and his publishers, Oliver and Boyd.

Suppose one draws twenty pairs, and that the correlation coefficient for these twenty pairs is r = 0·415. This actual value of r is then compared with the value the r must be, for 19 degrees of freedom, in order not to happen by chance more often than 5 times in a hundred draws. The above table shows that at the 5 per cent level, r should be at least 0·433. The obtained value is less than this, so we cannot assert with any degree of confidence that this value is significantly different from zero. Suppose further that in three more draws of twenty pairs one got correlation values of −0·216, 0·101 and 0·538. The first two values are clearly not significant, and it makes no difference that the first value is negative and the second positive. They are both too small to mean anything at all, for this degree of freedom. The third (imaginary) value, 0·538, is larger than 0·433, but smaller than 0·549. Such a correlation would be said to be significant at the 5 per cent level, but would fail to reach significance at the 1 per cent level.

It is vitally important to distinguish between the statistical significance of an observed correlation, and the meaning of the correlation. When a correlation is found to be significant at either of the two conventional levels, it means that there is presumed to be some real connection as distinct from a random association between the two sets of observations. But this says nothing about the amount of association.

Establishing that a correlation is significant is merely the first step. Unless the value is significant we cannot take the study further at all. If it is significant we can then go on to estimate the degree of association presumed to exist between the two sets of scores.

Connolly and Sluckin (1957, p. 154) give what they call 'a rough but useful guide to the degree of relationship indicated by the size of the coefficients':

0·90 − 1·00   very high correlation; very strong relationship
0·70 − 0·90   high correlation; marked relationship
0·40 − 0·70   moderate correlation; substantial relationship
0·20 − 0·40   low correlation; a definite relationship but a small one
0·20 and less   slight correlation; relationship so small as to be negligible

If one is going to predict from one set of scores to another, the correlation values need to be high or very high. This is what we are after in estimates of reliability and validity. For instance in estimating test-retest reliability, the nearer the correlation approaches 1, the more closely the scores on one testing occasion predict the scores on the other occasion.

Similarly, for pragmatic validity, the higher the correlation between criterion scores and test scores, the more accurately we can predict from scores on one to scores on the other. And so, if the criterion is valid the test must be valid. But in other cases we do not get, or indeed need, such high correlations. For instance when the IQ of parents and children are correlated, r is usually in the region of 0·50. This indicates a substantial relationship between the parents and children and amounts to a solid piece of information. But it forms a very slender basis for predicting. And even in testing one does not always want very high correlations. Subtests should correlate moderately with each other. If one had for instance three subtests in a foreign language test, vocabulary, grammar and comprehension, and the intercorrelations were in the 0·8s and 0·9s one could predict very closely from one to the other; they would all be doing the same job and so two of them would be superfluous. What one wants are moderate correlations. This is because one assumes that language skills are highly complex characteristics, and therefore that any assessment of them should include tests which tap different aspects of the total skill. Subtests correlated with total test score, of which they form part, will necessarily show higher correlations than with one another. This is shown in the following table drawn from a small preliminary try-out of some item formats on 45 Japanese learners of English.

	Grammar	Comprehension	Phoneme discrimination	Total
Grammar	–	0·68	0·49	0·89
Comprehension		–	0·59	0·89
Phoneme discrimination			–	0·76

The number of items in each subtest were Grammar: 40; Comprehension: 30; Phoneme discrimination: 30.

4 Norm-referenced versus criterion-referenced testing

Nearly all discussions on the concepts and practices of testing have concerned themselves with what has recently come to be termed norm-referenced testing as distinct from so-called criterion-referenced testing (Pilliner 1973). In norm-referenced testing the purpose is to compare the level of performance of an individual with the general standard of performance which is shown by the total group that he belongs to and can be compared with. In criterion-referenced testing the emphasis is not on how a student stands with reference to his peers, but on whether or not the individual student knows something rather specific that he is supposed to know, or can perform something rather specific that he is supposed to be able to perform. In one formulation, norm-referenced testing compares the behaviour of an individual with the behaviour of others, while criterion-referenced testing describes the behaviour of an individual with reference to externally predetermined and specified objectives.

As so often happens, the terminology is confusing. In norm-referenced usage 'criterion' is the term used to designate the other norm-referenced measure with which a new test is correlated in order to establish pragmatic validity. In the context of criterion-referenced testing, the criterion is also some externally defined object, but it is not itself norm-referenced, it is the specified objective itself. The objective can be specified in terms of content: does the learner know, or does he not know how to construct a question in English using 'do':

Mary loves John → Does Mary love John?

The criterion can also be specified in terms of degree of skill or levels of performance: for instance, does the learner possess the skills which would allow him to function adequately as a tourist, or as a student of current affairs? This kind of performance criterion is much harder to define. A specification of language content—vocabulary and structure—is not adequate, because though one might be able to predict some of the words and phrases that are likely to be used in actual, real-life communication situations, the native speaker or writer can and often does select from the total resources of the language in unpredictable ways. Also, though language is a very important part of a communication situation, it is only a part. It is for instance notoriously difficult to understand foreign newspapers, even though the words are known or can be looked up, because the writers presuppose all kinds of knowledge in the reader which a foreigner is unlikely to have.

There are many similarities between tests that are constructed so as to be norm-referencing and those which are constructed to be criterion-referencing. First let us consider those tests which take their content from a teaching syllabus. Norm-referenced tests which do this are called achievement tests. Achievement tests seek to answer the question: How much of what is supposed to have been learned has actually been learned? When the objectives of criterion-referenced testing are defined in terms of content, and when that content is specified in terms of a syllabus within an educational system, then criterion-referenced testing amounts to diagnostic testing, or more precisely, to diagnostic testing plus mastery testing. Both diagnostic and mastery testing have direct educational purposes. In diagnostic testing the purpose is to discover the educational objectives that the students have missed out on, so that remedial teaching can be directed where it is needed. Mastery testing, which is a closely allied but more recent concept, is related to an ongoing teaching programme, and enables teachers to determine whether a currently taught objective has been learned by each student, so that the programme can proceed to the next objective.

The difference between achievement tests on the one hand, and diagnostic and mastery testing on the other is that performance on an achievement test is evaluated in terms of a total test score, or on subtest scores. The principle is the same, namely that successes on individual items are summed and it is the sum that is important, not the individual tasks. We ask: 'Does a student score 70 per cent or 50 per cent or 30 per cent?'; We do not ask: 'Does he know that abstract nouns often have zero article in English?' In criterion-referenced testing the chief concern is not the total score that the candidate accumulates over the whole test, but his pattern of success or failure on homogeneous blocks of items which specifically set out to test mastery of a particular teaching objective.

Not all tests have their scope and content defined by a syllabus. Some tests are based on an independent selection from language and language behaviour, in accordance with what the test constructors judge to be important areas to test, and according to their views of the nature of language activities and the processing underlying these activities. Norm-referenced tests of this kind are called proficiency tests. As Davies (1973a) points out, a syllabus is a sample of the totality of language, and a proficiency test represents another and independent sample from the same totality. Proficiency tests, like achievement tests, provide an evaluation of the capacities of the candidates in terms of a sum of successes, over a large number of items, testing a variety of points, and this enables the administrators to place the candidates on a ranking scale, with the high scorers at the top and the low scorers at the bottom. In addition to providing this comparative assessment, in terms of the test itself, proficiency tests often provide indications of the level of performance, in real life situations, which can be expected from people who fall into various score intervals. For instance, by comparing the test scores obtained on the TOEFL test with the ratings provided by universities for more than 600 newly arrived foreign students, the test constructors could provide 'tentative' interpretations of what each score level meant, in terms of the ability of the students to follow academic courses.

TOEFL score	Recommendations
550 and above	No restriction on academic course load. No remedial English necessary.
400–549	No restriction on academic course load. Some remedial English desirable.
300–399	Reduced study load. Considerable remedial English required.
200–299	Not ready for academic courses. Full time intensive English required.

(D. Harris 1965)

When proficiency tests provide indications of the expected level of performance, they are analogous to those criterion-referenced tests which specify the criterion in terms of those components or parameters which make up complex language skills, at various levels of command. For instance one might hypothesize that in any real-life communication situation, a foreigner will always encounter new and unknown words, and that therefore his level of performance will in part depend on his ability to deal with previously unknown vocabulary. One would therefore set out to test directly a learner's ability to deal with previously unknown language items. This could be done by giving him a passage to interpret, where nonsense words had been substituted for real words in the passage. Alternatively one might give him a cloze test, where certain words had been deleted, and ask him to insert the deleted words. This would, if the theory was right, be a direct test of the learner's ability to cope with unknown elements in a passage. In a test of this type, there would be other sections designed to measure directly other facets of the performance situation.

The difference between the performance indications provided by proficiency tests and those which might be provided by criterion-referenced tests, is that the proficiency test indications can only be pragmatically established. One would test a number of people, observe their performance in an academic or professional setting, and establish the correspondences between scores on the one hand and estimated levels of performance in real-life situations on the other. In a criterion-referenced test the interpretation of success or failure on a block of items intended to assess mastery of any particular objective, e.g., inferring the meaning of new words, would rest on the validity of the theory of language use which asserts that this ability is a relevant part of successful communication, in other words, construct validity.

Criterion-referenced testing is heavily dependent on the *a priori* non-pragmatic forms of validity—content validity for when the criterion is specified in terms of content, and construct validity for when the criterion is specified in terms of kinds and levels of performance. Both content and construct validity have been established concepts in testing for some time, but it is only with the emergence of interest in criterion-referenced testing that really energetic attempts are beginning to be made to explore the nature of these concepts, and how to exploit them for practical testing purposes. Even so, most of the attention is being given to content specification. The study of performance specification and validation can hardly be said to exist.

There are great problems in the construction of criterion-referenced tests. For norm-referenced testing we have a set of sophisticated procedures for establishing the degree to which a test does what it is supposed to do, and how efficient it is in doing so. The problem in criterion-referenced testing is to establish how far the accepted procedures are applicable, and to what extent new procedures must be devised, to serve analogous functions.

The *a priori* concepts of content and construct validity are relevant to both norm-referencing and criterion-referencing testing; they are indeed central to criterion-referenced testing. When it comes to the statistical techniques for establishing the usefulness of items and the reliability and the pragmatic validity of tests and subtests, there is considerable doubt about their applicability. Some writers fall back on the *a priori* concepts, particularly on content validity. This seems to me insufficient, for two main reasons. First, it is well known from constructing norm-referenced tests that items sometimes behave in peculiar and unpredicted ways—that is to say, the candidates behave towards the items in peculiar ways. Two items deliberately constructed so as to be entirely parallel can easily turn out not to receive correct answers from the same set of individuals. Some items are more idiosyncratic than others, and it is essential to have some procedure to detect these.

In addition to item variability, human variability also has to be taken into account. Even if, by some means, we had managed to establish that a block of six parallel items was entirely homogeneous, that is, that they tested the same objective in the same way, there would still be some variation in the scoring pattern, because people do not always perform at the same level. Sometimes they function near the top of their capacities, sometimes considerably below. And, what is particularly important for criterion-referenced testing, such fluctuations of behaviour are typical for those who are engaged in the process of learning. This is particularly true for language learning. The process of learning to carry out a specific language operation is typically marked first by the students getting it right occasionally, then by getting it right more often. However, a nearly perfect performance over all occasions can be quite slow in coming. While this poses no particular problem for norm-referenced testing, where the aim is to achieve a ranking order based on all-over performance, it is one of the main problems in criterion-referenced testing, where the aim is to distinguish those who know from those who don't know; that is, to achieve a correct dichotomy.

The value of items in norm-referenced testing is judged in the first place by item difficulty and by item discrimination. Item difficulty is a simple matter of finding out the percentage of people in a try-out group who got the item right (see Appendix I). This is something that one also wants to know in criterion-referenced testing, but the use one makes of the information is different. In norm-referenced testing, where the primary purpose is to discriminate, one rejects items that are too easy or too difficult because these items do not contribute very much to the total discrimination. If many items were relatively easy, most of the scores would be bunched at the top end, as in the following diagram:

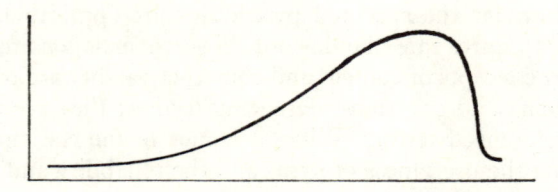

Similarly if all the questions were rather difficult, most of the scores would be bunched near the lower end.

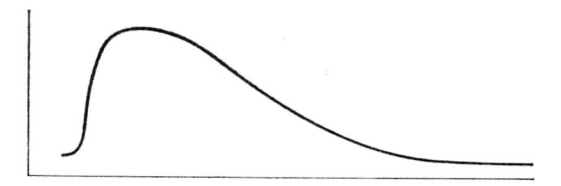

When a lot of people score within a few marks of each other, it is very difficult to make any distinctions between them.

Establishing the discrimination value of items in norm-referenced testing is a matter of comparing those individuals who succeed on a given item with those who score highly on the test as a whole. If many or most of those who score highly on the test as a whole answer a given item correctly, and many or most of those who score low on the test as a whole fail the item, then that item distinguishes between people in the same way as the total test (or subtest) does, and therefore it contributes to the desired discrimination. So, items that discriminate in the same direction as the total test are retained, those that do not are rejected. The assumption is that the test, however indifferent, is bound to be a better measure than any single item, and since it is the sum across items that is important, the procedure is entirely appropriate. But in criterion-referenced testing, since we are trying to find out whether items testing for example the *do*-construction are efficient, it is not appropriate to use the information that comes from the answer patterns on items testing *some/any*, *this/that*, negation, articles, prepositions etc. We are not interested in the global sum, but in each objective taken one by one.

Another difference between norm-referenced and criterion-referenced testing is to be found in the assumptions made about the characteristics of the population for whom the test is intended. In achievement testing, which, like mastery testing, is content based, we assume that in the population there are some who can carry out most of the operations tested, some who can do not quite so many, and so on downwards in a more or less continuous distribution. And when we draw a sample from the population we try to get one which mirrors the characteristics of the population, including the differences between the individuals. And we trust the information we get about difficulty levels and about the discrimination values that we get from the try-out group, because we believe that, within more or less narrow limits, the information is the same as we would have got from any other sample properly drawn from the population.

But for criterion-referenced testing we make different assumptions about the characteristics of the population. We assume that there are two kinds of individuals, those who can carry out an operation and those who cannot. And what we are interested in is dividing them up into two entirely separate, discontinuous groups. However, we must also accept that there is a third group of people within that population: those who are currently engaged in the process of learning to carry out the operation. And in this group there will be a continuous rather than a yes/no distribution, because even if the items were completely homogeneous, the individuals in this group would still pass some and fail others. It is the job of items in a criterion-referenced test to reflect a dichotomy. Finding the dichotomizing power of criterion-referenced items is analogous to finding the discrimination value of norm-referenced items. And while we have several ways of finding the discrimination value of norm-referenced items, there are as yet no widely known practical techniques for finding the dichotomizing powers of criterion-referenced items.

5 Tests and experiments

Although tests and experiments are most often used for giving information to the external world about what school or university leavers are supposed to be able to do, tests play a central part—or should play a central part—in any experiment on language learning processes or instructional practices. Without detailed and accurate knowledge of what actually has been learned, one cannot hope to specify those factors which lead to successful learning. This holds equally whether one is interested primarily in what the students contribute, or in what the educational system offers, or—and this is the real area of investigation—in the interaction between the two.

Teachers and educational institutions are in general very willing to try out new classroom techniques. As teachers we are all concerned with finding something which works, or works better. Good teachers are to some extent those who have found out what works for them as individuals, and for the classes that they teach. No testing apparatus is needed for this. Although it is a truism that the most important variable in teaching success is the individual teacher (ignoring for the moment the individual learner) it is also important to try to discover some generally applicable principles. It is for this purpose that reliable and valid tests are essential. Any educational research project must build in testing as an intrinsic part if it is to have any value beyond the immediate and specific situation in which it was carried out.

The problem is twofold: first, those who plan and carry out experiments must make adequate provision for the research and development of appropriate tests and, second, the administrators and teachers in the educational system where the experiment is carried out must be convinced of the crucial importance of giving ample time for testing, both before and after the experimental teaching has taken place. Many projects have been rendered trivial because the investigators did not realize the need for constructing accurate tests until too late. And quite a few have foundered because the administrators did not, when the time came, see their way to providing the necessary testing time. In particular, if the experiment is set up so that there is one group where something new and exciting is tried out, and another group which just carries on in the traditional way, and the plan calls for both groups to be tested before and after a specific period of time, it is quite remarkable how often the post-testing of the control group cannot be fitted in because of pressure of time. This ruined an experiment of my own (Ingram 1968), as it has ruined those of many others. The problem is that however much one tries to inject similar amounts of enthusiasm for each method under investigation, there is nearly always one method to which more prestige accrues. After all, most experiments are set up because somebody has a specific hypothesis they want to prove, and sufficient energy and enthusiasm to undertake the considerable amount of work which is needed.

An example of the weight which must be given to the construction of assessment tests is provided by Davies in his final report on the LAPP project (Davies 1973b). Davies directed a survey aimed at developing an aptitude test, consisting of a battery of indices for predicting success in language learning among school children in Britain. The project lasted for three years, and during this time approximately half the energy of the researchers was devoted to developing proficiency and achievement tests, i.e. tests for measuring what and how much the individual learners had managed to learn within a given period of instruction.

This was a testing project, so it is not surprising that assessment was taken seriously right from the start. What is surprising, however, is that often the organizers of large-scale experiments, involving major expenditure and huge planning efforts, appear not to have taken the measurement aspect seriously enough in the early stages. Two examples come to mind. The first is the Colorado experiment, reported by Scherer and Wertheimer (1964), the other the Pennsylvania experiment on high-school students, reported by Smith (1970). Both projects investigated current methods of language teaching viewed as packages, and both sought answers in terms of the traditional language learning skills. The Scherer and Wertheimer investigation is in my opinion largely without value, because it violated a number of basic experimental rules. For example, the allocation of students to groups was biased; the experimenters allowed the students to select which method they wanted to be taught by, and they even allowed people to change from one group to another between the first and second year. Equally grave, and more relevant to this discussion, they assumed that there were tests in existence which would suit their needs. When they found out how wrong they were, they had to scramble around trying to construct tests half-way through the project.

The designers of the Pennsylvania project paid much more careful attention to experimental design and to the necessity for testing; they were, after all, in a position to profit from the comments on the Colorado project. But even so, they found it necessary to commission a supplementary test half-way through. This was a test on sound discrimination, by Rebecca Valette; the relevant statistical information has not been published, at least not in any form accessible to me. In general, however, the experimenters relied on standard all-purpose tests. And so when they obtained a result which some people did not like, namely, that the traditional reading and translation method produced better listening comprehension than those methods which paid more attention to the spoken language, this could be explained away by the fact that the particular listening comprehension test being used demanded quite a lot of vocabulary, and so—it was argued—those classes who had done more reading had acquired more vocabulary. This, of course, might be a good argument for having learners do a lot of reading, since it seems to pay off for listening comprehension as well. But as far as the experiment is concerned, there would have been a lot to be said for specially constructed listening comprehension tests, with a controlled vocabulary.

The best strategy for investigations of this sort would seem to be to use both well-established, well-researched norm-referenced tests, and also such specially constructed tests as can be devised to answer in greater detail the questions the experiment is designed to elucidate. The custom-built tests would be constructed with particular reference to the setting of the experiment, the teaching materials used, and the particular variables the investigators wish to examine. For example, if one of the objects of an investigation is to find out the effect that varying amounts of speaking practice has on listening comprehension, one does not want to have a situation where size of vocabulary, however acquired, makes the interpretation of results uncertain. The main purpose of the established tests is to provide the validation criterion. If a specially constructed test, designed to yield very specific information, correlates highly with an established test, then the chances are that the specific test possesses a measure of pragmatic validity, in addition to whatever content or construct validity it may have.

There is another type of experiment which typically focuses on very specific educational objectives. The objectives are specified in terms of content, the teaching period is relatively short, and the numbers of students and teachers involved are much smaller. An extreme example of this is provided by Oller and Obrecht (1969). The material consisted of two sets of four elementary sentences in Spanish. One set was arranged in a natural conversational sequence, the sentences of the other set had no internal cohesion. There were 22 learners. The two sets of sentences were:

Set A	*Set B*
¿Cómo está?	¿Qué es esto?
Estoy bien.	Voy después.
¿Y usted?	¿Quien es?
Muy bien.	Pues voy.

Clearly, in this situation there is no question of sampling the material and so no question of testing in the usual sense. Learning is measured by asking the subjects to reproduce the full text, and then counting errors and omissions. Text A, in which the material was arranged in natural conversational sequence, proved easier to learn.

A more typical example of the kind of experiment which concerns specified educational objectives, rather than broad over-all skills, is the one reported by von Elek and Oskarson (1972). This experiment set out to investigate the role of grammatical explanation in the teaching of grammatical structures of English to adult students. The experimenters chose five 'structural objectives': some/any, adjective/adverb formation, preposition followed by -ing form, possessive pronouns, and passives. These were taught during ten sessions, in the middle of an ongoing course of 60 sessions. In addition to the ten teaching sessions, no less than four sessions for pre-testing and six for post-testing were provided, making ten testing sessions in all. This emphasis on testing is quite unusual but it is what makes the experiment valuable. The investigators used both standardized and specially constructed tests: standard tests rather than the equally useful random allocation method to sort the students into two groups of comparable ability, and specially written tests to assess (a) the general English proficiency of the students, and (b) the students' skill in handling the five chosen structural objectives. The authors do not give much information in the paper about the test construction processes, but as the experiment was carried out under the auspices of GUME (Lindblad 1969), it is virtually certain that the standard statistical procedures appropriate to norm-referenced testing were carried out.

In experiments of this type, with closely specified educational objectives, criterion-referenced tests could be a valuable addition to the currently used norm-referenced tests. But until we have developed more sophisticated techniques for evaluating criterion-referenced tests, it is unlikely that they will contribute much to the experimental design.

6 Practical work

Study the following questions and answer 'Yes' or 'No'.

Sections 1 and 2
 1 Written examinations were introduced because oral examinations were found not to be valid.

2 'Objective' tests were introduced because it was found that traditional examining techniques lacked reliability.
3 Because of their format, objective tests can be assumed to possess reliability and validity.

Section 2

4 The ordinal scale of measurement is used when we want to rank people as first, second, third, etc., in respect of some characteristic like height or command of a foreign language.
5 When we are measuring on the equal interval scale, the mean is the appropriate statistic for expressing the central tendency of a collection of data.
6 If we can find the right statistical method, this can do a lot to compensate for lack of rigour in collecting information.

Section 3·1

7 Tests, unlike examinations, give accurate information about a student's abilities.
8 By eliminating marker variability, validity is ensured.
9 A more efficient test should always be used in preference to a less powerful one.
10 When a statistical technique is said to be robust, this means that it is a rough and ready sort of test, to be used if nothing better can be found.
11 A measuring device is reliable only to the extent that any variation in the readings represents a true variation in the individuals measured.
12 Some people are more variable in their performance than others. This has the effect of reducing reliability estimates.
13 Some test tasks are more vulnerable to inconsistent behaviour than others. This means that one should avoid testing such tasks.

Section 3·2

14 If a testing procedure has *a priori* validity, it is superfluous to examine pragmatic validity.
15 One of the most useful criteria for estimating validity is the judgement of experienced teachers.
16 The problem with ultimate validity is that good operational definitions are hard to establish.

Section 3·3

17 The value of correlation coefficients varies between $+1$ and -1. In order to get a correlation of $+1$ two sets of scores must be identical.
18 In order to predict accurately from one set of scores to another, the correlation must be very high.
19 In a good test, subtests correlate very highly with each other.

Basic Concepts in Testing

Section 4

20 Until very recently nearly all tests were norm-referenced.
    (a) In norm-referenced tests an individual is compared with other individuals.
    (b) In criterion-referenced testing an individual is rated with respect to a particular objective.
21 Construct and content validity have only marginal relevance in criterion-referenced testing.
22 Items that are too easy or too difficult are usually rejected both in norm-referenced and criterion-referenced testing.

Section 5

23 The informal trying out of procedures in the classroom has no value.
24 Making adequate provision for assessment is vitally important in all educational experiments.
25 Among the many published tests available we can usually find one suited to a particular experiment.

3 ALAN DAVIES
The Construction of Language Tests

1 Introduction

A good deal of thought and work has gone into language testing materials in the last fifteen years or so, influencing and being influenced by the so-called revolution in language teaching. It has long been a truism in language study as in other school subjects that the examination often dictates what is taught; it has also been realized by many teachers that some method of evaluation is necessary in order to establish goals and check progress. Both these ideas have served to change and to streamline examinations. The first has led to the realization that it is no good throwing out translation as part of the curriculum unless at the same time some other method of testing is incorporated in the examination, and the second to the realization that it may well be necessary to spend rather longer preparing test materials, trying them out and ensuring that the items they contain 'work'. This has led, on the one hand, to a greater interest in the matching of one examiner's marks with another's, perhaps by getting a variety of impression marks of an essay; and on the other hand to a feeling that the kind of information that the translation or the essay or the oral have always been intended to provide may be more accurately obtained by spending longer on the preparation beforehand and less on the 'standardizing' afterwards.

Language study seems an obvious candidate for this kind of change. Progress is, or appears to be, inevitable; the student starts at zero and progresses until he has become fluent. This is, on the face of it, easier to describe and to assess than, say, the somewhat artificial target we assume for the study of physics or English literature, where there is no obvious way of deciding what should come before what, and no time when it can be said to the student: 'You can stop learning now because you know physics or English literature'. In language study we know what we mean by a fluent speaker and we know what we mean by a beginner. For example, I am a fluent speaker of English because it is my first language, and I am a beginner in Thai because I have never seen any Thai written down and never heard any Thai spoken.

But this apparent suitability of language study for curriculum arrangement and for ease of obtaining results is really an illusion. Although we know very well what we mean by a fluent speaker, it is by no means easy to say what it is that he possesses which we wish to learn or teach. Is it a body of knowledge which can be summarized in a book?—Presumably not. Is it a set of behaviour patterns?—Well, perhaps, but can we list the set exhaustively? Is it certain patterns in certain situations?—Perhaps, but again, how can we decide what are the appropriate situations? We accept that a knowledge of physics is implied in the remembering and comprehension of a set of materials in a physics textbook. There is, in other words, no native performer in physics as there is in English or in Thai. What is more, the grading or sequencing of language learning is equally illusory. Is there any reason why one item or language feature, say the verb *be* plus complement or the modal *can* should come before *have* or *belong*; or the present tense before the past? We impose this arrangement on the language because of our own assumptions of difficulty and order. It has been suggested that current investigations into first language acquisition will be of direct relevance to the problem of ordering materials and presentation in second language teaching; but this may well be another illusion because it is again an assumption that a second language is learned in the same way as a first language.

The implications of what we have said so far for language testing are as follows. At first sight it may appear to be easier in language than in physics to say to a student 'Now you know this subject'. In fact it is not so easy; it is more difficult in language than in physics to devise suitable tests of proficiency which are intended to establish degrees of control in the subject. This difficulty is felt both at the intermediate stages and at the terminal stage. As will be argued later, the difficulty in the intermediate stages is more a problem for the materials than for the tests since the arrangement of the materials is based on assumptions about the sequence of learning, and the intermediate tests accept these assumptions and are based on the teaching materials. But the test at the terminal stage has to make the further assumption independent of the teaching materials that performance in the test is directly relevant to proficiency in the language whether or not the materials are equally relevant. At the terminal stage, then, the tester has the crucial problem not only of testing learning of the materials, which may of course be of many kinds, but also of giving some indication of the 'validity' of these materials. For this purpose he needs some criterion outside the materials themselves; such a criterion is difficult to establish and here we come back to our original point about the difference between learning physics and learning a language. For physics we can say that this student now knows enough physics to enable him to do postgraduate research, but we have no such obvious criterion for adequacy of performance in language.

The purpose of this chapter is to set out this argument in some detail; to discuss an approach to language testing which gives it a central role in teaching; and to suggest ways in which the teacher may set about constructing

tests. But first it seems necessary to set out some of the views on
that have influenced teaching and inevitably testing as well. The
ews of language' are rarely found in an extreme form, but for the sake
icity we shall refer to them as the traditional, the structural and the
mational view, and we shall discuss them here as if they can be
differentiated from one another.

group who hold the traditional view see language as a thing in itself.
ge exists primarily in the form of texts and there is little interest in
ken language. Teaching is by the grammar translation method and
e student is expected to do is to translate in a 'literary' manner. Test-
ows the teaching and typically involves translation, lists of vocabulary
nd inflections of nouns and verbs. The position outlined here involves
l-known tendency to accord exaggerated respect to classical languages,
'great literature of the past', which has carried over into both foreign
ge and mother tongue teaching. The associated linguistic theory is
onalist and since little attention is paid to the needs of the learner there
sychological theory involved.

group who hold the structural view see language as a kind of machine
acts as a stimulus-response mechanism. Learning, according to this
consists of conditioned responses to the environment. But since a
ne goes on under its own momentum it provides its own environment;
is no need to look to the world outside for meaning. This view, then,
tempted to discuss language without recourse to meaning. Linguistic
sis proceeds, at least in theory, from sound to sentence and it has some-
been assumed that learning proceeds in this way too. According to
iew, in order to teach a language we must analyse it into its constituent
or structures. Concepts such as 'structural drill', 'pattern practice', and
udio-lingual method' have been associated with this approach. Learning
l to take place by generalization on the basis of the learned responses.
view is in linguistic terms structuralist and in psychological terms
iourist. Testing follows by providing dialogues for completion, sentences
gaps which have to be filled in, and multiple choice items where the
ct answer has to be selected from a number of possibilities.

e group who hold the transformational view see language as creative
ule-based. Language and learning are interdependent because no-one
tops learning his own language. The linguistic theory involved tends to
from Chomsky's work in transformational grammar and the psycho-
l theory is cognitive. Attempts to relate this view to language teaching
so far been rather tentative. But the implications for language teaching
r-reaching: first, that cognition is central, hence the importance given
aning-based instruction, realized in notional syllabuses; second, that
ep structure relationship between sentences which may differ consider-
n surface structure should be made explicit; and third, that there is a

need for grammatical explanation which may often involve the presentation of further examples.

As far as testing is concerned we can sum up the three approaches by suggesting a representative test for each of the three views of language: for the first, an essay; for the second, a set of multiple choice responses to spoken stimuli, the responses being written; for the third, a problem of some kind which demands a solution, spoken or written, and which will force the student to make language connections that may not be automatic. As for test presentation, the typical essay is an open-ended task, and a decision has to be made after the student has taken the test as to what is right, what wrong and what partially wrong. In the typical multiple choice question someone has already worked out what is to be accepted as right before the student takes the test. In devising a problem we may well try to combine the freshness and open-endedness of the essay and at the same time decide what are a number of possible right answers.

What is being suggested here is that there is a connection, not necessarily causal, which links the linguistic and psychological theories current at any one time with the teaching and testing which follow on from these theories. Of course there are time lags and many overlaps so that it is possible for the good teacher to select bits from all these different views and to incorporate them into a satisfactory whole. The sections which follow do not attempt to maintain any one of the three views of language; but it is hoped that enough has been said for the reader to make the necessary links with the different linguistic and psychological schools. A good deal of what is said will be seen to stem from the structuralist approach as far as testing is concerned. However, we will attempt to take situation rather more into account, to give proper due to the traditionalist approach, and to look forward to the problem type of language test.

The plan of the chapter is as follows: sections 2, 3, 4 and 5 discuss the more theoretical considerations, section 6 the more practical ones. Thus in section 2 the aims of testing are discussed together with the kind of information to be expected from a test. In section 3 various kinds and uses of test are described and a distinction made between examinations and tests. In section 4 there is a discussion of the demands made on language tests, the standards, internal and external, which they must match up to. A language test analysis follows in section 5. Finally, section 6 discusses the practical application in terms of item writing for teachers.

2 Aims and purposes of testing

2.1 Research

The first aim of language testing is that of research. Whether mother tongue or second language situations are being considered, whether the research is being conducted among the orderly surroundings of the laboratory or in natural settings, tests will at some point be necessary to check on the learning that has taken place so far. Whether it is theories of learning or theories of language, methods of teaching or teaching materials that are being investigated, at some point it will almost certainly be necessary to compare 'experimental' and 'control' conditions in order to examine one's research hypothesis. For this purpose it will be necessary to characterize or identify the two approaches, the new and the old, in some way. Tests are useful and necessary ways of doing this. Language tests, then, must be seen first as tools of research in experimental work in education.

2.2 Progress

Most language teachers are not likely to be involved in full-scale research work. This is true both of the teachers within one school and of the teachers in a total educational system. Tests or examinations (for the distinction between these see below 4.2) are just as necessary but for a different reason. The point of a test in research is to compare materials, methods etc., with the possibility of changing them; the point of tests with a progress aim is to compare pupils not with one another but with an already determined standard. This is the ideal aim; in practice pupils are often compared with one another and the already determined standard is a fiction. However, whatever faults there may be in the use of tests to measure progress the need for them is clear and the procedure well known and well understood. All teachers want to know how their pupils are getting on, and to have some idea of whether what they have been taught has been learned.

It would seem wise to take a fairly common sense and liberal approach to tests for progress and to include all kinds of test methods. Thus the whole range from the final degree examination, lasting several days or weeks right down to 'What is the meaning of *professeur*?', or 'Which tense should we use here?' are all progress tests, inasmuch as the teacher or examiner wishes to assess how far learners have gone.

2.3 Guide to curriculum

In education all language tests and examinations exert an influence on the curriculum and on the teaching. This wash-back effect is often bemoaned by teachers, but if we accept that exams are unavoidable, then we should at least try to ensure that the exams are good ones. We should try to ensure that the wash-back is beneficial and that far from stultifying the curriculum and petrifying the teaching, exams give students a real sense of purpose by describing exactly where they are meant to be going. A closely detailed and wide ranging syllabus is an essential partner of a good exam which itself needs to be illustrative of tried and defined proficiency levels (see 2.4). Current practice, however, does not always acknowledge this partnership. One traditional method is to provide no syllabus at all, but simply to make vague announcements: e.g. 'There will be a translation into French/a summary/an oral interview/an essay', etc. This is no help at all; it is as bad as saying: 'Learn French'. What the teacher wants to know is whose French, how much, what sort, and so on. A second traditional method is to 'teach the child not the subject', where the teacher is expected to provide variation in his syllabus sufficient to meet the needs and interests of every single child. This may work for skilled and gifted teachers, not for the ordinary teacher whose job is a job and not a vocation. A third traditional method is based on the idea of 'teaching through experience of France and the French'. This method is fine, especially in the hands of very good teachers, but it depends on a close relationship between the experience that is taught in the classroom and expectations as to what the pupil will actually be able to do when the teaching is over. This leads on to the fourth aim.

2.4 Representing terminal behaviour

The point of learning a language is to gain control of some kind over that language. Since the kind of control projected will presumably be over performance, however limited (and it could be argued that anything less is not worth having) then the terminal behaviour aimed at is performance, i.e., such and such control in such and such situations. But what does this mean? Some realization of so vague a notion is needed if syllabus and teaching are to receive the definition they need. A test, then, whether along the way or at the final stage of language learning, is a representation in actual terms of these vague notions of terminal behaviour. It stands in their place and at the same time acts as an adequate sample of them. The universe of discourse postulated for the learner's control is too vast ever to be completely tested. The test samples the situations, the items and the features which the learner should have grasped. Of course, the adequacy of the test itself in its sampling is another problem, and a serious one. This is a problem of validity and will be dealt with later (see section 5.2).

3 The influence of programmed instruction

Programmed instruction, involving an analytic step-by-step procedure and constant overt knowledge of success deserves to be used more widely. Whether language teaching makes much use of teaching machines or of programmed textbooks it will always have the advantage over other types of teaching of being able to make use of the language laboratory. The incremental step-by-step nature of such teaching/learning is central whether we are using a teaching machine, a textbook or a language laboratory; so is the validity of the teaching/learning in the sense that the method has been tried out sufficiently to show that it works. The step-by-step procedure may involve reinforcement by the presentation of correct responses in a special frame, on a certain page, etc. Doubts have been cast on the need actually to show such answers. What is perfectly clear is that whether responses are shown or not the reinforcement, the knowledge of success, is built into a good programme by its analysis of content into steps and by the experimental try-out and consequent item analysis. Thus the content of what is to be taught and its presentation have been incorporated into a form of self-tuition. In this sense progress in learning is being tested from step to step, so that while mastery of each step is ensured, incremental learning is tested at each step. Each step is, from this point of view, both teaching and testing at the same time. Mastery over the content of a programme is thus insured by going through it; there is no need to test for learning afterwards. It may, of course, be necessary to test for retention. It may also be useful to get students to write in responses to each frame, to ensure that they have worked at the programme right through.

What is being suggested here is that programmed instruction has radical implications for testing, and that since each frame is a test in miniature the need for after-testing (what we will call achievement testing) decreases. This is, of course, admirable. Testing is not an end in itself; its essential aim is to provide information which will help us to make intelligent decisions about possible courses of action (Carroll 1961:31). The more testing and teaching can be integrated and the less the ostensible demands of the external test or exam, the better for learning.

4 Types of test

4.1 Uses of tests

There was at one time a fashion in educational psychology to group human abilities in various ways, either together as one general ability, or into clusters belonging together, as group abilities, or into quite separate special abilities. Language enters into very many activities and it may best be seen as a group ability or a special ability, although some would see it as equivalent in status to general intelligence. The fact is, of course, that where language does enter into other abilities it may well be indistinguishable from intelligence. For present purposes what matters is language as a special ability since we are concerned with various types of control over language (especially second languages) and how to evaluate them. Naturally there is no clear-cut division between language as a special ability and language as it enters into other abilities and so it must be remembered that although we speak of language as a special ability no assumption is made about its isolation from other abilities and activities. Often enough it is only in the other activities that language can be observed. As a skill it may be said to exist for these other activities. But we call it a special ability because as far as possible we wish to separate it from those activities in which it plays a part.

Language tests may be distinguished in different ways. We shall use three taxonomies and the first is that of *use*. At this point the reader should be warned that not all writers use the same terms, and even when the same terms are used by different writers they do not always mean the same thing. For example, 'aptitude' will be used here where other writers may prefer 'proficiency'.

Four uses may be distinguished: achievement, proficiency, aptitude, diagnostic. These uses, since they refer to types of control may, in themselves, be regarded as special abilities.

4.1.1 THE FOUR USES

The four uses are distinguished firstly in terms of time (past and future) and secondly in terms of subject matter. Thus, if we use a left-pointing arrow to represent past time and a right-pointing arrow to represent future time, and if X is the point at which the test is taken, then we may symbolize the differences as in Figure 1:

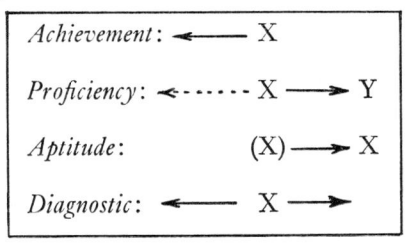

```
Achievement:  ←——— X
Proficiency:  ←·····X ———→ Y
Aptitude:            (X) ———→ X
Diagnostic:   ←——— X ———→
```

Figure 1

Achievement

Achievement or attainment tests are concerned with assessing what has been learned of a known syllabus. This may be within a school or within a total educational system. Thus the typical external school examinations ('Ordinary' level or 'Advanced' level in England, 'Highers' in Scotland), the university degree exams and so on are all examples of achievement tests. The use being made of the measure is to find out just how much has been learned of what has been taught (i.e., of the syllabus). Achievement type tests end there. Although the primary interest is in the past, i.e. what has been learned, very often some further use is made of the same test in order to make meaningful decisions about the pupils' future. It would, presumably, be possible to be interested entirely in the past of the pupils; Carroll's 'meaningful decisions' then would refer to the syllabus, i.e., to any necessary alterations to it that might be necessary or to the teaching method to be used for the next group of students. But achievement tests are almost always used for other purposes as well. It is important to recognize this and to account for it in one's test construction. But, as will be maintained later under validity, this is essentially a function of the syllabus. All that an achievement test can do is to indicate how much of a syllabus has been learned; it cannot make predictions as to pupils' future performance unless the syllabus has been deliberately designed for this purpose.

Proficiency

Proficiency tests, as we see it, are concerned with assessing what has been learned of a known or an unknown syllabus, hence the broken arrow in Figure 1. Here we see the distinction between proficiency and achievement. In the non-language field we might consider, say, a driving test as a kind of proficiency test since there is the desire to apply a common standard to all who present themselves whatever their previous driving experience, over which of course there has been no control at all. In the language field there are several well-known proficiency exams and tests of the same journeyman kind: the Cambridge Proficiency Exams, the Michigan Tests, the Test of English as a Foreign Language (TOEFL) and English Proficiency Test Battery (EPTB). These all imply that a common standard is being applied to all comers. More sophisticated proficiency tests (sophisticated in use, not in design) may be constructed as research tools to determine just how much control over a language is needed for certain purposes, for example medical studies in a second language.

If proficiency tests differ from achievement tests with regard to uncertainty about previous instruction, it is in their relation to future needs or control purposes that they are distinguished from aptitude tests. Some writers do not make this distinction. However it seems a useful distinction to make, and one we shall elaborate below in the section on aptitude. Here we will only say that proficiency in a language implies adequate control over language skills for an extralinguistic purpose.

Aptitude

Aptitude tests assess proficiency in language for language use. This is how we distinguish them from proficiency tests. Hence, in Figure 1 the arrow relates the language test under proficiency to something else (Y), and under aptitude to itself (X). Thus, as we have suggested above, we can think of a proficiency test as assessing adequacy of control in a second language for studying other things through the medium of that language. An aptitude test is generally conceived of as assessing the amount of linguistic skill needed for learning languages. Generally speaking, this will mean for learning a particular language. A number of problems, of course, arise: is it just linguistic skill that is involved; if so, what is linguistic skill? It is here that considerable research is needed. Presumably it is not just linguistic skill that we are concerned with. What an aptitude test should incorporate is that area of skill which may be termed linguistic and which is separate from the other obvious factors such as intelligence, motivation, and the whole teaching situation. It may be that once these factors are accounted for then nothing is left; hence the need for research.

In Figure 1 we have represented the aptitude test as (X), in brackets. We know where the arrow leads—to proficiency; and so in aptitude research we must set up our goals first. We must decide what is meant by particular language proficiency or accept ready-made goals which are commonly used in an educational system, for example external school exams, 'O' level and the rest. The proficiency measure is the criterion. But what is not known is how this may be predicted, for example how success in learning, say, Chinese may be predicted before any Chinese has been learned. Naturally, except with very young children, there is always the mother-tongue to fall back on. But it does seem that even if the mother-tongue is used for predicting success in foreign language learning, here is an important area for research, inasmuch as it will serve to break down into component parts those skills in present linguistic control which relate to future control. If in fact that can be done, then it seems immaterial that it is being reached through the medium of the mother-tongue. The importance of work on aptitude is not so much to predict future successful learners as to indicate what is fundamentally involved in language learning.

The distinction we have drawn between proficiency and aptitude may not always be a real one. Is a pilot's proficiency test really an aptitude test? Such a proficiency test could be looked on as a battery of aptitude tests (e.g., manual dexterity, sensitivity to lights, etc.) which together have been shown to predict performance as a pilot. But in language terms it seems sensible to make this distinction and to think of the proficiency test as facing both ways, as taking place at some point after learning has started, and as relating to future non-language performance. An aptitude test, in these terms, is concerned with inherent aptitude for language learning.

Diagnostic

The diagnostic use differs from the others in that it relates to the use of the information obtained and to the absence of a skill in the learner. Achievement, proficiency and aptitude are all concerned with both use and skill. A diagnostic test is a use made by a teacher of the information provided from the presence or absence of part of one of the skills. A diagnostic test may be constructed for itself or it may be an additional use made of an achievement or proficiency test. If it is specially constructed it could perhaps be argued that some element of learner's skill, or rather absence of skill, is involved because the tester is concerned with discovering what might be termed non-achievement.

Like the proficiency test, a diagnostic test may look before and after; before to find out what is wrong with the previous learning, after in order to do something about it in the form of remedial work.

An alternative name for a diagnostic test might well be a non-achievement test. Just as the achievement test is built on a sampling of the syllabus that has been taught, so the diagnostic test is built out of what experience or present evidence suggests has not been learned. It may be exploratory in that it sets out to predict the occurrence of error, based either on syllabus content like an achievement test, or on the content of some language description which indicates certain points of contrast or interference between the mother-tongue and the second language being learned. If the language description is satisfactory the syllabus content will certainly relate to it. Once such exploratory work has been done and the likely errors uncovered, future diagnostic tests can be, at least partly, made up out of expected errors. We say 'at least partly' because there is a danger in such 'error analysis' work in that it may concentrate on language interference and ignore learning problems of other kinds. An approach based partly on syllabus content—where the syllabus is related to future needs as well as to interference—avoids this danger.

4.1.2 SUMMARY

We have been discussing some of the uses of language tests. They can be distinguished, as we have suggested, in two main ways, in their connection with a known syllabus and in their relation to the time scale. An achievement test has a known syllabus and concerns the past; an aptitude test has no past[1] and concerns the future. Proficiency and diagnostic tests both concern the past and may or may not refer to a known syllabus. Both types of test relate to the future — a proficiency test, unlike an aptitude test, to the use of language to undertake a non-language task; a diagnostic test, like an aptitude test, to language performance itself.

But if these are distinct *uses* they do not necessarily imply distinct tests. The same test could very well be used for achievement and diagnosis; if it is based on a 'favoured' syllabus then it could be used for proficiency also. By 'favoured' here is meant a proven satisfactory course which not all students will necessarily have followed. In practice what starts off as a proficiency test often ends up as an acheivement test, simply because particular teaching-groups may adapt in preparing themselves for their 'proficiency' test, which then becomes their 'achievement' test. If this all-purpose test is given very early on in a language course, say at the end of three or six months in a school course, then it could also be used for aptitude purposes if any predictions are made as to likely future language learning success. A use then is not a test:

[1] Except, of course, that it must relate to the learner's previous experience, but that is not the point here.

it may (as aptitude almost always will) need a separate instrument, but not necessarily so. What matters above all is that the user should be fully aware of his purposes.

4.2 Examinations and tests

Another way of looking at language tests is to make some attempt to resolve the test/exam distinction. How does a test differ, if at all, from an examination? The notion of test conjures up vague ideas of psychology and of intelligence whereas an exam suggests the end-of-term multi-subject ordeal. Is a test more objective, more reliable, more specific, more realistic than an exam? We shall try to show that it is all these but that an exam may have an advantage in its influence over the curriculum. We shall also suggest that while these distinctions should be taken into account there is no reason at all why an exam should not incorporate whatever virtues a test may have.

In common usage the terms 'test' and 'exam' are often used synonymously. The famous 'eleven plus' test in the United Kingdom was sometimes called an exam; and all school children are well acquainted with class tests which occur once every week or fortnight and so on. Typically the examination is a more full dress affair than the test: thus we talk about the 'O' level exam, the end of year exam in school, and the university degree exam. Also the examination is, in our terms, usually concerned with achievement; not always, though—the university scholarship examination is more a proficiency or even an aptitude type test. And the type of achievement test referred to above is certainly not most clearly seen as an examination.

One simple solution would be to make the term *examination* refer to the whole area of language measurement and the term *test* to a specialized part within it, so that a test would be seen as a kind of examination. But since this is not how the terms are used and since specific examples of the two types are sometimes so different that they cannot be drawn together, what we shall do is to look at four levels and suggest ways in which examinations and tests are becoming more similar to one another.

4.2.1 EXAMINATION/TEST LEVELS

We are suggesting four levels; no suggestion is made as to hierarchy:

1. Examinations (traditional)
2. Ad hoc tests (teacher made)
3. Standardized tests
4. Examinations (new type)

We shall make a start with standardized tests since it is in relation to them that we wish to consider the others, and it is because of them that much of the testing mystique has arisen.

4.2.2 STANDARDIZED TESTS

A standardized test is objective; by this is meant that it has been tried out on a proper sample of the population for whom it is intended and that on this sample it has been shown to work, i.e., it is both reliable and valid. Most tests of this type are made up of items each of which is discrete in itself and has been shown to contribute towards the total performance of the test. As well as being objective a standardized language test will rest on some adequate linguistic basis, that is, according to its use, it will be made up of items which are linguistically meaningful. So a standardized language test has two qualities: it is psychometrically objective and it is linguistically realistic. Of course it may be argued that the second point is subsumed in the first, since under objectivity we have already mentioned validity, and presumably by validity is meant linguistic validity of some kind. In the achievement test situation objectivity would be sufficient since the syllabus is assumed to be linguistically realistic. We are thinking more now of proficiency and perhaps aptitude tests. Here the objective validity and psychometric quality relates to the linguistic content of the syllabus (which itself should embody an acceptable theory of language). That is to say, in the proficiency situation the proficiency test must, as it were, assume its own syllabus (this is its content or linguistic rationale) and it must also make itself objective on the basis of this syllabus.

There is a further problem about objectivity: if a test is objective does this mean that all the items must be objective too? Does it mean that the essay, for example, cannot be used in an objective test? All items, since all must contribute to the test, must be objective. This does not necessarily mean that the objectivity must be incorporated in the form of multiple-choice answers, but many items will be multiple choice because it is easier to design a test in this way, and because the analysis of trial items will have shown whether they work. But the essay type question is not precluded. The essay is best seen as a type of open-ended question; it is possible to administer such questions and then attempt objectivity in their scoring. This is more difficult than the multiple choice method; it introduces a further source of unreliability, that of examiner unreliability. However, research has shown that even in essay type questions examiner unreliability can be accounted for. A diagram may show the connections between objective and subjective type questions:

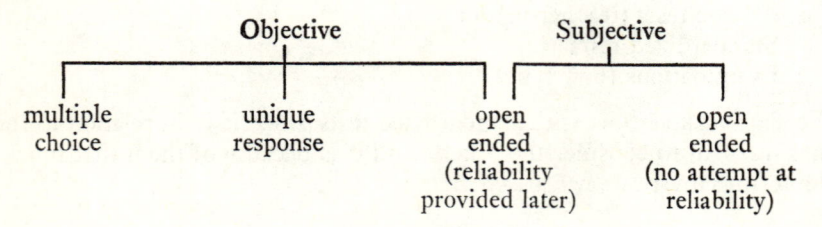

```
                    Objective                         Subjective
         ┌──────────────┬──────────────┐         ┌──────────────┐
    multiple        unique          open                    open
    choice          response        ended                   ended
                                    (reliability            (no attempt at
                                    provided later)         reliability)
```

The problem of a language proficiency test which is to be widely used in education is that reliability and validity are inextricably intertwined. That is to say, as reliability is raised by objectivizing through, for example, the use of multiple-choice questions, so validity is lowered because of the influence on the classroom; and this happens for two reasons. First, some skills, which cannot be reliably tested, are very often bypassed: examples are oral production and continuous writing (e.g., the essay). Second, the influence of the objective item test is to force the teaching which necessarily precedes the test into practising such items. As we have seen above, this becomes a problem when a proficiency test is looked on as an achievement test. But if standardized test techniques are introduced into educational examining then it is essential to prevent the deterioration of real validity, i.e., to ensure that all the meaningful skills are included and that the teaching does not become item practice of another sort. One argument against the traditional exam is that it gave no help other than itself as a syllabus model; if standardized tests influence the new types of exam they must do much more than this. To say that a test is valid is no answer to critics of this kind if what they mean is that they do not like the educational aims that such validity imposes on them.

4.2.3 AD HOC TESTS

These are quickly dealt with. All that is meant by ad hoc tests is those tests which any teacher may wish to construct and use himself in his own teaching. Since he is generally concerned with a whole 'population' and not with just a sample (i.e., his 'population' is his class and he is not concerned to generalize from it) he is not concerned so much with item analysis, but he is concerned with reliability and validity. The latter he will know about; he will obviously be concerned to test what he has taught and he will not make use of any special techniques of testing (e.g., multiple-choice items) unless he can cope with their backwash in the teaching. But he should also take reliability into account by using techniques likely to provide reliable results within his own orbit of validity. The more the test approaches the nature of a standardized test (while, of course, remaining under his control) the better for him it will be. What the designer of ad hoc tests can learn from standardized tests is, first, the importance of reliability, second the value of item discreteness, and third the importance of a thorough linguistic analysis of the content to be sampled for the test.

Teachers have always made use of such tests. They have always made use of versions within their own classrooms of standardized tests. Such tests may be more readily accepted if teachers agree that they are nothing more than generalizations based on the experience of a large number of teachers.

4.2.4 TRADITIONAL EXAMINATIONS

In the past, a typical foreign language examination consisted of various types of exercise such as comprehension of passages in the foreign language, translation from (and sometimes into) the foreign language, an essay in the foreign language. These were, of course, all reading/writing tests. There might also be an 'oral' examination of some kind given either by a visiting examiner or by the candidates' own teacher.

What is notable about such an examination from the testing point of view, and in terms of the criteria we have been discussing, is not that it lacks initial objectivity (all exams do) but that it lacks linguistic realism in terms of current attitudes to language learning. If languages are learned in order to be spoken (though of course they are also learned to be read) then the teaching must emphasize this. But so it does: or is supposed to do. It is the traditional examination which seems to be out of line in that it over-emphasizes certain skills at the expense of others. There are, of course, other kinds of doubts about translation and about essay writing. Here there are three arguments: (a) the purpose of language learning has changed from entirely reading to mainly speaking; (b) translation in any case (whether the purpose has changed or not) is a specialized kind of exercise and perhaps best not tested in this way; (c) essay writing needs special care in order to be reliable as a test of the written language. These are all kinds of validity argument. What must be stressed here is that the traditional examination was highly valid as a test of what was once regarded as the sole purpose of language teaching.

4.2.5 NEW TYPES OF EXAMINATION

The distinction between traditional examinations and 'new type' examinations is, of course, an artificial one. Two distinct types do not exist and no one sets out to construct a traditional examination. However, there are signs that a new kind of examination is certainly emerging. The new type of exam is characterized first by its approximation to the standardized test, i.e. by its attempt to build in psychometric objectivity and linguistic realism; and second by its attempt to work with detailed reference to a syllabus. This second feature is the clear answer to the problem of a proficiency test having to assume its own syllabus for which it then becomes a kind of achievement test. What is needed is for aim, syllabus and examination to be blended in together, for the exam to relate to the content of the agreed syllabus so that, in fact, it is possible for a test-like exam to retain its achievement use. Apart from this most important feature the special characteristics of the new type of exam are seen in its attempts to incorporate testing strategy. An example based on an Alternative French 'O' Grade Examination designed by the Scottish Education Department in the 1960s may make this more clear:

Traditional type	New type
1. Aural comprehension with open-ended questions	1. Oral reading
2. Reading comprehension with open-ended questions in English	2. Responses to questions in French (open-ended)
3. Translation: French into English	3. Oral comprehension based on pictures (open-ended)
4. Reading comprehension with open-ended questions in French	4. Aural comprehension based on four voices (open-ended)
5. French essay	5. Reading comprehension

Figure 2

As Figure 2 shows, the new type of examination abandons the essay and the translation, and omits the oral interview. It retains only one sub-test similar to the traditional exam, the reading comprehension. The other four are all concerned with the spoken language and all are recorded on tape for later scoring. The first is a general assessment of reading aloud; the second is an attempt to simulate a question-answer situation in which candidates must respond in French to questions in French; the third provides an opportunity for structured oral composition with pictures used as stimuli; the fourth simulates a conversation situation with several voices after which the candidate must show that he has comprehended what he has heard.

The characteristics, we have suggested, of the new exams are that they bring in testing strategy (objectivity and realism) and that they align themselves to a syllabus, which is another way of saying that they demonstrate in detail their linguistic realism. So far as I know neither of the exam types set out in Figure 2 has a detailed syllabus associated with it. However, this is a lack which is more apparent in the traditional type than in the new type. Both should have a syllabus: but what the new type has done is at least to look at the needs of the pupil and the ways in which the schools are setting out to meet them; it has attempted, in fact, to be linguistically realistic. The traditional exam was 80 per cent reading/writing; the new type is 80 per cent speaking/listening. Why? Because it is assumed now that these skills are more suitable for the learner to control; and, in fact, it is on these, more and more, that some schools concentrate. This is not true of all schools, however, and it should be emphasized that the new type of exam remains an alternative which schools are free to adopt or reject as they see fit. The new type may not provide a syllabus; but it does test what seems to be necessary. We would claim, therefore, that it is linguistically realistic and likely to be beneficial in its effect on the educational system.

But what of the objectivity of the new exam? If it is linguistically realistic then it must have some objectivity, i.e. it must be at least partially valid. All its items are open-ended: objectivity of one kind of reliability can be built in after the test has been taken. Each tape was heard at first by two or more trained examiners in the pilot experiment. Later on only one examiner scored each tape; by then, of course, they had had plenty of practice. But there are two remaining sources of unreliability: the usual problem of examiner unreliability which we see in the marking of written essays, and the more specifically spoken language problem where different examiners often cannot agree on what they have heard or on what response is expected of them. It is hard to find fault with so serious an attempt to meet all demands. The only criticism we would make on the theoretical side is that of doubtful reliability: this, as we have suggested, may be unavoidable in order to retain validity. But there seems no reason why at least some of the items should not be constructed with multiple choice responses. Even if half the items were constructed on this basis it would go a long way to meeting the problem of reliability without interfering with validity through washback in the schools.

This particular 'new type' exam was widely tried out experimentally and its items and mark scheme altered accordingly. A statistical analysis of the results was made. Here again there is a serious attempt at objectivity. Generally speaking, the new types of exam go a long way towards answering language learning needs and towards meeting the criticisms of the traditional exams. Whether or not such a sophisticated instrument is practical or not is another matter which we shall take up below.

4.3 Levels and skills

A third taxonomy of types of test, and the one most perhaps in common use, is division by level and by skill. Thus we speak of oral and aural (or listening) tests; of reading tests and writing tests: tests, in short, of anything which is itself simply because it is not something else. Other terms included in this category are grammar, reading (and listening) comprehension, and reading speed. It should be pointed out that while comprehension refers to a skill, grammar belongs to linguistic theory: the appropriate skill might be grammatical sensitivity. We shall not attempt a detailed analysis here since we shall set out a matrix with many entries later on (see p. 72). Our purpose at this point is merely to demonstrate that the naming of exercises is another way of considering different types of test.

5 Demands on language tests

5.1 Test criteria

From this point on no attempt will be made to distinguish between tests and exams, that is to say we shall use the terms 'tests' and 'testing' to refer both to tests and to the new types of exams.

Any large-scale testing operation is bound to influence very widely the educational system into which it is introduced. Except for the research use there are a number of criteria which must be met before accepting a particular test or indeed accepting the need for a test at all, or for making a test a compulsory instrument.

Some years ago I visited parts of West Africa for the purpose of advising on the testing of Spoken English at the 'Ordinary' or School Certificate Level. A test named after its originator, Mrs Cath McCallien (known as the McCallien Test), had been in voluntary use there for some ten years. For various reasons it had been decided that an oral test should, if possible, be made compulsory. I had been asked to make a feasibility study. In the course of my report to the West African Examination Council I suggested that there were three criteria to be taken into consideration before making such a test compulsory. These criteria are of general application in language testing and the relevant section of the report (Davies 1968) will be quoted here in full.

Purpose
 The writer takes it as axiomatic that a test should have a firm educational purpose. This seems especially necessary of a subject like spoken English in a situation like West Africa where the needs are so great and the problems so many. A good test is needed. This test should, above all, have an educational, not an administrative, purpose. The issue is therefore seen as an educational/social one rather than as an administrative or even a linguistic one.

Approach
 This issue must be approached from three sides: that of aims, that of demands and that of constraints.

Aims
 It seemed to the writer that those professionally involved in Spoken English in West Africa who were specially anxious for a new test had three aims in mind, and these aims were not always kept distinct. They were:

  (a) to produce a streamlined version of the present test
  (b) to exercise a strong influence on spoken English in secondary schools, encouraging the teaching of the subject and acting as a goal for that teaching
  (c) to raise the standard of spoken English throughout West Africa.

It was this third aim which seemed least distinct and which kept emerging as the real purpose of the whole operation and as equivalent to the second aim. It is not, of course. A good new test would assure aims (a) and (b) (since it would build on the virtues of the present system and, because compulsory, it would have an important educational wash-back) but it would not meet aim (c), at least not for a very long time, since it would be taken only by the highly selected General Certificate of Education entry. However, if this word of caution is accepted, it can be said that a good test, competently applied, would be one step towards the all-round improvement everyone wants. It is, of course, in teaching and the supply of well-trained teachers, that the real answer to this third aim lies.

Demands

There are three demands that must be met by every good educational test, and the syllabus associated with it. These are:

(a) the test should be simple
(b) the syllabus should be teachable
(c) the effects should be beneficial.

By *simple* is meant that the test should be easy to administer, that there should be no doubt in the mind of the teacher about what is being tested, so that a detailed syllabus can be provided; and that there should be no doubt as to its results, i.e. it will contain all the virtues of a sound objective test.

By *teachable* is meant two things:

(i) that the syllabus leading to the test should be sufficiently detailed to enable it to be effectively taught.

(ii) that it should be teachable by the average English teacher in the ordinary secondary school, not only by the phonetically trained teacher in the old established urban schools. In this sense the syllabus must be realistically based on what teachers can do and what equipment is available to them. It might be argued that in attempting to devise a spoken English syllabus that can be taught by every teacher, we would be in danger of permitting an unacceptable reduction in standards. In considering the question of what goal it is reasonable to set up, we should remember that spoken English is not like other subjects. It may be possible to devise a new syllabus and examination in physics or mathematics, and assume that all the teachers will have learned enough by the time new teaching methods are introduced, but if the teacher of English does not have a good command of the spoken language, there is very little he can do about it. We have to accept that there are many teachers whose spoken English is weak, and we can scarcely expect them to impart to their pupils those features of the spoken language which they have not fully mastered themselves. This argument is relevant to all discussions about how to teach and to test the production and discrimination of spoken English. We would certainly question the educational value of setting up unattainable goals; and the teaching of an RP, or even an approximately RP accent, might well be an unattainable goal in West Africa.

By *beneficial* is meant the influence the test has on the teaching of spoken English in the secondary school. It would be hoped that this beneficial influence would extend in two directions:

(i) to the primary schools and to the teaching-training colleges, especially the latter, for if the teacher trainers' speech is improved, that of the primary school children is likely to improve also.
(ii) to the rest of the teaching in the secondary school, including all the teaching which takes place outside the English class.

The implications of this demand for beneficial influence are that the test should deal extensively with valid problems, that it should set up a goal which is both realistic (i.e. teachable) and appropriate (i.e. necessary), that it should discriminate meaningfully, so that those who do well really do possess a certain control over spoken English which those who do badly do not possess; that it should, in short, possess both content and predictive validity, content validity in that it looks back to what are the linguistic problems of communication and predictive validity in that it looks forward to what effective teaching in spoken English will do.

Constraints

These are heavy demands. They would apply to any educational test which is used as a compulsory instrument. They are even further burdened by the constraints on the setting up of an oral test in West Africa.

Assuming that a desirable test which meets the demands outlined above could be produced, there still remain a number of constraints. They are:

(a) Supply of trained examiners.
(b) Administrative problems: distances and number of candidates.
(c) Use of machinery (e.g. tape-recorders) in tropical conditions. It is not clear how serious a difficulty this is but it was one widely mentioned. The supply and servicing of electrical equipment are certainly problems which must be faced.

Practical and theoretical

These three constraints are all practical. The assumption (which the writer does not share) is that a complete oral test of both production and comprehension could be designed. If the theoretical problem of designing a valid production test were overcome it would be immediately absorbed into the practical problem of making every examiner a professional phonetician.

5.2 Test virtues

Validity and reliability have been mentioned on various occasions, and it is time to make them explicit.

5.2.1 RELIABILITY

A reliable test possesses consistency of results. An inconsistent test would give meaningless, random results. Before looking at the meaning of results it is important to ensure that they are reliable. Unreliable results can have no meaning apart from their own randomness. The implication here is that although validity is far more important than reliability, which is in fact rather an obvious concept, it is essential to establish reliability first. Otherwise there is no point in considering validity.

This suggests that the two virtues are, as it were, imposed on the test afterwards, one after the other. This is not of course so. It is simply a matter of logical order of consideration; there is no point in considering validity if the reliability is poor. There are ways of increasing reliability; lengthening the test is the most obvious. The Spearman-Brown correction formula shows exactly what effect lengthening a test has on reliability. The formula is

$$r_n = \frac{nr}{1 + (n-1)r}$$

where r is the original reliability, and r_n is the reliability of a test n times as long.

But reliability is most happily seen as a form of validity; and so what matters for reliability, as for validity, is adequacy of plan, analysis and sampling of content, and relationship of test to purpose. The best way of ensuring reliability is through a good test; and at the reliability level one method of ensuring a good test is homogeneity of items, and as large a number of items as possible.

5.2.2 VALIDITY

Homogeneity of items may produce reliability; it will not necessarily affect validity. Why should it? A tape measure will be good for measuring cloth and always reliable but hardly valid for language. Yet the 'items' on a tape measure are highly homogeneous. Similarly a test of homogeneous grammar items (e.g. Give the past tense of *She loves me/She doesn't love me*) will be very reliable, but not necessarily valid in terms of the natural communicative use of language.

If the reliability of a test ensures its consistency, validity ensures its meaningfulness. A test is meaningful within the terms of what is wanted from the test. It has been customary to ask what has been called the 'old validity' question, that is: 'How far does a test measure what it purports to measure?' The old approach, then, is the common sense one; it relates a test to its already determined purpose. The only problem here is that it assumes that the exact purpose of the test can be known. In order to determine in fact whether a test is measuring what it purports to measure it is necessary to relate it to a criterion of some kind. The criterion, of course, represents what the test purports to measure, i.e. this is a measure or a statement of what it is all about. Different types of validity demand different kinds of criteria; these will be considered next.

5.2.3 TYPES OF VALIDITY

It is customary to distinguish five types of validity: face, predictive, concurrent, content, and construct validity. These will be dealt with separately below, but by way of illustration consider the following table (Cronbach 1961):

	Question asked	Procedure	Principle use	Examples
Predictive	Do test scores predict a certain important future performance?	Give test and use it to predict the outcome. Sometime later obtain a measure of the outcome. Compare predictive with outcome	Selection and classification	Admission test for medical students compared with later marks
Concurrent	Do test scores permit an estimate of a certain present performance?	Give test. Obtain a direct measure of the other performance. Compare the two	Tests intended as a substitute for a less convenient procedure	Group mental test compared to individual test
Content	Does this test give a fair measure of performance on some important set of tasks?	Compare the items logically to the content supposed to be measured	Achievement tests	A test of shorthand ability is examined to see whether the content is typical of office correspondence
Construct	How can scores on this test be explained psychologically?	Set up hypotheses. Test them experimentally by any suitable procedure	Tests used for description or in scientific research	A test of art aptitude is studied to determine how largely scores depend on art training, experience in Western culture etc.

Figure 3: *Types of validity.* From L. J. Cronbach, *Essentials of Psychological Testing* (p. 106), New York: Harper & Row, 1961.

Face validity

Face validity does not appear in Cronbach's table. There is good reason for this in that it is not a theoretical concept. It answers the question: Does this test look right? Does it seem right to the lay eye? (Hence so much of the criticism of intelligence tests—they just don't look right; hence too the opposition to multiple choice items.) But whatever may be theoretically trivial is not necessarily trivial from the practical point of view. In education it is often important to seem to be teaching, learning and testing as well as to be actually doing so. Public relations are important both for the pupils and for the public in general. And so a case may be made out for face validity. This may mean giving tests of, say, oral production as well as listening comprehension, simply because they are expected; this is not a bad reason. Nor is it bad to give a test to encourage the teaching of a particular activity or skill, for example essay writing. It may be that both oral production and essay writing are not very reliable tests, and they may not contribute very significantly to an estimate of total language control; but, often enough, what is desired is an estimate of specific essay performance.

The problems of face validity are, however, serious ones; experts often disagree but laymen even more so. Which lay opinion should be taken? This may be a small problem when the audience is small and fairly homogeneous, for example when we are dealing with a single school where the 'laymen' are the pupils themselves. But a greater problem arises when we try to determine just what the lay opinion is in the wider world; often enough in language learning, it represents outmoded, traditionalist attitudes. Thus a test of language to the traditionalist's eye should look like a run through a set of Latin paradigms: decline this, conjugate that. If this is face validity, then it may be more difficult to satisfy than in the more acceptable form of evaluating an essay.

Predictive validity

Predictive validity, like its partner, concurrent validity, is established by a statistical procedure, the common one of correlation, usually of the product-moment variety. (See Appendix I, p. 187). The correlation relates the test scores to an acceptable criterion which is predicted and which is quantifiable.

The test then is the predictor: it shows its predictive validity in its relation to its future criterion which it predicts. Examples are 'eleven-plus' selection tests and school certificate results; or scores at entry to higher education related to academic degree success.

Language aptitude tests will necessarily use predictive validity because they must relate present skill to future performance. Language proficiency tests which are used for selection will also use predictive validity.

Achievement and diagnostic tests are based on other types of validity but for them too predictive validity is extremely useful, though, of course, at one remove. Even though differing test uses (such as achievement) may not be concerned with prediction, it is probably true that prediction is a factor in all uses; all tests are used partly for prediction. But this is a different point from predictive validity. All tests must show validity, but a test may predict, or be used for predicting, without containing very significant predictive validity. The establishing of predictive validity is a purely statistical relationship.

Concurrent validity

In a similar manner to predictive validity a statistical procedure establishes concurrent validity. The correlation this time relates the test scores to an acceptable criterion which is concurrent and which is quantifiable. The only difference between concurrent and predictive validity, therefore, is one of time and since a predicted criterion becomes a concurrent one as soon as it is arrived at (and since, in some sense, it is possible to speak of a concurrent criterion as itself being predicted) there is no difference in the nature of the two criteria.

As Cronbach points out (Figure 3) the value of a test established by concurrent validity is its convenience. A group test, say of oral production, is more convenient than an individual test. A criterion such as teacher grades may be available but difficult to obtain for more than a restricted sample, and so a test which establishes its concurrent validity by means of these grades would be more convenient.

The most usual criterion is an already validated test. This is, of course, acceptable, but it does have the danger of regressiveness, i.e. if test X is established by concurrent validity on test Y which was itself validated against Z, then a certain drift is engendered. From time to time it is important to go outside existing tests as criterion measures. Concurrent validity is a useful check on a test's validity and all types of test can make use of it. Concurrent and predictive validity, then, are established by statistical correlation. They need criteria which are quantifiable. But all criteria cannot be quantified. What is more a purely statistical approach assumes that either there is one and only one criterion for a test (i.e. that the tester knows exactly what he is about) or that any criterion which provides acceptable coefficients will do. The remaining two types of validity indicate a different approach.

Content validity

If face validity is an appeal to the lay observer, content validity is an appeal to the subject expert. No statistical procedure is appropriate here. What is required is a rigorous analysis by the expert (who may, of course, be the language teacher) of the material which it is desired to test, a sampling based on that analysis and then an item writing operation based on the sampling. After that it is necessary to carry out the internal statistical analyses, item analysis, reliability and inter-test correlation. But the validity is established by an expert appraisal of the test content as a sample of the subject to be learned.

Content validity is particularly suitable for achievement tests. They are concerned with previous learning of a syllabus. Content validity of an achievement test shows that it is properly so related. What remains necessary is to show that the syllabus itself has validity and it may be that its relation to the desired terminal behaviour can be shown by predictive construct validity.

An achievement test, however adequate its sampling of the subject matter, will say nothing of the value of the syllabus. Teaching materials themselves need their own validation and it may be that this is best done by extensive trials on appropriate native speakers so that it can be demonstrated that they at least can cope with the subject matter. The dilemma will still remain of the relevance of such teaching materials to foreign language learners. Another way out of the dilemma is to employ predictive validity for the achievement tests in order to validate the materials. But content validity must first be established for the tests themselves, otherwise there will be no certainty that they are tests of this specific material.

Proficiency tests may also make use of content validity. Here the content of the test is shown to be acceptable in relation to the expectations of the learner. This may involve a two-pronged approach: the language itself needs to be fully represented and appropriate job sampling needs to be done. That is to say, an assessment must be made of just what the learners whose proficiency is to be tested need to do with the language, what varieties they must employ and in what situations they must use those varieties. This is an arduous task, and one largely based on guesswork, but it can be intelligent guess-work and it is essential for constructing a proficiency test. An achievement test has the advantage, or should have, that this preliminary groundwork will already have been done for the syllabus.

Construct validity

If concurrent validity is seen as another form of predictive validity, so content validity may be represented as being, in the event, based on construct which the test is based; the theory may be psychological, describing what learning is like, or linguistic, giving some view of the nature of language. The test, then, is constructed on the basis of the theory; and for this reason the most obvious testing purpose where construct validity may be employed is in research where the test may very well be a method of underpinning the theory, of finding out (as the representation in concrete form of a hypothesis) just how fully the theory stands up. The most obvious test use will therefore be in language aptitude work. Language aptitude must use predictive validity, of course, but this does not help in the construction of the test. For construct validity is essential; the tester is saying that this is what language and language learning are like and he embodies his construct in his aptitude test. Whether he is right or not will come out, at least partially, in the correlations (i.e. in predictive validity) with the proficiency test at the end of the learning.

Achievement tests, as we have seen, depend on content validity. But this is on the assumption that the materials are themselves valid. We have suggested that the materials may be validated on predictive validity. Another approach is to use construct validity for the materials. An achievement test in this situation will be valid on construct validity at one remove.

Another approach is to start where all proper research on language learning and teaching should start, at the twin points of beginning and end, and attempt to relate them. Thus work on proficiency (by construct and perhaps content validity) produces proficiency measures which are used as criteria for the tests produced by aptitude work (by predictive validity and constructed on construct validity). From the relationship so established is produced the teaching material which leads from aptitude to proficiency; and this is assessed along the way by achievement tests (by content validity) based directly on the teaching material.

5.2.4 SCHEMA FOR EDUCATION

Thus we have the schema shown overleaf which attempts to show these relationships between uses and types of validity:

Figure 4(a) suggests the relationship between test uses and types of validity and represents them in what is considered the proper ordering. Figure 4(b) is more ambitious in that it incorporates language theory as well and suggests the possibility that the theory itself may be supported by test series (themselves types of hypothesis) proceeding in the manner shown. It is, after all, the theory on which all else rests; it is from there that the construct is set up and it is on the construct that validity, of the content and predictive kinds, is based. It is, of course, true that work on proficiency gathers material as to what is proficiency in sample situations—i.e., here is control of the language at work, in this textbook to be read, this lecture to be understood, this letter to be written, and so on. But an adequate theory of language must incorporate some notion of situation; so that all idea of proficiency must, in the event, rest on a fully comprehensive language theory.

It is at proficiency that work for educational purposes should start. How much of a language has to be taught to students, which varieties and which registers for different purposes? What arrangement and order of material should be made? What does knowledge of, or control over a language involve and how can one tell whether a student has this control? These are all essentially proficiency questions. They can only be answered by basic research in proficiency and only from such work can proficiency tests be constructed. Such proficiency tests aim to provide adequate goals for and

64 Testing and Experimental Methods

complete information about the student whose language proficiency is in question. For example: Does student A have enough French for a particular situation, job, or course of study? For this type of question other information about student A is irrelevant at the time of testing. But if we ask: 'Is his

(4a)

```
Proficiency considerations
        ↓
Proficiency tests
(construct/content validity) ←┐
        ↓                      │
Aptitude considerations ───────┘
        ↓
Teaching materials
        ↓
Achievement tests
```

(4b)

```
                        Language theory
                       ↙              ↖
Construct validity                    
        ↓                              
Content validity              Predictive validity
        ↓                              ↑
Proficiency considerations    Achievement tests
        ↓                              ↑
Predictive validity           Content validity
        ↓                              ↑
Aptitude considerations ───→ Teaching materials
```

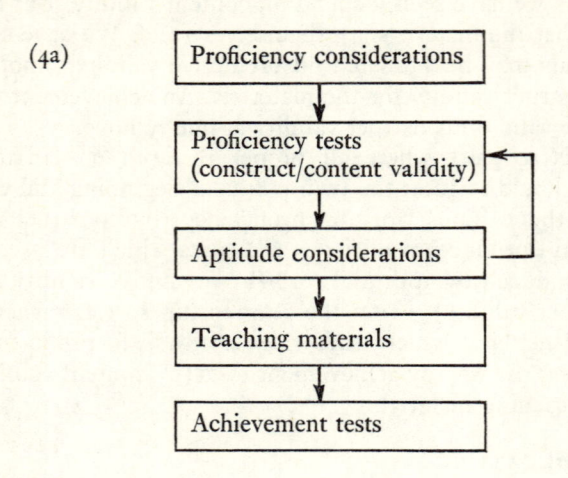

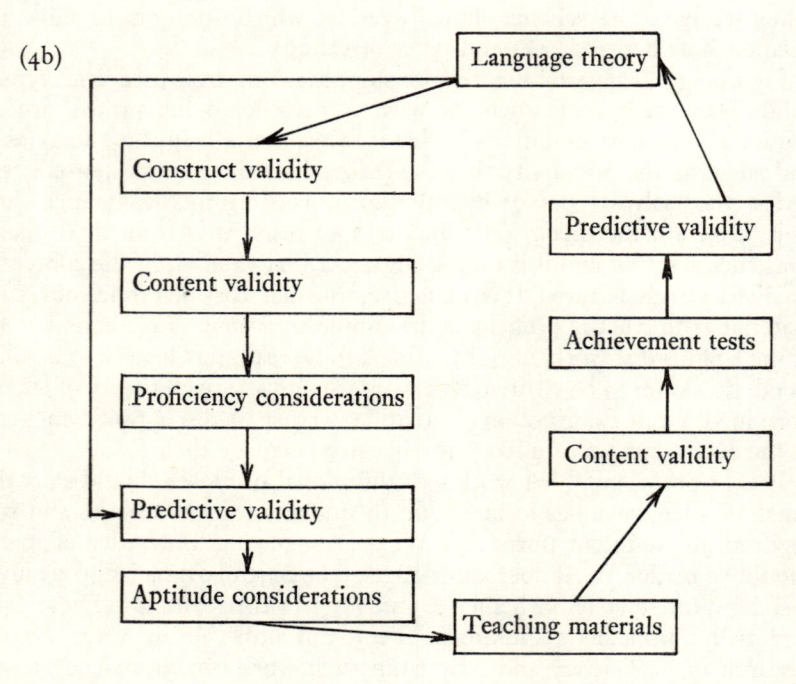

Figure 4: *Schema for education*

proficiency likely to increase after three months' exposure in a native speaking situation?' then student A's aptitude also needs consideration. And for all the other proficiency questions (e.g., what teaching materials should be used) aptitude must also be looked at. Aptitude, proficiency and achievement are, after all, only ways of looking at ability and for decisions as to what is to be taught and whether it has been learned, some concrete view of ability must be obtained. As well as individual ability, research must look at the other variables, such as the teaching, and the learning situation. But it is only by isolating the aptitude-proficiency relationship that it may be possible to make judgements about these other variables.

Achievement, in this view, is based on the aptitude-proficiency relationship. It is this relationship that makes use of the fundamental sampling, and of the theoretical construct; it is from this relationship that the syllabus needs to be drawn. Achievement tests need to incorporate all the requisite testing techniques of objectivity but linguistically they are parasitic as long as they have sampled adequately. An achievement test can do no more, can be no better than the syllabus which it samples; the only validity it need show is of the content type. It seems to me that too often achievement tests are mistakenly used as proficiency measures and that proficiency type expectations are raised so that an achievement test is somehow expected to provide information that is not allowed for by the syllabus which has been taught and whose content it samples. No achievement test can improve on its syllabus. 'Ordinary' level French, for example, does not give predictive evidence of control over French which is not provided for in the 'Ordinary' level syllabus.

6 Language test analysis

In all the discussion of types of language test, of breakdown and analysis by use and by purpose, little mention has been made of the analysis by level and skill. This may not be as theoretically important as analysis by use but it is certainly practically more important. Most language teachers who wish to construct their own tests are concerned either with proficiency or achievement uses (usually with the latter). What they want to know is what needs to be tested, and by 'what' is probably meant the combination of language element and individual control or skill. Naively put, the questioner is probably asking: Should I test grammar, and if so, how? Or: Should I test reading, speaking, dictation, précis, essay, vocabulary, comprehension, spelling and so on? How can testing techniques help me get at skills in language?

A distinction must be drawn at once between testing techniques and language skills. Reading, speaking, listening and writing are obviously kinds of skills, though it will be suggested later that they are not entirely adequate as categories of language skills. On the other hand dictation, précis, essay, spelling are testing devices for getting at language skills; they are therefore appropriate if they are considered to provide useful information and valid if they do in fact test language skills. The arguments against such devices as précis and dictation are twofold: firstly, they are umbrella type tests and do not analyse sufficiently, so that a 'mistake' in, say, précis cannot easily be related to a particular skill such as reading or writing; and, secondly, they take on (as tests must, of course) the aura of language goals and so become taught as if they were themselves skills. In consideration of this harmful wash-back effect it may be desirable to abandon such well-worn and suspect techniques for less familiar and less coherent ones.

Vocabulary and grammar were also mentioned; what place do these linguistic concepts have among techniques and skills? Most linguists would regard grammar and vocabulary as two different 'levels' and, indeed, one satisfactory method of test analysis can be provided by correlating the 'levels' of linguistic analysis against the four basic skills of reading, writing, speaking and listening. Into the boxes made in this way we can put the language testing techniques, so that we can see what can be done and where each technique fits in the general scheme. Such a scheme is illustrated below in the first language testing matrix:

Levels	Skills			
	Reading	Writing	Listening	Speaking
Phonology				
Grammar				
Lexis				
Context				
Extra-linguistic				

Figure 5: *Language testing matrix 1*

It should be noted, first, that such techniques as essay writing, giving an interview, giving a talk and role acting, really come outside language proper since they involve other important variables such as imagination, style and so on. This does not deny that these techniques are interesting both for themselves and for their content validity in relation to the curriculum, since often enough it is for just such activities that teachers believe, quite rightly, they are preparing their pupils. It might be argued that the use of such techniques implies too individualistic an approach, an attempt to get beyond general linguistic control to features of individual idiolect or style and that these are not the proper concern of language teaching or testing.

It should be noted, secondly, that while every box in the diagram may be provided with a testing technique it is more sensible to take an economical approach and to accept that if the receptive skills (both listening and reading) are easier to test than production from both the reliability and the practical point of view, then it is sensible to concentrate on reception. For similar reasons the level of grammar, though it can be reached both through production and reception, is much easier to test through receptive tests of comprehension (i.e., the tests are more reliable, practical and efficient).

It should be noted, thirdly, that even though it remains an ideal language testing maxim that the different language features or skills should be tested one at a time, this is not always possible and compromises have to be made. Thus the data provided by the tests will not always be as clear-cut as we might like it to be (for example, it might not always be clear exactly how we should categorize an error) but it does allow for wide coverage. This compromise is explained further in the discussion of language testing matrix 2 (see below).

The division into skills above is not entirely satisfactory since it makes too many unusable distinctions. It is possible to combine the traditional skills and the language elements or 'levels'. Here the balance is provided by the channels of production and reception. Thus we have the following matrix:

Skills	Channels	
	Production	Reception
Motor perceptive		
Organizational		
Semantic		
Extralinguistic		

Figure 6: *Language testing matrix 2*

If we take a traditional skill such as reading, where do we locate it in matrix 2? It will be found in one of the boxes linked to reception. The value of the new skills analysis is that it attempts to make even finer distinctions between techniques and skills. It is clear that for testing purposes a skill must be considered as either receptive or productive. Thus reading comprehension may be a technique for eliciting control over the skill of reading. But reading is now well recognized as a group of skills; is it any longer appropriate to regard it as a unitary skill? Reading itself then may be better regarded as a technique for approaching a more basic skill such as semantic or linguistic organization.

As was mentioned above, the maxim of one feature at a time is usually frustrated and matrix 2 well illustrates this; although production and reception are separated in the matrix it is virtually impossible to keep them separate in practice. The reason is simple: knowledge that comprehension is present in the pupil is difficult to obtain without some overt behavioural manifestation on the part of the pupil, i.e. he has to go into production to signal his degree of comprehension. Even an apparently straight test of production involves similar problems, for example 'Read this passage aloud'. Apart from the problem of deciding whether this command has been understood there is the further problem of deciding exactly how comprehension of the text affects the speaker's production of it. Reading aloud is inevitably influenced by the sort of understanding the writer of the text aimed at evoking. Thus given the sentence 'The constitutional experiments of the Puritan Commonwealth pioneered more experiments in government than any comparable period before the twentieth century', the reader needs one kind of understanding, i.e. of grammatical categories and the way in which they interrelate in order to make any production at all. And given the sign

SLOW
WORKMEN
AHEAD

the reader needs another kind of understanding; he needs to know what punctuation is appropriate in the situation to which the sign refers. In both cases he needs greater experience of the language than the text itself affords him. The linguistic context can provide this experience, of course; for example the SLOW WORKMEN AHEAD sign can be contained in a much longer text about road safety. But the problem of punctuation still remains, as does our uncertainty about whether the reader has understood the whole text. The inescapable conclusion is that the channels of reception and production cannot be isolated from one another in practice, and consequently we cannot hope to isolate them from one another in testing.

Any matrix such as those presented here is at best a loose approximation to what can be done. It cannot provide a testing scheme better than the linguistic theory on which it rests. Thus the testing techniques rest for their validity on the skills and levels suggested by some linguistic theory, incomplete and inadequate though this may be. For example, suppose we base our testing techniques on a model of grammar which contains no semantic level. In this case, how should meaning be tested? Should we assume that meaning is involved at every level and does not need to be separately tested? One thing certain is that language theory has a profound influence on what is tested and therefore on what information is provided by the tests.

It is always possible, of course, to use tests for research purposes, i.e. as a means of checking on the language theory. For example, we can devise tests of the projected skills and then perform statistical correlation procedures on the relationship between the different tests. Thus the initial analysis may suggest that reading comprehension and reading speed are different skills; a statistical analysis may suggest that there is so much overlap that it would be better to regard them as different representations of the same skill.

When a test blueprint or matrix (e.g. those presented on p. 66-7) has been selected there still remains the major problem of deciding just what the content of each item is to be. Which bits of information are to be drawn out and sampled for item writing? One answer is 'All bits'. This is perhaps just possible for phonology, but difficult for grammar and impossible for vocabulary. In an achievement test such an approach may be possible because we are able to say what we mean by 'all bits' i.e. everything that is in the syllabus. Whether these are the right bits is a question of proficiency, i.e. of the validity of the syllabus.

The problem of item choosing is essentially one of sampling. This problem is obviously more acute in a proficiency test than in an achievement test. In the second, the syllabus is known and the decision has been made as to selection from all possible language items; in the first the tester must make his own selection and so his sampling is both statistical and linguistic.

In the next section we shall go into the more practical considerations of test construction for the teacher. How should a teacher go about making his own tests?

7 Teacher made tests

7.1 Proficiency and achievement tests

The typical language test used in schools and the one most likely to be constructed by a teacher is an achievement test. In this section, however, we are still discussing proficiency tests. Teachers may want to use proficiency tests or to construct them for themselves. For example, a teacher may want to construct a test for placing pupils who have just entered a school and who have all done some French; but even this should be an achievement test based in some way on the syllabus which will be taught. Our reason for discussing proficiency rather than achievement is simply that achievement tests are entirely dependent on the syllabus and that therefore discussion of them must take the syllabus into account, otherwise such discussion is a trivial consideration of testing techniques. Discussion of proficiency tests, on the other hand, does not assume a syllabus, and we can legitimately make use of linguistic reasoning for balance of sub-tests and inclusion of items.

What needs to be stressed here is that achievement test construction in language work is easier than proficiency test construction, because there is less to do. The achievement tester has his corpus of language, the bits to be taught and learned, ready made; and so his job starts a stage further on than that of the proficiency tester, who as well as constructing and sampling items has to decide which bits of language should be known. Therefore, in concentrating on proficiency tests we are not evading a more difficult problem. At the same time we shall not do more than give suggestions as to which areas of language should be sampled for proficiency purposes. We shall discuss the areas of vocabulary and describe the construction of vocabulary items but we shall not say how many words or which words shall be tested, as we shall not give any vocabulary counts. This we take to be the job of those who construct the syllabus for schools while the prior descriptive work is the concern of the linguist.

7.2 Selection of language areas for testing

We assume further in the discussion which follows that the teaching is taking place somewhere between the third and fifth year of second language teaching. In other words, the learner has started and has become acquainted with reading and writing as well as speaking and listening. He has also been shown the importance of meaning as well as the mechanics of organization. We hope by this assumption to take into account different methods of teaching as far apart as audio-visual and traditional grammar translation. We will also take into account the different starting ages of learning according to the local system; i.e. the scope of the discussion covers third year English in French or German schools as well as fifth year English at the start of the secondary school stage in West Africa. It also covers, for example, third year French or German in the British secondary school.

The problem of selection for test areas is a sampling problem. This in itself raises the question of population, i.e. of learning outcome. What do we as teachers expect of our pupils (a) when they come to the end of their school language learning and (b) when they leave our class, whichever year they are in? It is easy to say that they should possess all the skills. But should they possess them in equal degree? Here the teacher can only use his own judgement. For an achievement test he has, or should have, the aims of the syllabus as a guide.

Let us assume that the teacher has decided on a wide ranging proficiency test. There are two basic areas to be sampled. The first is the language itself. What are the features, the levels, the skills which go to make up knowledge of the language and proficiency in its use? For instance, writing is clearly a necessary language activity but writing an essay is not, partly because this is something that we do with writing, not the skill in itself. It is a pity that in much preparation for school examinations essay writing is the only form of writing demanded. The second basic area concerns the use the learner makes of the language when he has learned it. This is very much easier in practice for second language teaching where the learner needs the language for study purposes. In the case of the British child learning French, on the other hand, it is less easy to define the goals. What is he learning French for? He may go to France on holiday, meet French people in Britain, visit France as a student at the Sorbonne, or he may do none of these things. Because of the difficulty of deciding exactly why he is learning French it may be necessary to include essay writing as a feature of the second area simply because this is the only thing that it is possible to be fairly certain about. It is likely that he will need French for essay writing at a later stage in his school career. This is a poor justification but it shows how difficult it is to say why languages are taught in schools.

7.3 Language analysis

We have already dealt with this in the discussion of the two grids (pp. 66–67). Although reception tests are much more satisfactory from an objective viewpoint than production tests, we shall deal here with both. At the same time there is no point in testing the same thing twice. For example, we shall deal with grammar under reading. We could also deal with it under listening, but it is more economical to deal with it once, at the point where it is easiest to do so.

Overleaf is matrix 1 with all the boxes filled in.

The fact that we can talk, for example, about 'intonation tests' still leaves us with the major problem of how much of each feature needs testing. This again is a sampling problem and it is one for the teacher himself. It is more difficult for intonation than for, say, vocabulary, simply because of the greater difficulty of deciding what are the relevant intonational features and in what order to teach them. We have to assume that by the third year of English the learner will be familiar with some part of a description of English intonation and so it is on this that we should test him.

7.4. Work sample analysis

The learner will possess something when he has finished learning; we need to determine what it is, how it can be made known to others, of what use it will be to him, and what he will do with it. As we said above, the second language learner will use the language as a study vehicle. The foreign language learner may never make much use of it; the British learner of French may never go to France, and never speak French to a Frenchman in this country.

Levels	Skills			
	Reading	Writing	Listening	Speaking
Phonology	phonemes through rhyme	—	intonation	stress, weakening and rhythm
Grammar	sensitivity to deviance	sentence completion	pronoun replacement	transformations
Lexis	synonyms	collocations	picture vocabulary	names for objects
Context	text with questions	summary	rephrasing	question-answer
Extra-linguistic	reading speed	free composition	conversation	completing a story

Figure 7. *Completed language testing matrix*

But we have to assume that a good learner will still have benefited from learning French, that he will retain something of practical value so that he would have an advantage if he ever decided to take up the study of French again. If he retains nothing of the French he learned at school, then presumably the time spent on French might have been more usefully employed on studying French history, or on reading French literature in translation – or on another subject altogether. It is sometimes argued that the point of learning foreign languages is that the learning in itself, and not what it might lead to, is of value, so that a child who might never speak French in a real-life situation and who may never read a French book will still have derived some benefit, in a general educational sense, from following a course in basic French at school.

Work sample analysis is basically a question of selection. As has been pointed out, this involves an examination of the external factors which are relevant in making a selection from the total language. No one knows the whole language. Native speakers differ in the areas which they know and control; this can be seen in the area of pronunciation, if we consider different accents, and it can be seen even more clearly in vocabulary. Which language variety should we set up as a model for our tests for foreign learners? Whose language should we teach?

Within a school this is not a question for the teacher at all. As we have already emphasized the school is essentially concerned with achievement testing. Decisions about syllabus, and therefore selection, have already been made. Of course the teacher still has to select for testing in the sense that he cannot test everything. But the proficiency tester has to select both from the total universe of discourse and within those areas selected for individual items. For him, external factors are important. They are more important at later stages of learning since the closer the learner is to the beginning, the more his language is limited to that part of it he cannot do without. The more advanced the level of language the greater the amount of choice. In other words, these external factors become more important in the later stages.

Let us now set up a work sample matrix (Figure 8). This must be a tentative procedure since it is a near impossibility for the teacher to know exactly what his pupils will need the language for. They may want it for holidays or for watching television, for living abroad or perhaps they will never need it. But it does have merit in that it distinguishes between a second language and a foreign language; in the case of a foreign language not all the operations need to be tested. No doubt the teacher will want to play safe and test as many kinds of activity as he can. From this point of view the larger the matrix the better. Hence the first skills matrix has an advantage over the second (Figure 9) and may well be preferred on this account.

External Factors	1 using the language for all official purposes	2 using the language for all educational purposes	3 learning the language for cultural and political reasons	4 learning the language as an academic discipline	5 learning the language out of interest, or as a hobby
Aims and Purposes					
Age					
Size of class					
Previous language learning experience					
Average educational level					
Previous experience of language					
Intensity of course					
Teacher proficiency					
Equipment					
Motivation					
Mother tongue					
Target standards					

Figure 8

74 Testing and Experimental Methods

The above matrix is insufficiently detailed. Even a third dimension here allowing for control over the different language skills, or for mastery of the various categories drawn from a linguistic analysis will not be enough because each of the external features itself needs a matrix. But let us take one example to investigate whether such an elaboration may be of help in making precise exactly what it is we are about when we teach a language. Let us take the age parameter (in the External Factors list) and select three ages: child, adolescent and adult. Here is the relevant part of the matrix (the numbers refer to the five columns in Figure 8):

	1	2	3	4	5
Child					
Adolescent					
Adult					

Figure 9. *Age parameter: all factors*

If English is our target language we have 15 boxes to complete on a world basis. But if English for immigrants in Britain is our concern then we might be able to limit the top row to numbers 1 and 2 (with the proviso that we may need a sixth category—to cover the use of English as a foreign language for only certain 'official' purposes such as reading road signs, shopping, and filling in government forms). If we limit our analysis further to the educational requirements of immigrant children and adolescents, then we reduce our top row to one column only, number 2. So we are left then with the following matrix:

	2
Child	
Adolescent	

Figure 10. *Age parameter: educational factor only*

We might even reduce the matrix to one box by combining the categories of child and adolescent if we take 'all educational purposes' to cover everything from primary school to University. Only when we know who the learners are and what are their needs can we determine which parts of the language matrix (Figure 7) relate to them.

For the achievement test work sampling will be a matter for the syllabus, not for the test. A good school syllabus should be related at each stage to what is expected of pupils at that stage in readiness to proceed to the next. This is commonly done, of course, with language courses which span two, three or even four years. The point of difficulty comes when there is a move from one institution to another, from primary school to secondary school to higher education. At those points the continuity often breaks down and if learners proceed satisfactorily from the lower stage but cannot cope at the higher that is the fault of the syllabus, not of the achievement test. What is lacking is more accurate work sampling in the syllabus, work sampling of the types of learner being catered for, as in Figure 8, and the kinds of performance expected of them in the higher stages.

Work sampling external to the syllabus is more properly the job of the proficiency test which, as we have suggested, provides its own syllabus to be sampled. What the proficiency test must first do, as was argued above, is to specify the type of learner as exactly as possible and then to sample the demands made on him when he has acquired that amount of proficiency. In point of fact, proficiency tests are likely only at certain critical points, namely when we want to check that the learner has enough of the language for certain extralinguistic activities. In practice this will probably mean that there are two levels of proficiency test, the advanced and the elementary. Again it is the needs of the learner that are being explored; the advanced learner of English needs the language, say, in order to study other subjects such as medicine or engineering. The elementary learner may need English in order to read simple instructions, or to work efficiently as a steward on an international air line. There are elementary proficiency tests which do not have this kind of specific extra-linguistic demand in mind. The well-known Cambridge Proficiency Examination is a good example. Such a test may be more usefully considered as an achievement test (more properly a pre-achievement test) since what it does is to base itself on the demands of the more difficult advanced proficiency test, in fact it can be regarded as a watered down version of the more difficult test. This is not to be seen as a criticism of either of these tests; the fact that a watered-down version is possible means that some fairly rigorous attempt is being made at a grading of material into simpler and more difficult. The argument is simply that both must be taken together as parts of a complete notion of proficiency.

The demands made on a learner are many and varied. What the work sampling does is to sample those demands. Such sampling can never be adequate but it can be random and, at least in part, purposive. The traditional oral interview in the British 'Ordinary' Level foreign languages examination is essentially an attempt to get at certain skills (oral production and aural reception) through a work sample. The interview represents a likely situation in which the learner is face to face with a native speaker of the target language. In other words, such a test has immediate face validity, since this is exactly the situation that the teacher wants his pupil to be able to handle when he has finished the course.

Simpler work sampling will have less face validity, perhaps, but may be more reliable. There is no need to illustrate work sample tests since, in practice, as we shall see below, language analysis and work sample analysis tend to go together, and both are reflected in the items that are constructed.

8 Item writing

8.1 The framework of a test

In practice, the same test items can meet both work sample and language analysis demands. Work sample texts, for example lectures or reading passages, can often be employed to get at language analysis skills. However, this will not always be possible; in a test of phoneme discrimination, for example, it is not clear what work is being sampled. A fluent speaker never has to tackle this type of task as an end in itself, but it is part of general language ability and may be a feature of our control which needs testing.

However, even for such a test it is possible to tap the ability to distinguish phonemes by means of a work sample text. For example, the McCallien Oral English Test for West Africa embeds a number of critical distinctions in a text to be read aloud. While the student may think he is being tested on general reading aloud ability, i.e. in comprehension of text, fluency and so on, in fact the examiner is listening only for those pre-selected points of contrast. It would be possible to do this for very specialized work sample texts. (We are speaking of production here; it is less easy to see how a listening phoneme test can be embodied in a work sample text.) What this does illustrate is that the framework of a test can be given reality even when what is being actually tested is an isolated linguistic feature. But more important than this, it points to the need to isolate features for testing from one another, so that the examiner knows exactly what specific area he is contemplating. If this is thought unfair to the student because he ought to know which skill is being tested each time then the answer surely is that in his preparation, as part of the necessary detailed syllabus referred to earlier, he knows that phoneme discrimination will be part of the test. The fact that he does not know exactly where in the test it comes may be all to the good because it makes the test more like real life, where successful performance does not depend upon learned stock responses.

We shall now go on to look at each box of Figure 8 in turn, suggesting kinds of test and kinds of item that could be employed. It must be stressed that this run-through of test types is not meant to be a comprehensive guide to item writing. Nor is it thought necessary to provide this, since the teacher should be able to write his own items as long as he asks himself these two questions: (a) Which specific language skill do I want to test here? (b) How can I get at this skill, i.e. by what technique or device can I be sure of validity and of coverage of the skill? His tests then need to be specific, practical and reliable. In effect the teacher is providing himself with answers to the demands of validity and reliability and the obligation to be practical. A test could be both reliable and valid but impractical because it would simply take too long; or it might demand access by all students to a language laboratory which might not be available, and so on.

The technique, then, is less important than the skill. At the same time, once the skill has been selected everything depends on carrying out the technique properly. Testees must be perfectly clear about what they have to do. If multiple choice items are being used there must be no doubt about what ticks, crosses, underlinings and so on mean. But even more important for the technique is the selection in a multiple choice test of the distractors. The distractors must be convincing; if they are not then no one will choose them except by mistake, and they might as well not be there. Let us give two simple examples. In a grammar recognition item we give choices at a crucial point as follows:

Example 1

I want to
1 gone
2 went
3 go
4 going
home now

Of these choices while 3 is right and 4 at least possible, 1 and 2 are impossible since neither *gone* nor *went* is ever used after *to*. Even more obvious perhaps is the second example from a reading comprehension test. Here the problem is that of making the distractors plausible while at the same time writing a right response which is not self-evident, i.e., one which depends on an understanding of the text rather than on general knowledge. Suppose that a text dealing with the history of Edinburgh is used as a test and that it contains the following sentence:

> Not every capital can boast a castle, a royal palace and three cathedrals as Edinburgh can; and yet the city is somehow less Scottish than Glasgow with no palace or castle but more so than Stirling which has all three types of building.

And then this question follows:

Example 2

The capital of Scotland is
1 Stirling
2 Edinburgh
3 Perth
4 Glasgow

The implication here is surely obvious; the item can be answered successfully without reading the text sentence.

Let us now rewrite the two items, this time employing acceptable distractors. Sometimes this cannot be done simply because the language selection is wrong (i.e. the wrong bit of text is being queried), and sometimes the language under inspection is not amenable to questions, except for a Yes/No response, though even this, with an added Don't Know, can be acceptable.

Here are the rewritten examples. But first we must ask what is being tested. Let us assume that in example 1 it is the *want* + infinitive construction. This being so, the example may be rewritten as follows:

$$\text{I want} \begin{cases} 1 \text{ going} \\ 2 \text{ go} \\ 3 \text{ to go} \\ 4 \text{ to going} \end{cases} \text{home now}$$

Now at least there are analogies which make all the distractors plausible while still testing *want* + infinitive; thus, *want going* can be compared with *like going*; *want go* with *can see*; and *want to going* with *see to going*.

Example 2 is a test of simple comprehension of the text. Here it is rewritten:

    Which one of these statements is true?
    1 Stirling has three cathedrals.
    2 Stirling is more Scottish than Edinburgh.
    3 Glasgow is less Scottish than Stirling.
    4 Glasgow is the most Scottish of the three cities.

What is needed, then, is to pay attention to the detail of the language under scrutiny, as well as to make sure that what is under scrutiny is worthy of close attention.

8.2 Examples of items

In Figure 11 which follows below we repeat the matrix for levels and skills. We shall now take each box in turn, starting in the top left-hand corner and reading down, referring by number and letter as in Figure 11. The techniques we suggest are no more than examples. As a very simple example we may cite a reading comprehension test. The skill being tested here is reading. The technique for getting at this skill may be a series of open-ended questions such as: What did X do? What kind of person did he meet? or it may be a series of multiple choice questions, each with four possible responses.

Levels	Skills			
	[1]Reading	[2]Writing	[3]Listening	[4]Speaking
[a]Phonology				
[b]Grammar				
[c]Lexis				
[d]Context				
[e]Extralinguistic				

Figure 11. *Numbered language testing matrix*

1a READING: PHONOLOGY

This is a tricky one to start with because it lands us straightaway in the uncertain ground of partial production, i.e., it makes use of the reading skill to simulate oral production. If this is so, then of course it is not reading that is being tested; reading is one of the techniques being used to get at something else. But it is convenient to consider partial production here.

Example 1: Phonemes through rhyme
The following words all rhyme, that is they have the same middle and last sounds: *sight, fight, bite*. In the following list tick all the words which rhyme:

>sit
>seat
>feet
>sheet

Example 2: Rhythmic groups
If you were reading the following passage aloud you would make pauses in certain places. The slant lines in the passage are there to suggest possible places to make these pauses. Only some of these are correct. You are asked to put a circle round those which you think are correct.
John's/ a / person / you can / really / re / ly on /.

Other language features which fit into this box and could be tested by similar partial production means are stress and intonation, unless it is preferred to test intonation as a grammatical rather than a phonological feature. We shall in any case deal with intonation under listening: phonology (3a), since there is clearly a need to avoid duplication of effort. Since intonation could be tested under each of the four skills we have to decide whether this is necessary or, if not, where it is most efficiently tested. This is less a problem for intonation (which is available under speaking only by the fiction of partial production) than for, say, grammar, where we have to decide whether we want to test it under reading, writing, listening or speaking.

1b READING: GRAMMAR

Grammar, as we have just pointed out, could be tested in any column. But since reading is the easiest place to do the testing it is in this box that we shall illustrate grammar tests. We are not claiming that ability in grammar is equally important for all the skills; but it does seem legitimate to argue that a literate person must at least have this ability in reading.

Example 1: Sensitivity to deviance

The following sentences contain a choice of four words or phrases. The native speaker of English would use only one of these. You must choose what you think would be the native speaker's choice and circle its number.

a For the last twelve years my brother
1 lived
2 has been living
3 is lived
4 was living
in Australia.

b We shall miss the train
1 if
2 unless
3 when
4 because
it's late.

Example 2: Grammar analogies

Part of the sentence A below is underlined. Look at sentence B and underline that part of it which you think corresponds grammatically to the underlined part of A.

A Without a moment to lose, she ran out to her car.
B He drove to his office feverishly, hoping to be there first.

Both types of test here can, of course, employ the open-ended method, so that example 1 becomes a sentence completion test and example 2 a sentence addition test. Notice that the use of the open ended method forces the constructor into much greater refinement and selection than we have used, for the very reason that the student does not know what is expected of him and may therefore provide an answer which is entirely meaningful but does not give any information about his grammatical ability. Thus in example 1(b) we might have:

We shall miss the train and it's late

which is adequate but tells us nothing about the student's control over subordinating conjunctions.

IC READING: LEXIS

Any kind of vocabulary test will do here. We shall suggest a synonym test and a network of relationships test.

Example 1: Synonyms

Underneath there is a sentence followed by some words in a box. Choose the word in the box that you think might most suitably take the place of the underlined word in the sentence without changing the meaning of the sentence:

a Our <u>tom</u> cat has been missing ever since that day I upset his milk.

```
1 wild
2 drum
3 name
4 male
```

b I must go to the bank today to <u>check</u> my recent bank statement.

```
1 investigate
2 play
3 cash
4 pay
```

Example 2: Network of relationships

Here is a word *cherry*. Below there is a list of other words. Try to decide how much connection each of these has with the word *cherry*. If it is very near (nearer than any of the others) put a figure 1 under it. Then put a 2 for the word next in order and so on. Some words may have the same amount of connection and so you may want to give them each the same figure.

Cherry: Red   Fruit   Vegetable   Blue   Cabbage
         Sweet   Stalk   Tree   Garden

It may be argued that these tests are testing intelligence, particularly example 2 which demands a very high degree of literacy, so high that it may be entirely intelligence that is being tested here. Language is very closely related to intelligence and the best known group intelligence tests are those of verbal reasoning in which vocabulary plays a major part.

Note that in example 1 the context is specified. It is not claimed that synonyms exist out of context; but in a context there must be synonyms which native speakers are aware of and make use of. Hence the point of puns and ambiguities.

1d READING: CONTEXT

This box in our matrix is one of the easiest to fill since it is here that the very well-known types of reading comprehension test fit in. The context can be one short sentence or it may be a number of paragraphs; the length and difficulty, which are not related to one another, will depend on the type of student for whom the test is intended. For our purposes we would expect the length to be moderate, say three to four paragraphs, though we shall use only one paragraph in each of our examples for illustration purposes. It is not easy to make a distinction between the context level and the extralinguistic level. Context obviously refers to what is going on internally within the test and this is the way we shall use it. But if something is extra-linguistic it is difficult to see how it can be tested in what is after all a language test, so the distinction must become somewhat blurred. We shall use extralinguistic with the sense of reference to the world outside, admitting that this may well turn the test into one of general knowledge. At the same time, such a test does seem parallel to one of free composition or of the interview/oral for the writing and speaking columns and both of these certainly make use of general knowledge even though they may be officially concerned with language ability.

For our examples we shall suggest a modified cloze procedure test and a typical test of questions on the text.

Example 1: Modified cloze procedure
In the text which follows certain of the words are indicated only by their initial letter and a dash. The dash does not indicate how many letters are missing. You must complete these incomplete words so that the paragraph makes sense.

> A wide variety o— crops i— now known t— t— West African farmer. T— a— a few peoples, mostly o— t— Jos plateau, w— still plant only a— inferior small grain. B— most o— t— savana peoples h— long depended o— varieties o— millet o— guinea crop. T— origin o— rice cultivation i— t— Mande areas o— t— upper Niger remains a mystery.

Notice that the words which have been mutilated are all 'structure words' rather than 'content words'. (The distinction is useful and has been widely used.) The structure words are relatively few in number and do not belong in one of the four major word classes.

Example 2: Questions on text
Read the following passage carefully and then answer the questions on it

The Construction of Language Tests 83

below. In each case there are three possible answers to the questions and only one of these in each case is right. You should select the right answer and put a tick by its side.

But the history of Western Christendom, too, is unintelligible within its own time limits and space limits. While Western Christendom is a much better unit than the United States or the United Kingdom or France for a historian to operate with, it too turns out, on inspection, to be inadequate. In the time dimension, it goes back only to the close of the Dark Ages following the collapse of the western part of the Roman Empire; that is, it goes back less than 1300 years, and 1300 years is less than a quarter of the 6,000 years during which the species of society represented by Western Christendom has been in existence. Western Christendom is a civilization belonging to the third of the three generations of civilizations that there have been so far.

In the space dimension, the narrowness of the limits of Western Christendom is still more striking. If you look at the physical map of the world as a whole, you will see that the small part of it which is dry land consists of a single continent—Asia—which has a number of peninsulas and off-lying islands. Now, what are the farthest limits to which Western Christendom has managed to expand? You will find them at Alaska and Chile on the west and at Finland and Dalmatia on the east. What lies between those four points is Western Christendom's domain at its widest. And what does that domain amount to? Just the tip of Asia's European peninsula, together with a couple of large islands. (By these two large islands, I mean, of course, North and South America.) Even if you add in the outlying and precarious footholds of the Western world in South Africa, Australia and New Zealand, its total habitable present area amounts to only a very minor part of the total habitable area of the surface of the planet. And you cannot understand the history of Western Christendom within its own geographical limits.

Western Christendom is a product of Christianity, but Christianity did not arise in the Western world; it arose outside the bounds of Western Christendom, in a district that lies today within the domain of a different civilization: Islam. We Western Christians did once try to capture from the Muslims the cradle of our religion in Palestine. If the Crusades had succeeded, Western Christendom would have slightly broadened its footing on the all-important Asiatic mainland. But the Crusades ended in failure.

Western Christendom is merely one of five civilizations that survive in the world to-day; and these are merely five out of about nineteen that one can identify as having come into existence since the first appearance of representatives of this species of society about 6,000 years ago.

(A. Toynbee, *Civilization on Trial.* New York: Oxford University Press, 1947.)

1 The narrow time and space limits of Western Christendom cause the writer to label it:
a unintelligible within its own limits.
b inadequate as a historical unit.
c a much better historical unit.

84 Testing and Experimental Methods

2 What does 'the species of society represented by Western Christendom' refer to?
a all kinds of Christian civilization.
b the western part of the Roman Empire.
c the third generation of human civilizations.

3 What is unusual about the writer's use of the term Asia?
a it contains all the other continents.
b it has a number of peninsulas and off-lying islands.
c it contains Western Christendom's domain.

4 If the Crusades had succeeded the most important gain for Western Christendom would have been:
a the cradle of Christianity.
b a foothold on the continent of Asia.
c the defeat of Islam.

5 What does the writer seem to conclude from the fact that Western Christendom is only one among many civilizations?
a civilization is constantly changing.
b Western Christendom is no more important or final than any other civilization.
c a proper historical perspective is necessary.

One of the major difficulties in a test of this kind is to provide enough linguistic information for more than a very few questions. For this reason there is a lot to be said for unique answer questions because they use up less information than multiple choice questions while having a unique answer and therefore provide the same kind of objectivity in scoring as the more usual multiple choice question. To illustrate what we mean, here are questions 1 and 4 again, this time without their multiple choice framework. It should be clear that in this format they are more difficult.

Example 2(a)

Answer these questions. In each case there is room for you to write in your answer. Note that the answer you require is contained in the text you have just read and that in each case only one answer is the right one:

1. The writer emphasizes the small-scale nature of Western Christendom. As a historian he finds it of minor importance, labelling it:
   ....

4. In terms of the writer's argument that Western Christendom has not been historically important, what would success in the Crusades have meant to Western Christendom?
   ....

1e READING: EXTRA-LINGUISTIC

As we have already suggested, it is not clear how to distinguish this box from the previous one except by taking context as referring to the language features themselves, and the world outside as involving the extra-linguistic relations. The problem that arises is one of distinguishing between language proficiency and knowledge of the world. It is a problem of sampling because, although we may feel capable of selecting and sequencing language material from a linguistic point of view, none of us will be so happy about grading situations simply because of lack of criteria on which to base our selection. Newspapers and the language of newspapers are of interest here. It is possible for us to grade the language of different newspapers in such a way that we can be fairly sure that *The Guardian* is suitable for some students and the *Daily Mirror* for others without looking at each issue. But we must still check that the use of language by the newspaper is not special and different from that in everyday use. What is being argued here, then, is that language tests proper end with the context level because beyond what is being tested is the student's awareness of other things in the world outside. If there is no control by the teacher at the extra-linguistic level, this becomes a general knowledge test; if there is this control then it becomes a test of history or politics or geography. It is exactly this which has been behind much of the criticism of production tests such as the essay and the oral examination. Because of the 'general knowledge' aspect of this kind of text we will give only one example of an extra-linguistic test. This is a test of reading speed which could very easily be fitted into the context box, but which we prefer to treat here since to a certain extent it does involve knowledge of the world outside.

Example 1: Reading speed

In the following passage some of the words are irrelevant ones which have been inserted into the passage. We have underlined the first two as examples. You must find these inserted words and underline them. Work as quickly as you can; you have one minute for the whole passage. The passage makes complete sense once you have removed the inserted words.

A number <u>yes</u> of assumptions about the <u>but</u> way of life in a yellow provincial university three are current yesterday today. We I used myself to hold a number of apples them fruit but in the temple course of an inquiry future in King's School College, Newcastle, river, on which this those paper is no based, I modified unhappy my your views considerably plural. It is was with a view to strongly seeing how now much truth lies there was in these King's assumptions that four an inquiry was will undertaken purple during under the through academic months years 1952–53 people.

It must be emphasized that this method of testing reading speed is somewhat idiosyncratic; however, it has the merit of testing reading speed during the actual process of reading. The scoring of the passage is easy and completely objective. All that need be done is to count up the total number of words correctly underlined and express this as a raw score for the test. It would be useful to know what effect on score the positioning of each distractor has but since we are concerned here with a more practical operation we can safely leave more sophisticated experiments to psycholinguistics. (Since underlining can lead to confusion by careless underlining of more than one word it is probably better to ask for the distractor to be crossed out rather than underlined.)

2a WRITING: PHONOLOGY

All of the writing skill tests necessarily involve some kind of creative writing ability. We are not interested in whether a student can make the appropriate graphic marks, i.e. whether he is able to write in the physical sense. What we are interested in is his language control and we make use of as many different approaches as we can to investigate this. Testing phonology through writing does not give us useful information about a student's language proficiency, since we may just as easily get at his over-all control in other ways. What his writing will tell us, of course, is whether he can write in the creative sense, but is this what we want to know? At a very high level of language study, say in the second or third year at university, we may want to know whether the student can write creatively in the foreign language, but before that we are probably better off testing his creative ability in his first language.

At the level we are discussing, a writing test will require little more than simply writing in some word or sentence. But for a phonology test it is difficult to see how this could be done. If we were to make use of the unique response then the student would need to write in a sound or a word with the correct phoneme or the intonation in question; this may be a case for teaching both a method of transcription and some system of indicating intonation. But such a test is surely little different from the one we have already discussed under reading/phonology and the one we shall discuss later under listening/phonology. In each case what seems to matter is the stimulus; we are anxious to find out the student's awareness of a particular sound distinction. His ability to write this down does seem rather trivial. We shall not therefore quote any examples for this box.

2b WRITING: GRAMMAR

The same comment can be made about possible tests in this box since the student's control over grammar has probably been tested under reading. Again we are not interested in his ability to write a grammatical sentence with minimal stimulus, in other words an open-ended or near open-ended type question. We shall suggest therefore two items of this kind here; the first will be a sentence completion test in which the student must complete from his own knowledge gaps in a sentence which have grammatical implications; the second will be an example of the well-known substitution type.

Example 1 : Sentence completion

Complete the following sentences so that they make sense. The number of letters required is indicated by the number of dashes:
a The map – – – roll– – up and the meeting brought – – an end.
b She drink– as much soup – – her three brother– and more milk – – – – her baby sister.
c In this play he murder– his mother, kills – – – dog and then – – – – – – – – the house.

There are problems here, particularly in (c), but we are presumably prepared to accept these in the interests of giving more scope to the student. The trick of indicating by dashes the right number of letters in the word is helpful (though it brings the test close to being a multiple choice one) but it will not prevent a student coming up with words which are grammatical but not semantically acceptable. For example, what shall we say if in (c) a student responds to the last part with the word *censures*. This is grammatical in a way but makes little sense in our sentence. The point would be even more clear if we had such a sentence as *They drank the* ——— in which we expected the student to insert 'milk' but instead he inserted 'cake'. Is this a grammatical mistake or not? It may well be, and some grammarians would treat it as such, but we need to be quite clear what we are subjecting the student to before we allow him such leeway in his responses.

Example 2 : Substitution test

Put the following passage into the plural (or into the past tense, passive, etc.):

A scientist lives by his wits and these are not always on the best of behaviour. A friend of mine who works in a chemical laboratory down the road from here has an office on the first floor; he says that he is often distracted by what is going on in the road outside his window but that he thinks this is helpful to him in his work as a scientist.

2C WRITING: LEXIS

Here we shall suggest two straightforward examples which involve the right selection of a word which has to be thought up by the student. The first example is a synonym test like that under reading except that it does not provide the student with a list to choose from, and the second is a collocation test which asks the student which grammatical sentences are acceptable on other grounds.

Example 1: Synonyms

Look at the following sentences and in the space at the end write in one or more words which have much the same meaning as the word(s) underlined:
a London is the capital of the U.K. ....
b The River Thames is full of tugs and barges ....
c Just now the men in the docks are on strike ....

Example 2: Collocation test

Some of the following sentences are acceptable English sentences; some are not. Indicate those which are not by putting a cross against them and then underline those words which lead to the unacceptability. In the first one, for example, we may speak of a bottle of gin but we rarely speak of a pound of gin; the student is therefore expected to underline the words *pounds* and *gin*:
a He has just drunk three pounds of gin.
b I've made my sofa very comfortable with lots of pillows.
c With all these dirty plates we should like you to help us polish the dishes after supper.
d I've tied the new black ribbon you bought me on my typewriter.

2d WRITING: CONTEXT

The two examples given here are both widely used; they are the summary, and the framework essay. In each case an attempt is made to provide the student with all the extra-linguistic information he requires, and to draw from him the language needed to express this in another way. It may be claimed that this is impossible and that such a division into language and situation is a theoretical one, useful perhaps in the analysis of the linguist but never valid in real life, and therefore not valid in a test which takes place in real life. What this claim is asserting is that any change in language will change the situation, and vice versa; it is no longer the same thing that is being talked about if the language is reduced, as in the summary, or extended, as in the framework essay. Now this may well be so; all we assert here is that while situations may never be the same, many of them appear to be similar and in real life we certainly act as if they were. What is more, we are usually prepared to accept a summary of a story or a set of events as standing for its original, and the extension as standing for its framework. This being so, it is perhaps not so far-fetched to claim that all we are asking the student to do in the following test is to change the language in appropriate ways. We shall give a shorter version in example 1 than may be needed in a full test; what we shall do is to provide a short paragraph and ask for a reduction to about one third. Notice that we do not make the stipulation (not often made these days) that the summary should be in the writer's own words.

Example 1: Summary
Read the following passage and then give what you think is the essential part of the meaning in a short continuous piece of prose which should contain about one third of the number of words in the original.

Convention would seem to possess two main real advantages, one primarily individual, the other social. The first lies in the fact that, in prescribing within narrow limits what has to be done, said, or worn, it saves us from the mental effort of thinking or deciding for ourselves and provides us, so to speak, with a number of formulae (which may, as Pear suggests, have value as social lubricants) for use on suitable occasions. In this it is like habit, but of course it shares with habit the disadvantage that it may lead us to behave in ways that, with changing circumstances, may have ceased to be appropriate. The second, social, advantage of convention consists in helping to preserve the solidarity of the groups or classes concerned. Our judgement as to its value in this last respect will largely depend upon how far we consider the retention of such groups and classes is desirable. Those who demand a classless society will rightly look upon many of our conventions with a certain suspicion.

Example 2: Framework essay
Here is the outline of a story. Use the outline in order to write the story for yourself. The outline contains about 60 words; your story should contain about 200 words.
Going home from school — friend suggests take an unusual route — see smoke coming from upstairs window of house — hear child scream — run off to phone Fire Brigade — difficult to find house again — no smoke now and Fire Brigade find the house empty — mystery of fire and missing child — Fire Brigade chief cross — but dog barking leads to kidnapper and child — mystery solved.

2e WRITING: EXTRA-LINGUISTIC

Here we are obviously concerned with free composition, with those aspects of the writing skill which are creative in some literary sense. The two items we shall suggest here are the familiar free composition and 'letter to a purpose'. Clearly the main problem with this kind of test is that of reliability, i.e. the difficulty of relating one type of answer to another on the same scale. There may also be a validity problem but we shall not go into that now. We argued in section 2d that language can be tested in a controlled composition but we would not claim so readily that this is the case here. In the free composition we are expecting not only language control but range and inspiration of ideas as well, and this is not strictly a language skill. Or is it? Many people feel that it is and that it must be tested since it seems to provide the most natural type of situation for using what language has been learned, which is what one has to do in a real life situation. There are exaggerations about this argument but we shall accept it and go on to look at our two suggested items.

Example 1: Free composition

Your headmaster has been asked to provide a full report on school life for a visiting inspector. He asks a number of students to write brief accounts of various aspects of school life. He asks you to write on your preparations for coming to school every morning, that is, everything you do from waking up until you arrive at your first class.

Example 1 is in fact very much to the purpose. But example 2 is meant to be even more so and to bring in notions of language in situation more directly.

Example 2: Letter to a purpose

You have just heard from your uncle that a large tree has blown down across the road leading to his house preventing him from taking his cattle and his van along the road. The tree belongs to your headmaster and you know that he and your uncle have had a long standing feud about rights of access. You and your headmaster get along very well and you are known as a hard working pupil. But you are fond of your uncle and you do, of course, have an obligation to him as a near relative. Write a letter to your headmaster stating the position and trying as politely as you can to persuade him to move the tree before your uncle takes the law into his own hands.

3a LISTENING: PHONOLOGY

The two items we shall suggest here are both more phonological than grammatical though there is some difficulty in keeping these two aspects of language structure apart. The first is a simple phoneme test; the second a test of intonation.

Example 1: Phoneme discrimination

Listen to the questions. In each one you will hear three words, 1, 2 and 3. You must decide if they sound the same or sound different. If they all sound the same put a line through all three numbers, if only two are the same then put a line through those two numbers only. If all three are different then do not put any lines.

The student then hears, for example:
a bit bit beat
b pain main lane
c share share share

and should respond as follows:
 a 1̶ 2̶ 3
 b 1 2̶ 3
 c 1̶ 2 3̶

This method of responding is preferred to the one in which the student actually sees the words written on his answer sheet because he is then being asked to do what amounts to a reading test as well, whereas here we have as pure a listening test as we can get, i.e. the student is being asked to identify what is different from what, phonologically speaking.

For the same reason it seems more satisfactory in an intonation test (i.e. one which is designed not to impinge on grammar) to deal with sound differences only. Again the student is asked to indicate if three choices are all the same, two different or all different. What he then hears is:

Example 2: Intonation

Here are three short sentences. Decide whether they are the same, all different or only two the same. If they are all the same put a line through the numbers 1, 2, 3; if two are the same put a line through those two numbers; if they are all different then leave the numbers blank.

What the student has on his script is as follows:
 a 1 2 3
What he hears on the tape is:
 a 1 It's five o'clock↗
    2 It's five o'clock↘
    3 It's five o'clock↘ (etc.)

3b LISTENING: GRAMMAR

Grammar, as we have pointed out, is most economically tested under reading. We could make use of the same kind of items here. Instead, we shall suggest a pronoun replacement test and a sentence-type test. Notice that both of these are kinds of translation test. What many sophisticated tests are in fact asking of students is subtle kinds of translation.

Example 1: Pronoun replacement

Listen to the following conversations and at the end of each put a tick against the correct answer:
 a The student hears but does not see written:
   Voice 1 My brother John works in London.
   Voice 2 What's his job?
   The student then hears this question:

Question: Which of the following words could replace *his*:
1 brother
2 John's
3 my
4 your

b *Voice 1* What's Scotland like to live in after sunny Africa?
Voice 2 My wife and I find it cold, of course, but the children are excited by the mountains.
Question: Which of the following words could replace *it*:
1 wife
2 children
3 mountains
4 Scotland

c *Voice 1* Mary, may I introduce my brother Peter?
Voice 2 But we've met before in Bristol.
Question: Which of the following words could replace *we*:
1 Bristol
2 Peter and I
3 Mary
4 Peter and Mary

Example 2: Sentence-type test

Listen to these sentences. After each one there is a question which asks you to choose the sentence on your script most like the meaning of the one you have heard.

a *Voice*: The farmer shot the rabbit.
  Question: 1 Who shot the rabbit?
  2 The farmer did not shoot the rabbit.
  3 Shoot the rabbit!
  4 The rabbit was shot by the farmer.

b *Voice*: Boil the egg for four minutes.
  Question: 1 Fry the egg.
  2 Do not boil the egg for four minutes.
  3 Have you boiled the egg for four minutes?
  4 You must boil the egg for four minutes.

3C LISTENING: LEXIS

Listening tests of vocabulary may often be repetitions of their writing counterparts. After all it is not vocabulary items separately presented that make listening comprehension difficult. To present them in a running spoken text must create other difficulties, for example, uncertainties as to what is being tested, whether it is the items or the connections between them. However, we shall assume that a listening vocabulary test is different from writing, and suggest two kinds. The first is a straight vocabulary test in which the student has to match pictures with single words; the second is a test of collocation in which the student must read a very simple sentence beginning and then choose the appropriate ending from a series of vocabulary items on tape.

Example 1: Picture vocabulary test
Below is a series of four pictures, 1, 2, 3, 4. Look at these carefully. Now listen to the tape. You will hear three words; each one is repeated. Each time choose the picture which the word best describes and write the word in the space under the picture.

1 ......   2 ......   3 ......   4 ......
Voice: umbrella
       shade
       shed

Example 2: Collocation in sentence completion
Below is a sentence. It needs one word to complete it. Read the sentence beginning and then listen to the tape. You will hear four words. Choose the one which best completes the sense of the sentence and write it in the space provided:
a The weather today is very ....
  Voice: white
         blue
         grey
         green
b Two pints of ...., please.
  Voice: coffee
         beer
         water
         tea

3d LISTENING: CONTEXT

In many ways this is one of the more satisfactory of the boxes to fill. Here we can afford to relax our attempt to keep the levels apart. Almost any test of listening comprehension seems to fit into this box and it is probably in tests of this kind that most progress has been made recently.

We shall suggest two well-known test types, the first a rephrasing test in which the student has to select the best written paraphrase of a heard sentence, and the second a question-answer test on similar lines. We shall not discuss the more common text-based test, useful though this is, since a test of this type has already been discussed as an example under reading (1d, example 2). Notice that the distractors present plausible paraphrases to similar statements or plausible answers to similar questions.

Example 1: Rephrasing test

Listen to the following sentence and then choose from the numbered sentences on your script (1–4) the one which has the closest meaning to the one you hear and put a cross through its number:
Voice: John hasn't returned to Bristol yet.
Sentences: 1 John is in Bristol.
              2 John has gone back to Bristol.
              3 Where is John?
              4 John is not in Bristol.

Example 2: Question-answer test

Listen to the following question and then choose from the numbered sentences on your script (1–4) the one which provides the best answer to the question and put a cross through its number:
Voice: What did John leave with you?
Answers: 1 In the afternoon
          2 With his brother
          3 A large parcel
          4 Yes he did

3e LISTENING: EXTRA-LINGUISTIC

As long as the responses are kept fairly short it is possible to be objective here in the sense that you know whether an answer is right or wrong. What you do not know, of course, in the case of a wrong response, is what is making it wrong—language, situation, general knowledge, or something else.

There does remain the difficulty of sampling at the appropriate level. For an over-all proficiency test this is less of a problem since, ideally, the 'proficient' student should be able to cope with any material from any area of general knowledge. But since we are concerned with intermediate students we cannot fairly go outside the language content they have learned. Consequently an extra-linguistic test must involve the use of some of this language in a situation with which they may be unfamiliar. Then, as we have seen before, the question remains of whether this is a language test at all.

The two examples we shall suggest are a conversation test and a 'what is the situation?' test. It has to be admitted that the dividing line here between context and extra-linguistic is far from clear.

Example 1: Conversation test

Listen to the following conversation and then answer the questions below by putting a tick against the choice you select:

Voice A: Tickets please!
Voice B: 6p, one please!
Voice A: Where to?
Voice B: London Road.
Voice A: Sorry, dear, that's 9p now. You see it's over two miles.
Voice B: Oh dear! I only have 6p.
Voice C: Here's an extra 3p for you.

    Questions: 1 Where does this conversation take place?
              in a car
              in a bus
              in a train
              in a plane

            2 Who is asking for the money?
              the driver
              the conductor
              the shopkeeper
              the inspector

            3 How far is it to London Road?
              2 miles
              3 miles
              6 miles
              9 miles

            4 How much has the fare increased by?
              2p
              3p
              6p
              9p

    5 What do you think the child will do?
     get off now
     stay on and pay later
     stay on and not pay
     stay on and use someone else's 3p

Example 2: '*What is the situation*' *test*
Listen to the following short dialogues, then look at the suggestions below each as to what kind of situation they occur in. Choose the one you think best and put a cross through its number:
a Voice A: It's not that time, is it?
 Voice B: Yes it is. 7.30. Must get up.
  Situations: 1 bed time
       2 early morning
       3 supper time
       4 closing time
b Voice A: Can I speak to Mr Brown?
 Voice B: Yes, I'll put you through.
  Situations: 1 a party
       2 an introduction
       3 outside a house
       4 on the telephone

4a SPEAKING: PHONOLOGY

A speaking test at the level of phoneme discrimination is not difficult to devise but it is difficult to be precisely objective about. Since a student is being asked to pronounce certain items (and, implicitly or not, make distinctions) it follows that the examiner must be able to hear what is said accurately, and what is more the student must be able to repeat the same sound any number of times. It is unlikely that he can do this and even more unlikely that the examiner (unless he is a trained phonetician) will hear accurately. Since the student will be asked to produce 'difficult' sounds and since we all utter allophones rather than phonemes, it will be difficult to determine whether the allophones of a number of students all belong to the same phoneme. Of course students may be asked to distinguish several phonemes, in which case the particular allophones no longer matter as long as they serve to keep the phonemes apart. There still remains the problem of which phonological system we are using. For example, if I pronounce *bit* as /biːt/ and *beat* as /bʌt/ I am keeping the words apart but to no purpose since the second is plainly wrong.

 Our two examples will depend on the examiner's skill and test, first, production of phoneme-like sounds previously prepared by the examiner so that he knows which sounds to listen for; and, second, production of word stress, weak forms and rhythm in the same text, which must therefore be read twice.

Example 1: Phoneme test
Read the following passage aloud so as to bring out the meaning:
Extract from text:

> The orchestra stopped playing but my neighbour went on beating time on his knee. The people in front who had finished clapping turned to one another.

The examiner listens for the pronunciation of the following sounds:
neighbour /ei/
beating /i:/
his /i/
people /i:/
another /ə/

Example 2: Stress, weakening and rhythm
The same instructions and text are given. The examiner listens for the production of the following:

the	(weak form)
orchestra	(stress placement)
neighbour	(stress placement)
who had finished	(no stress on *who*)
to one another	(no pauses between the words)

4b SPEAKING: GRAMMAR
All speaking tests must be administered individually, with one examiner to each student, or they must be recorded on tape for scoring afterwards, just like a written script. This being so it is possible to devise tests which assess grammatical control and which do not depend on reading or require too much lexical or contextual awareness. The first we shall suggest is a connectives test in which the student is given a list of three, four or five words which he must use to make up a sentence. The second example will be a transformation test in which the student must make certain grammatical changes in a heard sentence.

Example 1: Connectives test
Here is a list of four words. Use them to make up a sentence keeping the same order:

John
brother
hospital
crash

Example 2: Transformation test

Listen to the voice. When it has finished you must repeat what it says making the required changes:
  1 *Voice*: John came here yesterday. (I, tomorrow)
     Expected response: I will/shall come here tomorrow.
  2 *Voice*: It's raining now. (Question, yesterday)
     Expected response: Was it raining yesterday?

As will be realized the difficulty in tests of this kind is in procuring unique responses. Since this is not always possible the examiner has to work hard in his scoring in deciding just what is an acceptable response.

4c SPEAKING: LEXIS

This time we shall suggest two examples. In the first example the student must provide appropriate names for objects in pictures, and in the second he is asked to complete or add to a series of terms. In both cases, of course, the problem of assessing the appropriateness of the response rests with the examiner.

Example 1: Names for objects
What can you see in the picture?

Example 2: Words in series

Listen to this list of words and then complete the list or add to it by providing a word of your own:
  1 Grandfather, father, son, ...
  2 Tree, bush, shrub . . . .

4d SPEAKING: CONTEXT

The two examples we suggest here are, first, a question-answer test and, second, a picture-description test. Again, as with the earlier context examples, we see the greater ease of devising such tests and the more apparent relevance to the real-life demands of language use. Answering a question in particular is very much what is demanded of us in a real second language situation. Another possibility is a test involving secondary statements, that is, responses to something said which is not a question but which acts as a conversation initiator.

Example 1: Question-answer test
Listen to the question and then give what seems to you an appropriate short answer:
1 *Voice:* What time is it now?
  Student: It's about three o'clock.
2 *Voice:* Shall we stay in or go for a walk?
  Student: Go for a walk.

It is not necessary to use the same situation for all the questions.

Example 2: Picture description test
Here is a group of four pictures which tell a story. Describe briefly what the boy is doing in each picture.

4e SPEAKING: EXTRA-LINGUISTIC

This box is similar to writing/extra-linguistic (2e). Here again we are really concerned with free composition as opposed to the more restricted type we have just been dealing with. We shall suggest as our two examples, first a test of free conversation and, second, a test in which the student is given the beginning of a story, in written form, and then told to complete it. The free conversation example is nothing more than the traditional oral test in which the examiner confronts the student and seeks to engage him in simple conversation which he then assesses. We have discussed several times the difficulties of this assessment and we will not repeat the argument here. Since the free conversation may be on any topic thought to be within the student's knowledge it is not necessary to give an example.

Example 2: Completing a story

Read the following passage which is the beginning of a story. You will then have about three minutes to tell the rest of the story in your own words.

One day on his way home from school John saw something lying in the middle of the road. When he came closer he saw it was a man's hat, rather like a railwayman's flat peaked cap. It was blue and looked new. He picked it up and was examining it when his friend Henry came along. 'What's that you've got?' asked Henry. Just then a lorry rattled down the road towards them and stopped. The driver got out of his cab and spoke to the boys.

Now go on.

8.3 Conclusion

The purpose of this section has been to show that it is possible to devise tests for all the skills and at each of the levels. No strong claim is made for the particular division into skills and levels used here since other divisions can also be employed to produce a similar coverage of the language abilities. This is just one way of doing it. However, the earlier sections of the chapter, especially the discussions of validity, emphasized the importance of relevance in testing. Although tests of all kinds can be constructed they are often not relevant and therefore not useful. The most satisfactory tests are, undoubtedly, those that actually *look* relevant. For example the blanket-type tests of reading and speaking at the context level look relevant to most teachers and are, indeed, the most useful test types. True, they are too crude to be much help for diagnostic purposes; they provide no precise information on what is going wrong with language learning at various stages. But we cannot be sure that tests of the more discrete types (e.g. reading/phonology) can provide that precise information since our language learning theory is still so undeveloped. In the present uncertain state of knowledge in this area blanket-type or global tests are probably the safest and certainly the most valid for proficiency purposes.

9 Practical work

Exercise A: Constructing a grammar-morphology test

Write a 25-item test on English suffixes and prefixes following the model provided below. In a real situation you would probably need about 50 items in order to sample English suffixes and prefixes adequately. Note that the suggested instructions allow for the possibility of dummy items, i.e., items which do not need changing.

The Construction of Language Tests

Instructions

Fill in the gaps so that the phrases on the left have the same meaning as those on the right. You will find that sometimes the phrase is already complete and you do not need to add anything.

Examples

1 some taste . . . soup	some soup that has no taste
2 the wood . . . merchants	the merchants who sell wood
3 a land . . . strip	a strip where planes can land
4 a . . . war car	a car made before the war

Answers to examples

1 To give the meaning 'some soup that has no taste' you must add 'less' to the phrase on the left, so the answer will be: *some tasteless soup*.
2 To give the meaning 'the merchants who sell wood' you do not need to add anything to the phrase on the left, so the answer will be: *the wood merchants*.
3 To give the meaning 'a strip where planes can land' you must add 'ing' to the phrase on the left, so the answer will be: *a landing strip*.
4 To give the meaning 'a car made before the war' you must add 'pre' to the phrase on the left, so the answer will be: *a pre-war car*.

Now write 25 similar items.

Exercise B: Assessing restating and responding ability

Write a 15-item test to assess restating and responding ability. There should be 7 restatement and 8 response items. Each of the restatement items should consist of a statement consisting of three possible restatements, only one of which is correct. Each of the response items should consist of a question followed by three possible responses, only one of which is correct.

Instructions

In the items below you will find a statement or a question followed by three choices. When the choices follow a statement, tick the choice that gives the same meaning as the statement. When the choices follow a question, tick the choice that gives the best answer to the question.

Examples

1 When we reached the library this morning we found it closed for the holidays.
    a We closed the library.
    b We were able to find the library.
    √*c* The library was not open today.

2 What kind of lamp is it?
   a It's a lamp of the table.
√*b* It's a table lamp.
   c It's a table's lamp.

Answers to the examples
1 The choice that most nearly says what the statement says is (c). That is why there is a tick beside (c).
2 The best answer here is (b). Hence the tick beside (b).
Now write 15 similar items, 7 with statements and 8 with questions.

Exercise C: Reading comprehension
Write 8 reading comprehension items based on the following text. Vary the kind of items you write so as to test both points of detail and points of more general reference.[1]

Instructions
Read the text below and then answer the questions that follow.
Each question has three choices, only one of which is correct.
Tick what you consider to be the correct answer.

Having glanced at the historical origins of the principal concepts of human communication, let us now examine some of the modern technical work in which they have been treated mathematically. The material in this section must necessarily be rather technical and may be omitted at first reading.
5 It is in telecommunication that a really hard core of mathematical theory has developed; such theory has been evolved over a considerable number of years, as engineers have sought to define what it is they communicate over their telephone, telegraph and radio systems. In such technical systems, the commodity which is bought and sold, called *information capacity*, may be defined
10 strictly on a mathematical basis, without any of the vagueness which arises when human beings or other biological organisms are regarded as 'communication systems'. Nevertheless, human beings usually form part of telephony or telegraphy systems, as 'sources' or 'receivers'; but the formal mathematical theory is of direct application only to the technical equipment itself, from microphone
15 to headphones or loudspeaker, and is abstracted from specific users of the equipment. This is not to say that the mathematical concepts or techniques are completely forbidden elsewhere, but if so used, this must not be regarded as a simple application of existing 'theory of (tele)communication' by extrapolation from its legitimate domain of applicability.
20 Perhaps the most important technical development which has assisted in the birth of communication theory is that of telegraphy. With its introduction, the idea of speed of transmission of 'intelligence' arose. When its economic value

[1] See Volume 3, chapter 6.

was fully realized, the problems of compressing signals exercised many minds, leading eventually to the concept of 'quantity of information' and to theories
25 of times and speed of signalling.

In the year 1267 Roger Bacon suggested that 'a certain sympathetic needle' (lodestone) might be used for distant communication. Porta and Gilbert, in the sixteenth century, wrote about the 'sympathetic telegraph' and, in 1746, Watson, in England, sent electric signals over nearly two miles of wire. Thus
30 not only did the notion of distant communication, by invisible means, arise at an extraordinarily early date, but the first practical achievements were made at a date which astonishes many telecommunication engineers. In 1753 an anonymous worker used one wire for each letter of the alphabet, but in 1787 Lomond used one wire pair and some code. The introduction of 'carrier waves', during
35 the First World War, was made practicable by G. A. Campbell's invention of the wave filter. This principle of allocating simultaneous signals into 'frequency bands' has been the mainstay of electrical communication and remained unchallenged until the Second World War.

Related techniques which have greatly urged the development of general
40 communication theory are those of telephony and television. Alexander Graham Bell's invention of the telephone in 1876 (anticipated by Reis and Bourseul, it is believed) has particular significance in relation to the question of analogies between mechanics and physiology, to which we shall be making further reference later when discussing both the value and the dangers of anthropomorphic
45 or *animistic* analogy; otherwise the telephone is, from our present point of view, purely a technological development, setting up problems similar to those of telegraphy.
        C. Cherry *On Human Communication*. M.I.T. Press 1957 pp. 40–1.

Examples
1 What reason does the writer give for suggesting that the reader omits this section?
   a its technical nature
   b it has already been dealt with in the historical review
   c it is not about human communication
2 Do human beings have information capacity?
   a Yes, because they form part of a telecommunication system
   b No, because they are not bought and sold
   c No, because information capacity applies only to the hardware

Answers to examples
1 The answer here is (a) which refers to the 'rather technical' phrase in line 4.
2 The answer here is (c) since we are told in line 14 that the theory 'is of direct application only to the technical equipment itself'.
Now write eight similar items yourself.

10 Further Reading (Chapters 1–3)

Clark, John L. D. 1972. *Foreign Language Testing: Theory and Practice.* Philadelphia: Center for Curriculum Development. A useful guide written by one of the foremost American practitioners of criterion referenced testing.

Cronbach, L. J. 1961. *Essentials of Psychological Testing.* New York: Harper and Row. A standard textbook concerned with the construction and use of tests. It has to do with tests as experiments rather than with the use of tests in experiments.

Davies, Alan (ed.). 1968. *Language Testing Symposium.* London: Oxford University Press. An attempt to bring together practical language testing procedures and the underlying theoretical disciplines.

Guilford, J. P. 1942. *Fundamental Statistics in Psychology and Education.* New York: McGraw-Hill. This book is out of date in some respects but it contains all the statistics needed by the test constructor, presented in an accessible way.

Harris, David P. 1969. *Testing English as a Second Language.* New York: McGraw-Hill. An excellent guide which can be used as a teaching text.

Heaton, J. B. 1975. *Writing English Language Tests.* London: Longman. A good source book for item types, with suggestions for item writing.

Lado, R. 1961. *Language Testing.* New York: McGraw-Hill. A pioneering work which retains its value as a comprehensive guide and a check list of test types.

Magnusson, D. 1967. *Test Theory.* Reading, Mass.: Addison Wesley. This book, translated from Swedish, is particularly successful in presenting the mathematics underlying testing in a simple way.

Murphy, M. J. 1969. *Designing Multiple-Choice Items for Testing English Language.* Lagos: African Universities Press and The British Council. A simple and brief guide, with lots of examples.

Robson, C. 1973. *Experiment, Design and Statistics in Psychology.* Harmondsworth: Penguin. A guide to the essential statistics likely to be needed by applied linguists.

Valette, Rebecca. 1967. *Modern Language Testing: A Handbook.* New York: Harcourt Brace. Contains many examples of sample items in languages other than English. In some ways the book brings Lado up-to-date.

4 RUTH CLARK
The Design and Interpretation of Experiments

1 Introduction

We are accustomed nowadays to having the results of experiments thrust at us from all sides arguing in favour of various techniques at work and warning against various indulgences in play. In self-defence the educated man needs to know enough about experimental design to be able to resist false arguments and enough about statistics to be able to interpret valid arguments. In addition, the teacher may wish to try his own hand at controlled experimentation. He will need to know what types of experiment are feasible given the limitations of the classroom situation, and if he intends to seek the help of a trained statistician in planning his work he will need to have the basis of a common language with him.

The purpose of chapters 4–6 is not to make the reader into a statistician, but rather to present a number of useful techniques. It is hoped that they will help to make research reports more intelligible, and to make the reader less vulnerable to false claims. The chapters also aim to demonstrate the fundamental logic and simplicity of statistical concepts and to make it possible for the reader who so desires to approach a full scale work on statistics with confidence.

People are often put off statistics by the idea that one has to be good at mathematics. The only mathematics necessary for carrying out the procedures described in the following chapters are the basic operations of addition, subtraction, multiplication, division, squaring and finding square roots. If the reader wishes to perform some of the tests he will find it helpful to be able to use a calculating machine or tables of logarithms, but this is not essential. Often it is the use of symbols in statistical formulae that may appear to constitute an obstacle for the non-numerate. However, the formulae are not basically very complex and one soon gets used to the symbols.

One problem is that different symbols tend to get used for equivalent concepts in different textbooks. Variants of symbols and additional symbols have occasionally been included even when they are not essential on the grounds that this should make the transition to other books easier. Another problem is that different books sometimes contain formulae which though mathematically equivalent to the ones presented here are not always identically presented. The reader should not be daunted by this, but where necessary seek help in clarifying the relationship between different types of formula.

It will be necessary to introduce a number of technical terms; these are listed in the index together with page references. Symbols and computations will be introduced very gradually. The aim is to give the reader a feeling for different types of experiment, and to help him understand the part that statistical computation plays in evaluating experiments, before plunging him into arithmetical and algebraic activities.

Chapter 4 begins with a discussion of the problems of measurement of variables in research studies, and goes on to consider the role of the control of variables in experimental design. Then comes a section in which data are presented from four different research studies. These four examples have been chosen to illustrate six basic statistical tests, differing from one another in certain key features. The aim here is to illustrate how statistics works in various contexts to help us answer research questions. For this reason only a handful of tests is presented, but the reader is told where he can find further information about analysing data which do not conform precisely to the four models discussed.

Only the preliminary evaluation of findings is considered in chapter 4. Details of the computations associated with this preliminary evaluation will be found in chapter 5. The text concentrates on the reasons for performing these particular computations. Not until chapter 6 will the reader be shown how to carry the analysis of all four experiments through to their conclusion. Chapter 6 begins by presenting the statistical concepts of probability and significance which must be grasped before the complete analysis can be understood.

It is hoped that by going through various stages of analysis for all four experiments concurrently, the reader will get a clearer understanding of the basic similarities between all six statistical tests. It is also hoped that by considering the studies in relation to one another, the reader will become able to identify when a particular statistical technique is appropriate more easily than if he dealt with them one by one, without seeing them as a group.

Other aspects of experimental design and statistics are introduced in the course of the three chapters as they are needed to provide the basis for subsequent stages of the argument, or as the development of the chapters provides the background necessary for them to be understood.

2 Measurement

Research is concerned with recording the incidence of things and with seeking relationships between things. We may wish to know the proportion of literates in a community or the relationship between sex and literacy. We may wish to find out the number of examinees attaining each score in an examination and then to look for a relationship between the exam score and motivation or the exam score and the textbook used, or the exam score and the type of teaching.

We cannot go far in research without meeting problems of classification and measurement. Whatever phenomena we are interested in we are going to have to find ways of classifying them. In the first example above we can easily classify people according to sex but how are we to define 'literate' and 'illiterate', 'motivated' and 'unmotivated' or whatever shades of literacy and motivation we wish to deal with? Before beginning to discuss experiments, we shall have to consider some problems of classification and measurement.

2.1 The choice of an adequate measure

To illustrate some problems of measurement, let us look at an example. Suppose that we are investigating the hypothesis that the teachers who are satisfied in their jobs are the most effective in them. We must first choose a sample of teachers since we cannot include all teachers in our survey. More will be said about sampling later. The next step might be to question teachers as to their job satisfaction. Shall we say to them 'Are you satisfied with your job?' If we did this we might expect the answer 'Mind your own business' from some people. Those who did answer might fluctuate between expressions of deep satisfaction and profound dissatisfaction depending on whether they thought we were investigating them as candidates for promotion, considering the possibility of usurping their jobs or studying working conditions with a view to improving them. Others would probably say 'What on earth do you mean by "satisfied with my job"?'

We can learn several lessons from these hypothetical responses. Firstly we must be wary of antagonizing any of the members of our sample. It is chosen to represent the population we are interested in and the people who resent our questions are quite likely to differ in relevant respects from the rest of the sample. If they were to withdraw it would upset the representativeness of the sample. Any delicate social investigation has a category of refusers about whom little is known. This category must be kept as small as possible.

Secondly we must avoid putting those people who do participate on the defensive. We want their answers to be as truthful as possible and not to be modified by their interpretation of our purpose in asking. For example, if someone knocked on your door to ask if you had a television you might answer one way if you thought he was a salesman and in quite another way if you thought he was checking whether you had a television licence. Whenever possible we should base our measurements on concrete objective evidence rather than relying on people's statements. Where this is not possible we should try to make our questions matter-of-fact and prevent the sensitivities of the interviewee being aroused. In clinical studies this is achieved by asking questions about neutral traits known to be connected with the clinical syndromes in which the questioner is really interested but about which the patient may be reticent. Similarly in questionnaires buffer items about unrelated topics are often interspersed among the questions to distract attention from delicate material.

The third lesson to be learned from the example is that people's views as to what constitutes job satisfaction probably do not coincide. If we just relied on impressionistic replies to questions as imprecise as 'Are you satisfied with your job?' we would have very little idea of what we were actually measuring, and in fact we would probably be measuring a hotchpotch of things each with a different relationship to the effectiveness of teaching. We have all met with instances of parallel studies which have come up with conflicting results. One has proved that 'A' is related to 'B' and the other that it is related to 'not B'. Very often the reason for this is that the two research teams are working with different definitions of A or of B or of both. This matters less if we have clear information about how the characteristics, usually known as variables, were defined. We need operational definitions in research; that is to say, we need precise statements as to how the variables were measured or it will be impossible for another investigator to check whether replication of the experiment produces the same results. Furthermore, it will be impossible for the reader of a research report to interpret the findings. If, however, a researcher said 'I took the amount of voluntary extra work a teacher did in the school after hours as a measure of his job satisfaction and found this to be related to the proportion of pupils he got through their terminal examinations' the reader might not think the operational definitions of job satisfaction and effectiveness as a teacher adequate but he would at least know exactly what the claim was.

Thus, a first step towards getting an acceptable measure is to define what we take to be the components and criteria of job satisfaction so that we can be more confident that all the teachers are taking into account all the same aspects of the job in their answers and that they know what we want them to base their judgements on. Any researcher replicating the experiment can have the same confidence. Wherever possible questions should be specified in concrete terms. For instance if we decide that we need to know how long a teacher spends each week preparing his lessons we should not ask 'Do you spend a long time?' This leaves room for a considerable amount of subjectivity in the decision as to what constitutes a long time. It would be better to say 'How long do you spend?' or 'Do you spend less than two hours, between two and five hours or more than five hours?'.

Such operational definitions give some guarantee of consistency in the judgements reached by different participants in the study. To turn for a moment to the other variable, effectiveness in teaching, we may decide to use evaluations by headmasters as a means of classifying the teachers. They might be asked to classify teachers as 'highly effective', 'effective' or 'ineffective'. Since the teachers being rated will come from a number of schools and since headmasters have different criteria (not to mention different degrees of insight in judging people) we would not be applying a measuring instrument which could give consistent judgements throughout the study. This lack of consistency would be more evident if we had a number of people evaluating the same individuals. If we asked the teachers' colleagues (or even their pupils) to rate their efficiency and there was more than one teacher from the same school in the sample, we might well find that the different judges arranged the teachers in a different order of merit. The stability of a method of measurement and its capacity to produce the same results consistently whenever, wherever and by whomever it is applied, is known as reliability.

One of the advantages of the operational definition of job satisfaction suggested above is the ease with which it can be applied. It is relatively easy to get an objective measurement of how long a teacher spends in school after official hours. Since it is easy to apply, it is a reliable measure, i.e. different investigators would be unlikely to classify teachers differently on the basis of it. The criterion would have to be applied over a fairly lengthy representative period or another kind of unreliability would creep in. A teacher might be misclassified because in the particular month under study a close relative of his was ill and so he was prevented from taking as much interest as he normally did in extracurricular activities, or he might have been on bad terms with his wife and used school activities as an excuse for spending less time at home. Despite its convenience, however, the amount of time spent in school after hours could be regarded as a very limited and rigid criterion which did not do anything like full justice to the richness of the concept of job satisfaction. Similarly, the inadequacy of examination successes as the only measure of effective teaching hardly needs mentioning. The simpler and more reliable measure may not tell us what we really want to know. We have to be sure not only that we are measuring something consistently but also that we are measuring what we want to measure. In other words, the measure must not simply be reliable, it must also be valid.

2.2 Measurement: further sources of bias

The use of the above measures may have a further disadvantage. It is possible that using voluntary work after school hours as a measure of job satisfaction could build a bias into the very measurement of the variable which would favour the confirmation of our hypothesis. If we observed a relationship between amount of voluntary work done after school hours and proportion of examination successes by pupils we should infer that job satisfaction is related to efficiency. However, voluntary work and examination success might be linked indirectly in a way unconnected with job satisfaction. For example, pupils may do well generally in English literature examinations. Also, one of the chief extracurricular activities in schools is drama, which is likely to be organized by the English master. In this case by using the voluntary work after school hours as a measure of job satisfaction and the exam successes as a measure of efficiency we would find the association we expected between extra hours and exam successes, but it would be due to the special nature of English literature rather than to a general relationship between satisfaction and efficiency. Thus we should be in error if we inferred the latter. If we want to know whether satisfaction and efficiency are related, we must avoid prejudicing the issue by our choice of measurement and measure them strictly independently of one another.

On the other hand, our investigation would be vitiated in a similar way if the judgements of the effectiveness of teachers were to be contaminated by judgements as to their enjoyment of their job. Someone might reason 'He's a very effective teacher, he's so enthusiastic.' If this kind of reasoning were prevalent, the hypothesis could not help being confirmed. Many statements posing as research findings based on evidence are in fact statements of the way the writer defines a given variable. For example the statement 'Hot-tempered people are insecure' might mean that a relationship has been discovered between hot temper and insecurity or it might mean that whenever the author of the statement observes that a person is hot-tempered he judges him to be insecure.

It is often preferable in research for different people to make judgements on the different variables and for them to be unaware of the hypothesis. It is very easy for a research worker to be unconsciously influenced in the way he records events by his preconceptions about how they will occur. It is also possible for him to communicate these preconceptions in a subtle manner to the participants in the experiment (usually known as experimental subjects) and so influence their responses in the appropriate direction.

It has been found necessary, for instance, in experiments where the effectiveness of drugs is being compared, for the doctors or nurses assisting to be kept in ignorance of which drug, if any, they are administering to each patient, lest their own expectations as to its effectiveness affect the patient's confidence in the drug and hence his reaction to it. This is known as the double blind technique because both doctor and patient are unaware which treatment is being administered. Its aim is to reduce both investigator and response bias. Often the experimental hypothesis is one about which the subject himself may have views which would colour his responses to a questionnaire or prevent him from reacting naturally in a laboratory test so it is usually necessary 'in the interests of science' to keep him in ignorance of the main purpose. We have to avoid establishing in the subjects of experiments a mental set, a specific expectation of what the experimental material will consist of or what sort of response the experimenter requires. Here again buffer items, which were mentioned above in connection with emotive material, may be very useful, even in an emotionally neutral context.

At this point the reader's reaction may be 'Let's get rid of the human element altogether since it is so troublesome and settle for as objective a measure as possible in every case'. What could be a more objective measure of satisfaction in a job than the length of time a person remains in it? The difficulty is that to measure this we have to come in at the end, as it were, and look retrospectively at the other variable, the quality of the teacher's teaching at the time when he was doing the job. Many researches are built on this retrospective pattern but they suffer from the difficulty that earlier situations about which the investigator enquires may be fading from the subject's memory or distorted by intervening events. A person who left a job some time ago may be recollected more favourably by a headmaster than one whose faults have not yet mellowed through the passage of time. Later success may modify harsh judgements of the past since we tend to try to construct consistent images of other people. This tendency is known as the halo effect. For these reasons longitudinal or prospective studies may be preferable in the investigation of some problems. In such studies people are observed over a long period and continual records and judgements made about them. In this way the investigator has the advantage of knowing how things turn out eventually without the corresponding difficulty of studying earlier circumstances through the haze of time. The longitudinal study, of course, while it may reduce the halo effect, will not automatically eliminate it.

This long inventory of the pitfalls of measurement in research with human beings might be brought to a close with an inquiry as to whether some things are measurable at all. The spark that a good teacher can kindle in a student's mind is fairly intangible as are a person's degree of adjustment to his environment, the extent to which he can sublimate his antisocial tendencies, his creativity and the host of other variables which psychologists try to catch in their butterfly nets. Contrary to appearances, perhaps, it has not been the intention in this section to make the reader despair of the possibility of adequate measurement in psychology and the other social sciences. Rather, the aim has been to draw his attention to the limitations which have to be borne in mind and alert him to the lamentable naïveté of much, but not all, extant research in those fields. Reliability and validity have to be juggled when planning a piece of research in order to arrive at the right measure for the job. For instance, if we wished to know whether a room was warm we could use a thermometer or ask the people in the room whether they felt warm. For some purposes the subjective measure would be much more appropriate. There is no point in measuring something irrelevant because it happens to be measurable. On the other hand, there is no point in intuiting the inner reality of things if there is little chance that our intuitions will correspond to anyone else's.

Let me summarize briefly the points made about measurement. We need to define our variables operationally, preferably in terms of concrete criteria which can be corroborated objectively. We must try to ensure that the subject knows precisely what we mean by our questions and that they are not of a kind likely to provoke evasion of the truth or elicit responses based on preconceptions about the aim of the investigation. It is therefore sometimes necessary to keep the subject in ignorance of his role in the research study by methods such as the inclusion of buffer items and the double blind technique. We must make sure that the variables we are comparing are measured independently of one another to avoid the halo effect. Longitudinal studies are desirable since they often enable observations to be made more objectively and avoid the necessity of depending on distorted memories of past events. All these precautions should contribute to the reliability and the validity of our observations.

3 Control

3.1 The natural experiment

The hypothetical investigation into teachers' job satisfaction which we looked at in the previous section is of course not an experiment at all. The essence of experiment is that the experimenter modifies or varies certain conditions, holding other conditions constant; then he observes the effect of the variations on the performance of the experimental subjects. In our study of teachers we could not alter the subjects' job satisfaction to see whether this improved their teaching ability, nor could we alter their teaching ability to see whether this increased their job satisfaction. If we found, therefore, that these two factors were related we would not know why. The fact that the subjects were effective teachers might make them enjoy their jobs. On the other hand the fact that they enjoyed their jobs might make them effective teachers. Alternatively these two factors might not be directly related to each other, but might both be related to a quite different variable. A man with very wide interests might be very satisfied with a teaching job because the short hours and long holidays allowed him plenty of spare time, and his range of interests might contribute to his success as a teacher. This type of study where neither variable is under the control of the research worker has been called a natural experiment and always carries problems of inference as to the nature of the causal relationships involved.

The use of the natural experiment is quite widespread in the social sciences. We can take rats or pigeons and vary their early environments to see what happens but we cannot, or rather would not, do the same with human beings. Even where ethical considerations permit, practical ones may not. We may wish to test whether children who take up a second foreign language in the first year of secondary school retain throughout the school their advantage over children who do not take it up till their third year. The financial and administrative burden may make it impractical to plan and execute an entire teaching programme for the necessary period. We should therefore have to study the effects of existing variations in educational procedure.

Unfortunately much more would vary in this situation than the age at which study of the language commenced. Different schools have different policies with regard to foreign language teaching so that the pupils taking up a second language earlier would be in schools which differed in a multitude of other respects. Teachers take into consideration the policies of a school when choosing a job so we would expect the teachers of our 'early' and 'late' learners to differ in their attitude. They might also differ in enthusiasm, particularly if the introduction of a second foreign language at an earlier age was seen as a progressive measure and was at an exciting experimental stage. The headmasters may allow only the brighter children to become 'early learners'. Parents with a keen interest in languages may choose a school for their children where they know the maximum of language teaching goes on. Among the children themselves the more motivated ones would try to get more tuition in more languages. All these factors would make for differences between the groups we wish to compare and it would not be valid to attribute the superiority of one group solely to the effect of early introduction of the language.

We can call those factors which would invalidate such a study contaminating variables. The above study would be liable to contamination in two respects. First, there would be differences in the treatment received by the groups we are comparing. Ideally, we would prefer the treatment of the two groups to be identical except for the one variable we are concerned with, the age at which learning begins, but we have no influence over the schools or the teaching. Second, there would be differences in the two groups of subjects themselves, and these arise from the fact that we have no influence over their selection. It is these two kinds of contaminating variable that the controlled experiment is designed to exclude.

3.2 The controlled experiment
The essence of experiment is that the experimenter modifies or varies certain conditions, holding other things constant, and observes the effect of the variations on the experimental subjects. People and the treatments they can

receive may vary in many respects. If we are to understand the effects of any of these variations we must prevent them obscuring each other. It is essential to decide initially which variables we will concentrate on.

(a) *Varying certain conditions and observing the effect*

There are a variety of strategies we can adopt. Look at the following extracts of research reports (all hypothetical). They differ from one another in certain respects:

1. It was felt necessary to discover whether a large amount of expenditure on teaching a foreign language to children of poor general ability would be justified in terms of its results. An intensive French programme was therefore undertaken with no expense spared. The group selected was given expert teachers who had just received high quality refresher courses. The best available textbooks and other language teaching materials were provided, including films and tape recorded conversations. Every attempt was made to interest the children's parents in the programme and to keep them informed about it. Arrangements were made for the children to visit France during their holidays and for French children to spend some time with the group in Britain. The children's progress was measured over the course of a year.

2. An investigation was undertaken to discover whether available resources for the improvement of language teaching to less able children would be best spent on retraining teachers, procuring more up-to-date instructional materials or attempting to increase the motivation of the pupils by interesting their parents and providing direct contacts with France and the French. The teaching of three groups of children was enriched, each in one of the above ways, and their progress over the course of a year compared.

3. An educational body wished to discover whether the success of new French language teaching materials depended on the motivation of the pupils, the retraining of teachers or both. Accordingly a study was set up to examine the use of materials by three groups of children: (a) a highly motivated group of children without retrained teachers, (b) a group with average motivation and retrained teachers, and (c) a group which was both highly motivated and had retrained teachers. Children's attainment was measured before and after the study.

In the first study many aspects of the teaching programme were improved at the same time to see if their combined effect would be appreciable. The group's treatment was superior with respect to teaching, motivation and materials. In the second study these three areas of improvement in the teaching process were compared to see which had the most effect. In the third study a change in teaching materials was studied in terms of its inter-relationship with two other variables.

The first type of experiment can be called a gross comparison. If the improved teaching programme produced no effect we would know not to bother with any part of it, since it is unlikely that the different improvements would be cancelling each other out. However, if there was an effect we could not determine which factor was causing it without performing an experiment like the second. If we were fairly sure that each improvement would produce some effect or if money was not available for improving all aspects of the teaching programme in the school system at large whatever the results of the experiment it would be pointless to perform the gross comparison. In the second type of experiment each improvement is isolated and each is applied to a different group so its effects can be compared with the effects of the other improvements. The third type of experiment is said to have a factorial design, since it compares the interrelationships of more than one variable or factor. This kind of design allows for the study of interactions. An interaction occurs when the effect of a change in one variable is different for different values of another variable. For instance, the retraining of teachers might bring about an improvement with highly motivated children and no improvement with children not highly motivated. The design chosen will depend on what is known already and on the general purpose of the research, in other words, on factors specific to the problem in hand.

We have been talking about the effect of various modifications to the teaching situation without saying specifically what is affected or how the effect might be measured. Methods for assessing the pupils' progress would have to be devised to suit the above situations (see chapters 2 and 3). The measure used would be called the dependent variable. Its value for any subject depends—in part at any rate—on the modifications the experimenter has made. The variables which the experimenter manipulates—teacher training, materials and motivation—are called independent variables. Whether a pupil is assigned a newly retrained teacher or whether he is in a high-motivation group or a group provided with the most up-to-date teaching materials does not depend on anything but the decision of the experimenter. Compare the natural experiment discussed above where the relationship between job satisfaction and effectiveness was under investigation. In the natural experiment neither variable is clearly the dependent or the independent one.

(b) Holding other things constant

There is one marked deficiency which the above experiments share. None of them takes into account the possibility that the changes in treatment or motivation will have no effect at all. We need to include a group receiving none of the treatments as a standard of comparison. Otherwise if a change occurs we cannot know if it would have happened anyway without our intervention. Such a group would be called a control group. It may be that information is available about the basic rate of progress of pupils over the course of a year. It would nevertheless be preferable to check this again in the course of the experiment with a control group in case trends were altering because of special factors such as a particularly good series of French lessons on television. The practical work at the end of this chapter contains examples of a number of inadequately controlled experiments and if the reader studies these he will get a clearer idea of the role of a control group.

It would be important for the control group in such experiments to be aware that it was no less a centre of interest than the treatment group—otherwise the mere fact of novelty and special attention experienced by the treatment group might give the improvement conditions a semblance of superiority. This phenomenon is known as the Hawthorne effect after an experiment at Hawthorne in the United States in which effects due to novelty and special interest taken in the subjects were at first attributed to the independent variable. Some experiments use two types of control group, one called a placebo group which receives no specific treatment but has as much interest taken in it as does the treatment group, and one receiving neither treatment nor special attention. The word placebo is the term for the dummy drug used as a control in drug trials to ensure that improvement in the patient due merely to his confidence in the treatment is not mistakenly attributed to the drug on trial. The control group, then, holds other things constant by being a parallel group whose subjects, treatment and materials are as far as possible equivalent to those of the experimental group except with respect to the variables which are deliberately being manipulated.

More will need to be said about the design of experiments. So far we have concentrated on the way in which the controlled experiment eliminates bias, and we shall return to this in the section on sampling. Another important aim of experimental design is to allow effects to be manifested which do not show up in natural situations because too many other factors are at work obscuring them. It will be easier to develop this point after looking at some sample investigations which have actually been carried out.

Having looked at the problems involved in collecting observations we now need to consider how these observations can be made to answer our research questions.

4 Interpretation of results

We have been discussing problems of measurement, problems of inference in the natural experiment, and some features of the planning of controlled experiments. But the job is not over when we have planned and measured and amassed our date. We have to be able to interpret the data.

A first step in the process of interpretation is to represent the results graphically wherever possible, so that we can appraise them more readily. In this section we shall look at data from four simple studies. We shall consider firstly how the data may best be organized into a graph or tabulation, and secondly what aspect of the results might form the basis of an analysis. This section will concentrate on explaining why particular methods of analysis are appropriate for each study. Details of the computational procedures required for each analysis will be found in chapter 5. Not until chapter 6 will the final stages of the analysis be described, since an understanding of probability and significance is necessary before these can be understood, and these concepts are presented at the beginning of chapter 6.

The four experiments will be used to illustrate different types of measuring scale and different ways in which experimental groups may be constructed. The headings at the beginning of each section will indicate the new concepts to be introduced in the section.

It is important to realize that as well as exemplifying statistical techniques, the four studies also serve as examples of how simple experiments can be structured. Experiments need to be structured in such a way that they will be amenable to statistical treatment. When an experiment is planned, consideration must be given to how it will be analysed statistically. Otherwise the experimenter may find after he has performed his experiment that there is no suitable statistical model which can be applied to its analysis.

4.1 Spanish-teaching experiment: nominal data

In 1965 a report was produced of an experiment in which Spanish was taught to first-year students in a liberal arts college in Missouri solely through the medium of programmed texts. During the course of the study several of the students were dropped because of their poor progress or backed out of their own accord. On the basis of questionnaires one of the hypotheses investigated was whether there was any connection between a student's having had previous experience of automatic teaching methods and his failure to complete the course. Of 49 students who were still enrolled on the course 20 had and 29 had not used language laboratories before. Of 28 dropouts 15 had and 13 had not used language laboratories before.

In this experiment we are concerned with two groups of people, those who are still enrolled on a Spanish course and those who are no longer enrolled. Each person falls into one of two categories on another variable also, i.e. whether or not he has ever used a language laboratory before enrolling on the course. We can label these categories *yes* and *no*. The figures we have represent the number of people falling into the two categories on each dimension. The best way of arranging the figures so that the pattern emerges is in a table like Figure 1. This is called a contingency table. Scales which consist of a set of categories like 'still enrolled, yes/no' and 'used a language laboratory before, yes/no', are called nominal scales since each category is simply given a name. Categories on a nominal scale have to be mutually exclusive and exhaustive, i.e. we have to be able to put every subject into one category and one category only. Examples of nominal categories are nationality, school attended, of age/not of age, pass/fail.

		Still enrolled	
		No	Yes
Used a language laboratory before	Yes	15	20
	No	13	29

Figure 1. *Table showing previous use of a language laboratory by students still enrolled and students no longer enrolled on a Spanish course*

Looking at a contingency table we can study the relative frequencies of cases in the different boxes and see what relationship they reveal between the variables. It seems from the figures that being still enrolled is associated with not having had previous experience of language laboratories. This would suggest that it was the novelty of the technique that was commanding the interest and efforts of the students who were sticking it out. But how can we be sure that there is any genuine connection between the variables and that the imbalance in the figures is not produced by chance variations? If we took another group of 77 students and exposed them to a similar language programme we might get a set of frequencies which would give quite a different impression. This question will be taken up below and in chapters 5 and 6.

4.2 Training in the use of pronouns: ordinal data from independent groups

A student at Edinburgh University performed a small experiment to test whether explicit instruction on the appropriate use of pronouns in place of nouns helped ten-year-old children to avoid using pronouns ambiguously and nouns redundantly in a subsequent test. The thirty children in his instruction group achieved the following scores on his test (the scores are out of 18): 8, 5, 10, 7, 6, 5, 8, 8, 6, 6, 8, 4, 3, 8, 5, 4, 6, 8, 7, 9, 7, 6, 6, 10, 6, 7, 9, 9, 6, 3. The thirty children in his control group achieved the following scores: 3, 4, 4, 5, 5, 4, 5, 2, 4, 3, 2, 5, 4, 4, 5, 10, 5, 10, 6, 6, 3, 4, 3, 14, 13, 6, 4, 5, 5, 5.

Here the two groups are an instruction group and a control group. These are the two values on our independent variable, i.e. treatment received. For each member of each group we have a test score which is a value on our dependent variable. In this case the children are not simply classified into distinct categories like the *yes* and *no* categories in the Spanish-teaching experiment. A score of 8 is not only distinct from a score of 7, it is larger, just as it is smaller than a score of 9. This is not true of the categories on the nominal variables such as nationality and school attended referred to in the previous section. While the yes/no categories in the last example constituted nominal scales we may say that these test scores constitute an ordinal scale. Ordinal scales have the same properties as nominal scales plus the property that the values have an ordered relationship to one another.

In the results from the training in the use of pronouns our aim is to compare the positions of the children in the two treatment groups on the ordinal scale for proficiency in the use of pronouns. To do this we first need to write out the possible test scores in order of size and note how many children in each group achieved each score. We can represent each child as a block in the diagram overleaf.[1]

Looking at Figure 2 we can see immediately that the most typical score in the instruction group is 6 while the most typical score in the control group is 5. The score which is most frequently obtained or the category into which most members of the sample fall is called the mode of the distribution. Thus the modal score of the instruction group is 6 and the modal score of the control group is 5. This accords with our expectation that the instruction group would do better.

We can see on examining Figure 2 that the control group scores do seem on the whole to cluster round a different central point when compared with the scores of the instruction group and that this point is lower on the scale. Notice that if we were to draw a line across both boxes in Figure 2 at any point and count the number in each group above the line and the number below it we would have a contingency table like the one in Figure 1. We can conveniently draw the line in such a way that half the 60 scores lie above it and half below it. The score which divides the sample into two halves is called the median of a distribution. In this case the median for the total sample, instruction and control groups combined, lies between 5 and 6, and is taken to be 5.5. This line is shown in Figure 3a. The resulting contingency table is shown in Figure 3b.

We can now look for an imbalance between the groups in the relative frequencies above and below the joint median. This would give an indication of any tendency for the instruction group to have higher scores. If there were no difference between the groups we would expect fifteen scores from each group to be above the median and fifteen below. We will call these the expected frequencies and put them in brackets below the observed frequencies (see Figure 3b). In looking at Figure 1 we saw that we could draw no definite conclusions from the mere fact that there was an imbalance

[1] The reader will find instructions on how to construct such a diagram from a frequency table on p. 149.

between the frequencies in the different boxes. We have taken a further step here, because it is easy to see what frequencies we would expect if the instruction group was not superior. We can perhaps go on to examine the difference between the observed and the expected frequency in each box.

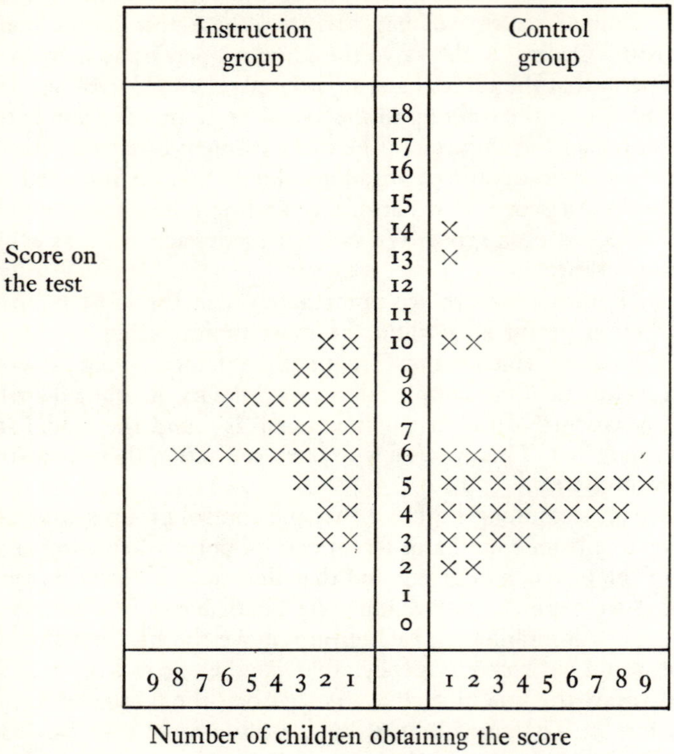

Instruction group	Score on the test	Control group
	18	
	17	
	16	
	15	
	14	×
	13	×
	12	
	11	
× ×	10	× ×
× × ×	9	
× × × × × ×	8	
× × × ×	7	
× × × × × × × ×	6	× × ×
× × ×	5	× × × × × × × × ×
× ×	4	× × × × × × × ×
× ×	3	× × × ×
	2	× ×
	1	
	0	
9 8 7 6 5 4 3 2 1		1 2 3 4 5 6 7 8 9

Number of children obtaining the score

Figure 2. *Instruction group and control group scores on test for use of pronouns (each × is a person)*

However, even if we were comparing two groups which had received the same treatment we would not necessarily be surprised if the observed frequencies did not correspond precisely with the expected ones. Even if instructions were not helpful, some chance variation between the performance of the groups might be expected. The question is how big do the differences have to be before we can ascribe them to our independent variable. We shall return to this question in chapter 6, having developed the concept of observed and expected frequencies further in chapter 5.

We have seen that by grouping the scores of the instruction and control groups in the training in the use of pronouns experiment into two categories,

Instruction		Control
	18	
	17	
	16	
	15	
	14	X
	13	X
	12	
	11	
X X	10	X X
X X X	9	
X X X X X X	8	
X X X X	7	
X X X X X X X X	6	X X X
X X X	5	X X X X X X X X X X
X X	4	X X X X X X X X X
X X	3	X X X X
	2	X X
	1	
	0	

Figure 3a. *Instruction and control group scores on test for use of pronouns split at median (each × is a person)*

	Instruction	Control	Total
Above median	23 (15)	7 (15)	30
Below median	7 (15)	23 (15)	30
Total	30	30	60

Figure 3b. *Contingency table of scores above and below the median in instruction and control groups. (Figures in brackets are expected frequencies)*

above and below the median, we can construct a contingency table. However, we saw above that in this experiment the test scores are in an ordered relationship to one another. By making a crude cut across the middle we are treating the data as if they were on a nominal scale and ignoring much of the information that we have about the relative positions of the scores of the two groups. For instance from Figure 3a we see that nearly half the scores in the control group which are above the median are scores of 6 whereas nearly half the scores of the instruction group which are above the median are scores of 8 or more. This information is lost in the contingency table (Figure 3b) but we can retain it if we give the score of each subject a value or rank in accordance with its position relative to the scores of the other subjects. We can then sum these ranks for each group as a whole and make a comparison between the groups using a measure to which each score contributes.[1]

We have now looked at two investigations, one of Spanish students and their prior experience of language laboratories in which the data were on a nominal scale, and one of use of pronouns by two groups in which the data consisted of test scores on an ordinal scale. The ordinal scores can be treated in one of two ways. They can be converted to nominal categories, which loses information about relative position on the scale, or they can be ranked, which preserves that information. We now need to look at ordinal data from a rather different experiment. In the training in the use of pronouns experiment we had data from two separate or independent groups, instruction and control. Each child belongs to only one group and we have only one score from each child. Similarly in the Spanish-teaching experiment each observation is independent of every other observation. Each person appears in the contingency table as an entry only once. We shall see that the understanding of logical connectives experiment differs from the first two in this respect.

4.3 Understanding of logical connectives: ordinal data from related groups

In 1967 a student at Edinburgh did a thorough study of children's understanding of logical connectives. He used a number of tests. In one of these the child had to choose from three connectives the one that fitted best into a given sentence frame. He called this controlled production. In another test a main clause followed by a logical connective was presented with three different sentence completions, only one of which fitted the sense of the connective. The child had to choose the right completion. This was called the selective completion test. One of the aims of the study was to see which of the tests the children did better at. The results from 36 nine-year-old children are as follows. (The scores are out of 18. The first figure in each pair represents the controlled production score and the second figure represents the selective completion score for the same child.) 17,16; 16,11; 11,11; 18,15; 18,15; 10,12; 9,11; 16,14; 18,14; 18,16; 15,15; 16,13; 17,15; 6,7; 14,11; 17,15; 16,16; 8,13; 10,11; 17,16; 18,16; 18,17; 18,18; 18,18; 12,10; 12,10; 17,14; 15,13; 17,14; 17,18; 17,17; 16,17; 13,14; 16,14; 14,13; 16,12.

[1] In chapter 5 we explain how a rank can be assigned to each person's score. The use that can be made of these ranks in assessing the effects of instruction is described in chapter 6.

Here again we have an ordinal measure as our dependent variable, namely a score on a test of logical connectives. This time our independent variable is the type of test; i.e. whether it is a controlled production test or a selective completion test. This experiment differs from the previous one in that the two sets of scores are from related samples rather than independent ones. In the use of pronouns experiment each child was in either the instruction group or the control group. We therefore had only one score for each child. In the logical connectives experiment, on the other hand, each child did both tests, and consequently we have two scores for each child. In the use of pronouns experiment no score in either group bore any special relationship to a particular score in the other group, but in the logical connectives experiment each score is related to a score in the other test, since the two scores come from the same child. If we wish to retain the information about which score in each set belongs to each score in the other set we should tabulate the scores as on page 124, since in diagrams like Figure 2 we cannot represent which of the scores are paired.

In the understanding of logical connectives study the experimenter wished to know which of the two tests the children did better at. In the last example we compared the two sets of scores as a whole. In this experiment, however, since we have related scores we can compare a child's score in one test directly with his score in the other, provided that both tests have the same number of items. We shall be discussing the advantages of this method in the section on matching. (In situations where each test is out of a different total we would have to scale down one set of scores so that the two were equivalent.) It is obviously relevant to know whether a child got a higher score on controlled production or selective completion and how much bigger the score was. This information is recorded in the right hand column of Figure 4. A plus represents a higher controlled production score and a minus represents a higher selective completion score (e.g. subject no. 1: $17 - 16 = +1$; subject no. 6: $10 - 12 = -2$). We can now simply sum the number of pluses and the number of minuses, ignoring the children who got the same mark on both tests. We have now placed each child into one of two nominal categories: did better on Test I/did better on Test II. This gives us 22 pluses and 8 minuses. It looks as if the controlled production test was easier for most of the children, but how can we be sure that this difference really means anything and that we would get similar results with another set of children doing the same tests? Again we need some procedure for deciding how unequal the measures need to be before we can draw any conclusions. Once more we shall defer further discussion of this point until chapter 6.

In discussing the training in the use of pronouns experiment we saw that there were alternative ways of using the available information, one of which was more wasteful than the other. Similarly in the case of related samples we have a choice as to how precise we shall be. We can merely look at how many

Sub no.	Con. prod.	Sel. comp.	Difference
1	17	16	+1
2	16	11	+5
3	11	11	0
4	18	15	+3
5	18	15	+3
6	10	12	−2
7	9	11	−2
8	16	14	+2
9	18	14	+4
10	18	16	+2
11	15	15	0
12	16	13	+3
13	17	15	+2
14	6	7	−1
15	14	11	+3
16	17	15	+2
17	16	16	0
18	8	13	−5
19	10	11	−1
20	18	16	+2
21	18	16	+2
22	18	17	+1
23	18	18	0
24	18	18	0
25	12	10	+2
26	12	10	+2
27	17	14	+3
28	15	13	+2
29	17	14	+3
30	17	18	−1
31	17	17	0
32	16	17	−1
33	13	14	−1
34	16	14	+2
35	14	13	+1
36	16	12	+4

Figure 4. *Table of controlled production and selective completion scores with differences between the scores*

children did better in the first test or we can see whether the differences which favour the first test are larger than those which favour the second. To do the latter we rank the differences in the way that we ranked the instruction and control scores in the pronoun test, then we sum the ranks of plus differences and the ranks of minus differences.[1] Once again the children who did equally well on the two tests will have to be excluded from the analysis. Just glancing at the last column of the table we see that most of the children who did better on the selective completion test only got 1 or 2 extra points whereas many of the children doing better on the controlled production test got 3 or more extra points. This shows that if we take the relative sizes of the differences into account we shall have a measure which is more sensitive to the difference between the tests.

So far in this interpretation of the logical connectives study we have been concerned with whether one test was easier than the other, but we can look at the findings in a quite different way (see Figure 5). We can examine the data to see whether the two tests are related to each other in the sense that children who do well on one are also likely to do well on the other. Since we have two ordinal scales here and a value for each child on each scale, we can enter each child on a graph in which one axis represents the controlled production score and one the selective completion score, e.g. the mark representing child no. 1 is opposite 17 on the controlled production axis and opposite 16 on the selective completion axis. This type of graph is called a scattergram. By looking at the general layout of the points we can see whether there is any relationship between what the two tests are measuring. Clearly there is some tendency for children doing well on one test to do well on the other one also, but the relationship is not perfect. If it were perfect all the points would lie on a single line. In order to quantify the degree of relationship rank positions once more come in useful. The greater the relationship the smaller the difference between the children's rank positions on the two variables. The measure of relationship derived from rank positions is called a rank order correlation. Correlation techniques are widely used and are central to the procedures for establishing the reliability and validity of tests. They are dealt with in chapter 2 and in Appendix I. Here we are concerned with the techniques for comparison between sets of scores. However, acquaintance with the concept of correlation will be necessary for an understanding of the section on matching (related-subject designs).

In the Spanish-teaching experiment we looked at nominal data where we could only count the number of cases falling in each combination of categories on the two variables. In the training in the use of pronouns experiment and the understanding of logical connectives experiment, we were dealing with test scores which were ordinal. We had a choice in each case of how to analyse the data. We could convert the test score to a nominal variable,

[1] See p. 154.

126 Testing and Experimental Methods

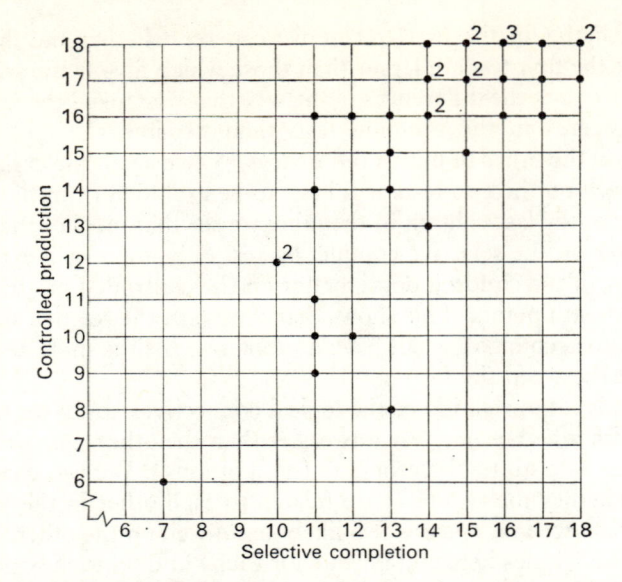

Figure 5. *Scattergram showing relationship between scores on controlled production and selective completion tests*
The number 2 or 3 above a point indicates that more than one child got that combination of scores.
⇐⌇⌇⌇⌇ indicates that an axis is not drawn from its origin.
  Note that in a scattergram the scores are marked on the line whereas in Fig. 2 they are marked in the middle of a column.

above or below the median for the pronouns experiment and better at Test I/better at Test II for the logical connectives experiment, but this wasted some of the information. Alternatively we could rank the scores and sum the ranks for each group in the pronouns study and rank the differences in score and sum the positive and the negative differences in the logical connectives experiment. We shall now look at measurements of a more refined nature which can be used directly without being converted to ranks.

4.4 Birth weight of normal and speech-retarded children: interval data from independent groups—subject variable

The following list provides information about the birth weights of 99 normal children and 60 speech-retarded children: Normal: 5 under 6 lb. 1 oz., 26 between 6 lb. 1 oz. and 7 lb., 35 between 7 lb. 1 oz. and 8 lb., 21 between 8 lb. 1 oz. and 9 lb., 11 between 9 lb. 1 oz. and 10 lb., 1 over 10 lb. Speech-retarded: 7 under 6 lb. 1 oz., 8 between 6 lb. 1 oz. and 7 lb., 21 between 7 lb. 1 oz. and 8 lb., 16 between 8 lb. 1 oz. and 9 lb., 7 between 9 lb. 1 oz. and 10 lb., 1 over 10 lb.

In this example we are comparing the birth weights of speech-retarded children with those of a control group of normal children. The data are already grouped in intervals of one pound weight and the frequency of cases in each interval has been counted.[1] The next step is to construct a table and then represent the frequencies in histograms. The horizontal axis represents the dependent variable (birth weight) and the vertical axis represents frequency. This contrasts with Figure 2 on p. 120, in which the vertical axis represents the dependent variable and the horizontal axis represents frequency. We shall superimpose one histogram on top of the other.

(a) *Frequency table*

Type of subject	Weight at birth in pounds						
	Under 6·1	6·1–7	7·1–8	8·1–9	9·1–10	Over 10	Total
Normal	5	26	35	21	11	1	99
Speech-retarded	7	8	21	16	7	1	60

(b) *Histogram*

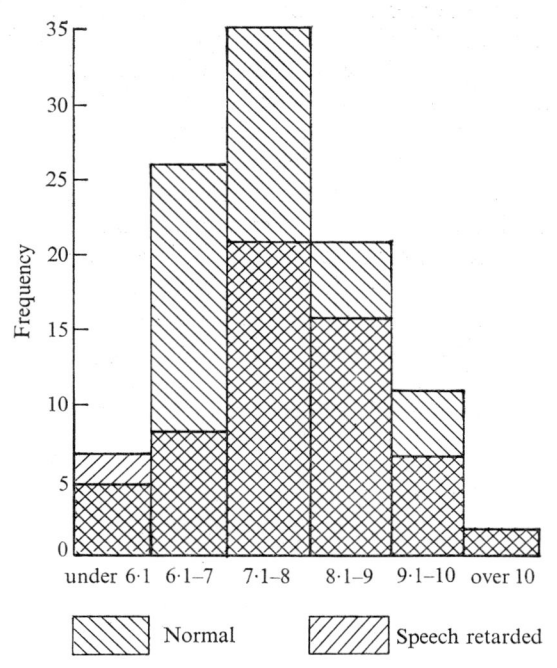

Figure 6. *Birth weights of speech-retarded and normal children in intervals of 1 lb*

[1] Recommendations regarding the choice of intervals when data are grouped can be found in Blalock, 1960, p. 34.

In the case of the pronouns test we noted the modal score for each group separately. We can see from Figure 6 that in this study the modal weight for both groups is between 7 and 8 lb. We then went on to calculate the median score for both groups combined. We could also have calculated the median scores for each group separately and then compared them. We shall follow the latter procedure for these data, which results in a median of 7 lb. $8\frac{1}{2}$ oz. for the normal group and of 7 lb. $11\frac{1}{2}$ oz. for the speech-retarded group.[1]

The mode and the median are both types of average, otherwise known as measures of central tendency, since they locate the centre of a distribution. We can calculate another type of average for these weights, i.e. the arithmetic average or mean which is obtained by summing all the observations in a group and dividing the result by the number of people in the group. The means of these groups were calculated from the original data before they were grouped into intervals of 1 lb. They are 7 lb. $9\frac{1}{2}$ oz. for the normal children and 7 lb. 12 oz. for the speech-retarded group. The means can now be compared to see if the difference between them is large enough to demonstrate a genuine tendency for speech retardation to be associated with a large birth weight. Details of the procedure used can be found in chapter 6.

The advantage of the mean over the sum of ranks which was discussed on p. 122 in connection with the previous experiment is that it makes use of information about the actual values observed rather than just their relative positions on the scale. The reader may be wondering why we did not compute the means for the pronouns experiment. The reason we can add the observations and compute their arithmetical average in this instance is because they are on an interval scale. An increment of one ounce in weight represents an equivalent amount at whatever point on the scale it occurs, and so we treat the units of weight as quantitatively equivalent by adding them up and dividing them. $10+9$ is only equal to $8+11$ if this equivalence applies. We have no assurance in the case of the test scores in the pronouns experiment that an increase of one point in score means the same at each point on the scale, although many people in practice act as if they do have this assurance. This point will be discussed further in chapter 6.

Furthermore, the statistical technique for comparing means which we referred to in the paragraph before last depends for its validity on the distribution of scores in the population at large having certain characteristics which, again, will be discussed in chapter 6. If scores are not on an interval

---

[1] The actual calculation of the median was simple for the pronouns experiment since exactly half the children got a score of 5 or less and half got a score of 6 or more. It is more complicated for these data since the middle weight for each group lies within an interval on the scale. Details of the calculation of a median in such cases will not be covered here since it is not necessary for any of the tests we shall meet. For the test which uses the median to construct a contingency table, if the exact median falls within an interval the division is made above that interval. The reader is referred to Amos, Brown and Mink (1965) and Blalock (1960) for further information about the median.

scale and if the distribution does not have the relevant characteristics, some technique based on ranking should be used.

This discussion illustrates the fact that different methods of calculating averages may lead to different results. The common practice of quoting a figure as an average without specifying what type of average is therefore unsatisfactory. This can be particularly misleading if the distribution of values on the variable is assymetrical, i.e. skewed.

We can demonstrate this latter point by means of the following information regarding the ages in months at which a group of 15 aphasic children acquired their first word: 23, 31, 32, 33, 34, 34, 37, 37, 38, 40, 43, 44, 45, 53, 56. These ages are represented in the following histogram, but they have had to be grouped into three-month intervals for reasons of space and to give a clear picture. The mean of these 15 ages is 38·7 months, the median is 37·25 months, and the modes 34 and 37 months. If we add an invented child who acquired his first word at the age of 70 months the distribution is markedly skewed. When we recalculate the measures of central tendency to include this additional child we find that the new mean is 40·6 and the new median 37·5 while the modes remain the same; i.e. the mean is increased by nearly 2 months, the median by only 0·25 of a month and the modes not at all.

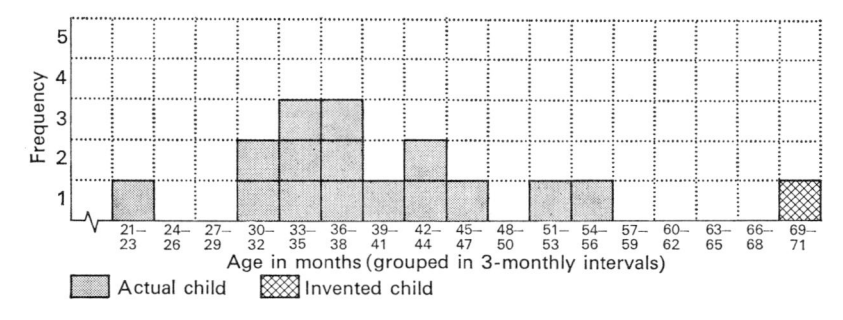

Figure 7. *Ages at which 15 aphasic children produced their first word with one invented case added*

A typical case of the questionable use of means as the average in preference to other measures of central tendency when a distribution is skewed, is in calculating the average wage in a commercial organization. A director with a very high income can inflate the mean so that the staff are quoted as having an average income which is in fact higher than anyone but the director himself actually earns.

Notice that the mode is the only measure of central tendency which is applicable to nominal data; the median, since it is a measure based on the relative order of scores, is particularly suitable to ordinal data and the mean, which depends on the legitimacy of performing the operations of addition and division on the scores for its validity, is suitable for data measured on interval scales.

To return to the birth weight study, it differs from the pronouns experiment not only in the type of measuring scale involved (interval rather than ordinal) but also in terms of the composition of the groups being compared. In the experiment on the effect of training in the use of pronouns it was the experimenter who decided which children would be given instruction and which would be controls. He could therefore ensure that the groups were equivalent in whatever respect he thought relevant. In this study ready-made categories of person comprise the independent variable. The researcher cannot choose to put a given child in the speech-retarded group or the normal group. It might be more accurate to call the variable a subject variable on that account. This point does not affect the statistical analysis of the results but it does affect the interpretation of the findings and will be discussed further in a subsequent section.

4.5 Summary of the four studies

In this section on graphic representation and preliminary analysis I have made a number of distinctions which need summarizing before we go on. The studies which we have considered differ in terms of the level of measurement (nominal, ordinal or interval), and whether the groups were independent or related. The topic of level of measurement will be considered again in chapter 6 and the relative merits of independent and related subject design will be discussed later in this chapter.

The Spanish-teaching experiment involved a study of the relationship between being still enrolled on the course and having had previous experience of a language laboratory. Nominal data from independent groups. Analysis would be based on the difference between observed and expected frequencies in a contingency table.

The training in the use of pronouns experiment involved a comparison of the performance on a pronoun test of a group which had had special instruction and of one which had not. Ordinal data from independent groups. Analysis would be based on the difference between observed and expected frequencies above and below the median or the sums of ranks of scores in each group.

The understanding of logical connectives experiment involved a comparison of a controlled production and selective completion test for the use of logical connectives. Ordinal data from related groups. Analysis would be based on the number of children with higher scores in one test compared with the number with higher scores in the other or the sum of ranks of differences favouring one test compared with the sum of ranks of differences favouring the other. (If information was sought about the relationship or correlation between the tests, the difference between each child's rank on the two tests would form the basis of an analysis.)

The birth weight study involved a comparison between birth weights of normal and speech-retarded children. Interval data from independent groups. Analysis would be based on the difference between mean weights of the groups.

	Independent	Related	
	Comparative	Comparative	Correlational
Nominal	Spanish-teaching experiment		
At least ordinal	training in the use of pronouns	understanding of logical connectives	understanding of logical connectives
Interval	birth weight study		

Figure 8. *The four studies classified by level of measurement and type of experimental design*

Research designs exist to occupy the boxes which are empty in the above diagram but we will not have space to consider them. Correlation techniques are dealt with in chapter 2, as has already been indicated. In the section on the controlled experiment we discussed experiments involving more than two treatment groups and factorial designs. The analysis of the latter cannot be considered in the space available but we shall see in chapter 6 that some of the techniques already mentioned are applicable to more than two groups.

We have seen that measures of central tendency, the mode, median and mean, play a part in the analysis of experimental findings. We also need to take account of the *dispersion* of scores in a distribution.

4.6 Dispersion

We have been concerned so far with variation between groups participating in an experiment. A difference in central tendency can be used as an index of how different two sets of scores are. However, it is also important

132 Testing and Experimental Methods

to know how much variation in score there is within groups. If there is a lot of overlap between the scores of two groups then a difference in central tendency is going to matter less. We shall return to this point in the next section and in chapter 6.

To see how the amount of dispersion among scores in a group can be quantified let us look again at the data on aphasic children first introduced on p. 129. The ages in months at which the 15 children acquired their first word were as follows: 23, 31, 32, 33, 34, 34, 37, 37, 38, 40, 43, 44, 45, 53, 56. Here once more is the histogram with the same age-groups (this time no extra child has been added). If we want to describe the way these scores are

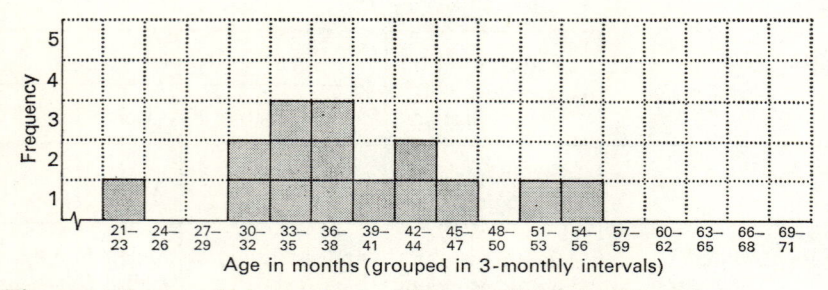

Figure 9. *Ages at which 15 aphasic children produced their first word*

dispersed we can merely quote the range of ages. This is simply the difference between the highest age and the lowest age, i.e. 56 months minus 23 months = 33 months (taking the original ungrouped figures). This measure is clearly very crude, taking into account only two of the ages. It is also very unstable since the two extreme scores may vary considerably in different groups drawn from the same population. There are measures of dispersion that use more of the available information than the range.

For simplicity consider the following two distributions of five ages, which are subsets of the above set:

(a) 31, 37, 38, 40, 44.
(b) 31, 34, 38, 43, 44.

Both distributions have a mean of 38 ($\frac{190}{5}$) and a range of 13 (44–31). Yet the distribution of scores about the mean differs. How can we express this difference in degree of dispersion in such a way that each child's age is taken into account?

This can be done by calculating the mean deviation. As the name implies, it is the arithmetical average of the deviations from the mean of the scores of a distribution. It is calculated by subtracting each score from the mean and adding up the results, i.e. the deviations, ignoring + and − signs, then dividing by the number of observations. In the case of distribution (a) it is 3·2, i.e. $(38 - 31) + (38 - 37) + (38 - 38) + (40 - 38) + (44 - 38) \div 5 = 7 + 1 + 0 + 2 + 6 \div 5 = 16 \div 5 = 3·2$. The mean deviation for distribution (b) is 4·4.

However, the standard deviation is a measure of dispersion that is much more generally used than the mean deviation, since it has a wider application in statistics, as we shall see in chapter 6. The standard deviation is calculated in a similar way to the mean deviation but instead of being the average of deviations from the mean, it is the square root of the average of squared deviations from the mean, i.e. each deviation is squared, the squared deviations are summed and divided by the number of cases, then the square root of this result is found. The standard deviation of distribution (a) is 4·24, i.e. the square root of $(7^2 + 1^2 + 0^2 + 2^2 + 6^2 \div 5)$ = the square root of $(49 + 1 + 0 + 4 + 36 \div 5)$ = the square root of $90 \div 5 = \sqrt{18} = 4·24$. The standard deviation of distribution (b) is 5·02. The reader might like to calculate the mean deviation and standard deviation of the group of 15 aphasics as a whole. The answers are given on p. 220.

5 The advantages and limitations of certain research designs

5.1 Related subject designs and the restriction of variation

As was pointed out in the discussion on the controlled experiment, people vary enormously in their responses to situations and this variation is determined by a multitude of factors. In an experimental situation we are manipulating a particular factor or set of factors to see if it contributes to this variation. If our result is to be significant, we must produce a difference between the groups on the dependent variable which is large enough to show up against the natural variation in the subjects' responses. For instance, we shall see in chapter 6 that it is not the size of difference between the means under experimental conditions which counts, but its size in relation to the standard deviation.

It follows that one way to have a treatment effect show up is to reduce the natural variability of the subjects' responses in the experiment. This can be done by restricting the type of subject used to a very narrow range or by restricting the experimental situation in such a way that a number of factors which would normally produce variations in response are excluded.

An example of restriction in the type of subject might be a comparison of the running speed of boys and girls where the experimenter concentrated on a restricted age range to avoid sex differences being swamped by age differences. An example of restriction of the variables which might operate in the experimental situation is Ebbinghaus's work on memory in which he served as his own subject. Anxious to study the pure mechanisms of memory he tried to eliminate the effect of efforts after meaning on his results by using nonsense syllables and deliberately averting his mind from any meaningful associations that these elicited in him.

The problem with restricting variation in this way is that it also restricts the relevance of our results to the limited range of subjects and situations covered by the experiment. An effect might happen to be specific to the particular type of subject who participated in the experiment. Similarly, while sizeable effects may be produced in laboratory conditions, these may not be relevant to real-life situations, in which the critical variables may in fact be the ones we have taken the trouble to exclude in our experiment.

However, there are methods of limiting the effects of intrinsic variability without restricting the relevance of the experiment. Supposing we wanted to compare the effect of equivalent quantities of two types of food on the weight of pigs. We would sample pigs to represent the relevant population and divide them into two equivalent groups. (See section on randomization below, p. 139.) We would then give food A to one group of pigs and food B to the other group and weigh the animals at the end of the experiment. The final weights are represented below. Food B is slightly superior but because of the wide variability among the animals the superiority does not show up very clearly. However, if we had arranged our pigs in pairs according to their initial weight and assigned one pig at random from each matched pair to each group we could then compare their final weights pair for pair. If initial weight is highly correlated with final weight, which it must surely be, we may get the following outcome (see Figure 11). The effect of food B is no greater here, but it shows up better since the variability between pairs can be discounted in the analysis.

Notice, however, that while in Figure 10 we would be dealing with ten

Figure 10. *Weights of independent samples of pigs (relative weights represented by size)*

weights in our analysis in Figure 11 we are dealing with five differences of weight. In restricting the influence of variability by matching, we have halved the effective size of our sample of observations and as we shall see in chapter 6 this reduces the sensitivity of a test. Whether this is worth while in practice will depend on how well the variable which we use initially to match the subjects correlates with the dependent variable, since this will determine the extent to which our final observations will be paired in order of size in the way the pigs are in Figure 11.

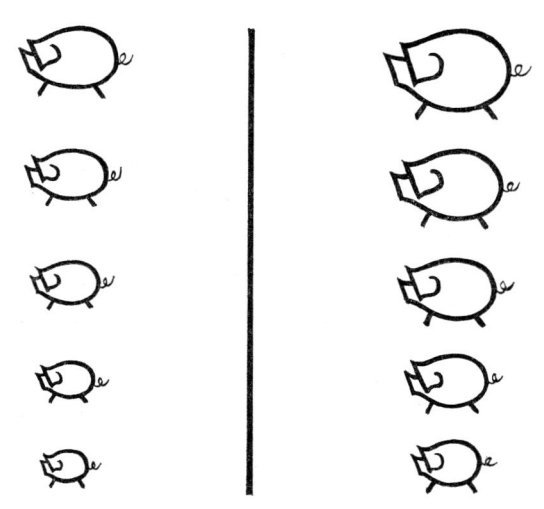

Figure 11. *Weights of matched pairs of pigs (relative weights represented by size)*

We have used pigs to illustrate the principle of matching since it is easy to represent weight diagrammatically by means of size. However, the principle also applies to the matching of attributes such as IQ and memory ability in a language learning experiment.

Matching is one method of establishing related samples. The other method we have already met in the logical connectives experiment. Here we had the same subject performing under both treatments. This is called an identical subject design. Clearly, to use the same subject for both measurements is the surest way of getting rid of differences on other variables which may affect performance. However, it is not possible to do this if a person's performance under one treatment is going to be affected as a result of his having already experienced the other treatment (as it would have been in the case of the pigs). For instance it would be impossible to teach a person a skill by two different methods and compare his speed of learning in each case.

Sometimes the adoption of an identical subject design will entail the construction of a second set of materials, equivalent to the first in relevant respects. For instance, if the comprehension of punctuated and unpunctuated texts is being compared, the same text can be used in both forms with independent or matched groups. With identical groups, however, it would be nonsense to give the same text twice. The correct procedure would be to have matched texts, A and B, and give half the subjects (chosen at random) A with punctuation and B without, and half B with punctuation and A without, this yielding two versions of the text. In the experiment on the understanding of logical connectives, the selective completion and controlled production tests were matched carefully, in terms of content and vocabulary. If they had not been, it would not have been valid to attribute any difference in difficulty between the tests to the testing method, 'completion' or 'production'.

Similarly, if an identical design is chosen some decision has to be made about the order in which the treatments are to be presented to each subject. If the same treatment is always presented first it will be impossible to determine whether the superior performance under one treatment is due to the effect of the treatment or to an order effect (e.g. practice or fatigue). If no systematic effect of order is expected it is appropriate to decide the order at random for each subject independently. If, however, some consistent effect is expected then it is appropriate to counterbalance, i.e. distribute that effect evenly between the treatments by ensuring that each treatment occurs first equally often. A similar procedure was in fact followed in the case of the logical connectives experiment. It was slightly more complicated since there were more than two tests but that need not concern us here. Subject to this constraint which of the individuals received treatment A first and which treatment B would have to be left to chance (see the section on randomization below). If matched texts are involved one might add the further constraint that half the group doing each version of the test should have one order and half the other, i.e. there would be four groups. Figure 12 illustrates the above example.

Groups	Order of presentation	
	1st	2nd
i	A+	B–
ii	B–	A+
iii	B+	A–
iv	A–	B+

Figure 12. *Order of presentation of punctuated and unpunctuated versions of matched texts (A and B are texts; + means punctuated, – means unpunctuated)*

Sometimes the experimental material consists of a number of separate short items of two types rather than two prolonged tasks. For instance one might be investigating whether it is easier to learn the translation equivalents of words referring to concrete objects than of words referring to abstract ideas. In this case the items should be intermingled throughout the test with the order decided randomly or counterbalanced according to some systematic scheme such as the following : ABBAABBA. The latter order ensures that an equal number of A and B items occur in each quarter of the session and that an A item follows a B item as often as a B item follows an A item.

The above procedures for controlling order will not succeed if order is likely to affect the different tasks differently. If there is a possibility that task A will be easier than B if done first but task B will be easier if done second, it is equivalent to saying that the subject's performance under one treatment will be affected as a result of his having experienced the other treatment. We pointed out above that an identical subject design is unsuitable in such circumstances.

We have seen that the success of matching depends on some knowledge of what correlates with the dependent variable and that in matching, while we have discounted variability between pairs, we have correspondingly halved the number of observations we deal with in the analysis. Another disadvantage of matching is that it may require the exclusion from the experiment of extreme cases for whom no close match can be found. This interferes with the representativeness of the sample. Furthermore, if an experiment continues over a period of time and one member of a matched pair happens to drop out, his match has to be dropped from the analysis also. The advantages of matching must therefore be weighed against the disadvantages in each particular experimental situation.

5.2 Designs with a subject variable

Designs with a subject variable can be considered to be a cross between a controlled experiment and a natural experiment, since if we are comparing different types of people, such as boys and girls, we are not in a position to choose which group to put them in but must take them as we find them. Therefore, if we found differences in some characteristics between boys and girls for example, the experiment would not tell us whether they were due to genetic factors or aspects of upbringing.

Matching procedures can be applied to subject variable designs in the same way as to independent variable designs. Samples would be selected to represent each of the relevant populations, then each person in the first sample would be matched according to the variable chosen with a member of the other sample. Sometimes, particularly in clinical studies, a small sample of people of a certain type is already delimited, e.g. the speech-retarded children in the birth weight study. Matching here consists of selecting from a large population of normal individuals persons matched on certain variables with the clinical group. It is in such cases as these that matching can be most successful, since there is every chance that people fulfilling the right requirements will be found. It is vital to prevent the control group varying in too many respects from the clinical group for useful comparisons could not be made in these circumstances. The problem is to know what variables to match on. For instance, matching aphasics with normals for chronological age in studies of perceptual skill will give quite different results to matching them for intelligence. A firm intuitive understanding of the phenomena concerned is necessary before decisions can be made.

The use of factorial designs with a subject variable as one of the factors allows the study of interactions between values on the independent variable and values on the subject variable. For instance, one might find that teaching a body of information by means of a branching programme worked better with more intelligent children while teaching it by means of a linear programme worked better with less intelligent children.

6 Sampling

It will only be possible to say a little about sampling in this chapter. The statistical tests we have been discussing are based on the assumption that the samples have been drawn at random from the relevant population. This is a requirement of experimentation which is not always met. In psychology, for instance, captive groups of naval ratings, students and rats are frequently used. Generalizations are made from these on the assumption that relationships which hold between variables for these groups will hold in the population at large.

Ideally samples should be representative of some defined population and there should be no bias in their selection. The larger a sample is, the more representative it is likely to be. (This point should become clearer after a reading of chapter 6.) The only way of avoiding bias is to remove the human element from selection of subjects by using a mechanical procedure such as shaking a dice or cutting a well shuffled pack of cards or drawing numbers out of a hat to determine who is chosen. In practice it is usually more convenient to use random number tables which are themselves constructed by such mechanical procedures. This presupposes that the members of the population are listed and numbered in some way, which is very often not the case.

Simple random sampling of this type is not the only valid kind of sampling. The reader is referred to Blalock (1960) for a fuller treatment.

7 Randomization

The concept of randomization has been introduced at various points during the discussion. Randomization is a device for ensuring that the selection of subjects and their distribution between treatments is left to purely mechanical procedures which exclude the unconscious bias that might result from human agency. It is important both in ensuring that samples represent the relevant population and that treatment groups are equivalent. Figure 13 summarizes a number of different designs for experiments which have been introduced in the chapter, showing that randomization plays a role in each. Figure 13 does not exhaust all the possibilities of experimental design. However, the general principles of randomization, counterbalancing and matching are applicable with very slight modification to more complex designs in which there is more than one independent variable (factorial designs) or more than two treatments. Anderson (1966) is recommended for a discussion of such designs. A very valuable discussion on how to carry out randomization procedures can be found in Cox (1958).

8 Conclusion

In this brief discussion much has had to be omitted. For instance, it has not been possible to discuss what variables might be used as a basis for matching in different circumstances, if subjects are to be matched. Nor has it been possible to discuss details of treatment or what variables need to be controlled in the construction of experimental materials in the language area. Such knowledge has to come from experience of an area of research and from study of the literature.

I hope that enough has been said, however, to indicate that the scope for experimentation in the classroom is limited. One requirement in particular is difficult to fulfil in a classroom situation, i.e. the criterion that subjects should be responding independently to the experimental treatment. Ideally, experimental treatments should be administered individually, and a great deal of care should be taken to see that the subject is put at his ease and that he performs to his full capacity.

Certain themes have recurred throughout this discussion, i.e. the need for representativeness, verisimilitude and equivalence. Equivalence applies to all three ingredients of an experiment—subjects, treatments and materials. As far as possible the groups compared should be equivalent in all respects except for the variable under scrutiny. Verisimilitude concerns the extent to which the skill studied in the laboratory represents some genuine process which is relevant to real life behaviour. Treatments and materials must take this need into account. We have discussed how the requirements of delicately poised controlled experiments can sometimes conflict with verisimilitude. In

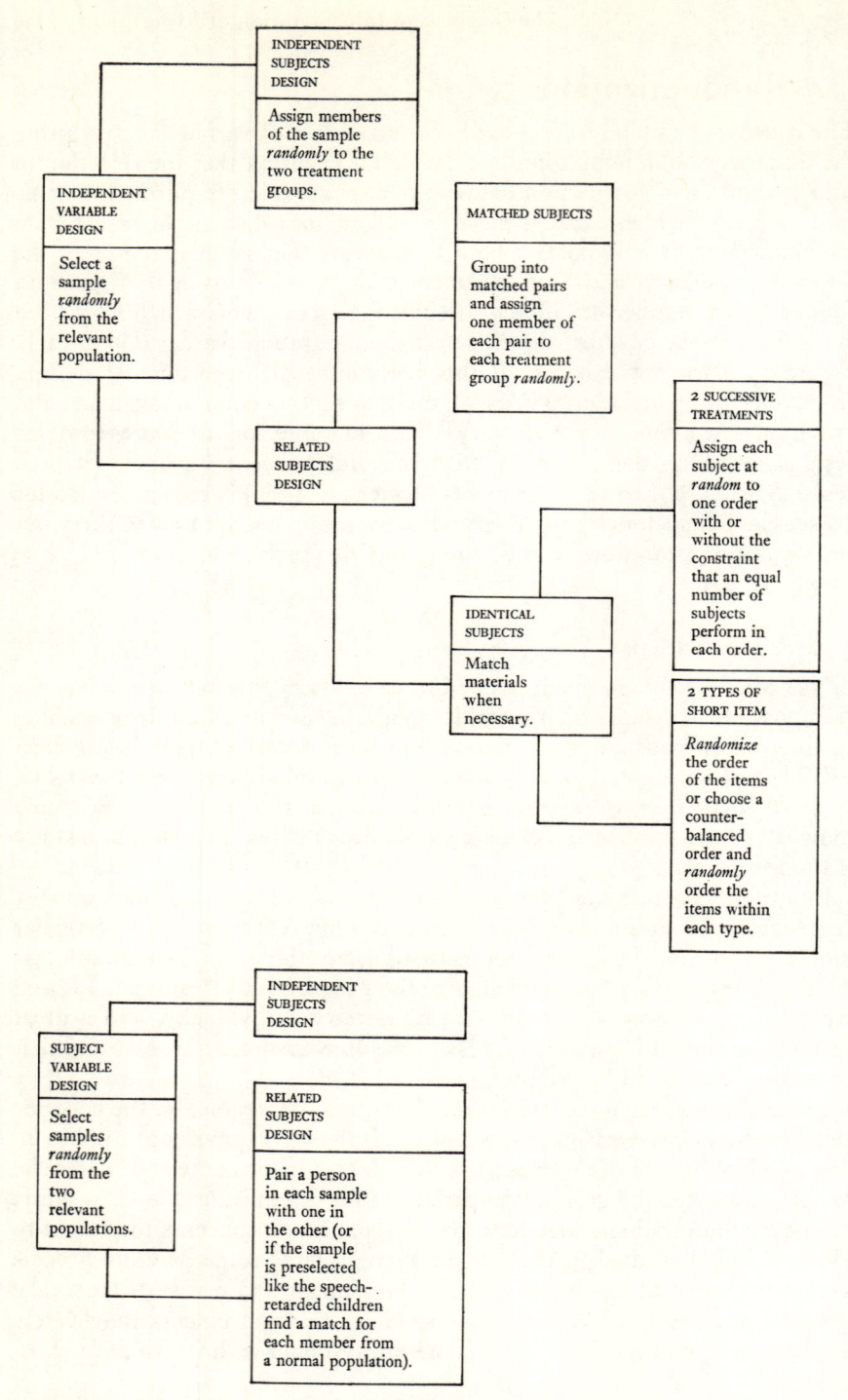

```
                          ┌─────────────────┐
                          │ INDEPENDENT     │
                          │ SUBJECTS        │
                          │ DESIGN          │
                          ├─────────────────┤
                          │ Assign members  │
                          │ of the sample   │
                          │ *randomly* to the│
                          │ two treatment   │
                          │ groups.         │
                          └─────────────────┘
┌──────────────┐
│ INDEPENDENT  │
│ VARIABLE     │
│ DESIGN       │
├──────────────┤                ┌─────────────────┐
│ Select a     │                │ MATCHED SUBJECTS│
│ sample       │                ├─────────────────┤
│ *randomly*   │                │ Group into      │
│ from the     │                │ matched pairs   │
│ relevant     │                │ and assign      │
│ population.  │                │ one member of   │
└──────────────┘                │ each pair to    │
                                │ each treatment  │
                                │ group *randomly*.│
                   ┌──────────┐ └─────────────────┘
                   │ RELATED  │
                   │ SUBJECTS │
                   │ DESIGN   │                    ┌─────────────────┐
                   └──────────┘                    │ 2 SUCCESSIVE    │
                                                   │ TREATMENTS      │
                                                   ├─────────────────┤
                                                   │ Assign each     │
                                                   │ subject at      │
                                                   │ *random* to     │
                                                   │ one order       │
                                      ┌──────────┐ │ with or         │
                                      │IDENTICAL │ │ without the     │
                                      │SUBJECTS  │ │ constraint      │
                                      ├──────────┤ │ that an equal   │
                                      │ Match    │ │ number of       │
                                      │materials │ │ subjects        │
                                      │ when     │ │ perform in      │
                                      │necessary.│ │ each order.     │
                                      └──────────┘ └─────────────────┘
                                                   ┌─────────────────┐
                                                   │ 2 TYPES OF      │
                                                   │ SHORT ITEM      │
                                                   ├─────────────────┤
                                                   │ *Randomize*     │
                                                   │ the order       │
                                                   │ of the items    │
                                                   │ or choose a     │
                                                   │ counter-        │
                                                   │ balanced        │
                                                   │ order and       │
                                                   │ *randomly*      │
                                                   │ order the       │
                                                   │ items within    │
                                                   │ each type.      │
                                                   └─────────────────┘

                          ┌─────────────────┐
                          │ INDEPENDENT     │
                          │ SUBJECTS        │
                          │ DESIGN          │
                          └─────────────────┘
┌──────────────┐
│ SUBJECT      │
│ VARIABLE     │
│ DESIGN       │
├──────────────┤          ┌─────────────────┐
│ Select       │          │ RELATED         │
│ samples      │          │ SUBJECTS        │
│ *randomly*   │          │ DESIGN          │
│ from the     │          ├─────────────────┤
│ two          │          │ Pair a person   │
│ relevant     │          │ in each sample  │
│ populations. │          │ with one in     │
└──────────────┘          │ the other (or   │
                          │ if the sample   │
                          │ is preselected  │
                          │ like the speech-│
                          │ retarded children│
                          │ find a match for│
                          │ each member from│
                          │ a normal population).│
                          └─────────────────┘
```

Figure 13. *Summary of a variety of experimental design*

so far as representativeness relates to the choice of subjects we have drawn attention to the fact that this requirement is often neglected. It is not always realized that representativeness is a relevant criterion in the planning of experimental materials also. If the study of language is to be useful then the type of language studied in the laboratory should relate to language as it is used in normal communication. Too often linguistic material in experiments is strained and artificial, in much the same way that the sentences studied by linguists often seem unnatural and sometimes perverse.

Circumstances may make it difficult to perform experiments which are fully rigorous with respect of sampling procedures and measurement but if the limitations are kept in mind when the results are being interpreted, the performing of even a small experiment can be of great value in sharpening observation and developing intuitions. However, large-scale studies which draw broad comparisons between teaching methods have a habit of being inconclusive.

9 Practical work

I: *Faulty designs*

Each of the following investigations has at least one flaw in design or reporting. See if you can detect the error in each case. Some are actual experiments and some have been invented.

1 Two students, Jack and John, could not agree about whether intelligent people tended to be popular or not so they decided to check this using their fellow students as subjects. They divided the students by putting all the names in a hat and picking them out one by one, assigning them alternately to two groups which they labelled A and B. John then arranged the names of the students in group A in order according to how popular he judged them to be. He arranged those in group B in order according to how intelligent he judged them to be. Jack did the rankings on popularity for group B, and intelligence for group A. They then looked to see whether the boys judged popular in each group were also judged intelligent.
2 To test the hypothesis that the best plays are written by young authors the research officer of a newspaper listed all the new plays that had been performed in Britain during the year and in each case recorded the length of the run in weeks. He then compared that with the age of the authors when they wrote the plays.
3 The distribution of autistic children registered at clinics in different social class categories was compared with the distribution of these social

class categories in the population at large. It was discovered that there was a significant tendency for autistic children to come from middle-class and upper-class homes.
4 A study set out to establish what the distance needs to be between two points of stimulation on the skin in order for the points to be perceived as distinct. Pairs of pins were applied simultaneously at points separated by varying distances and the subjects, who were blindfolded, were asked whether they felt both pins or only one.
5 Quotation from *The Guardian*, Monday 20th January, 1969: 'The best guarantee of intelligence whatever your social class is to be the first child born to a woman over 35.'
6 Teachers in Lanarkshire, Scotland, were instructed to divide their classes into three groups and to give one group ¾ pint of pasteurized milk per day, a second group ¾ pint of raw milk per day, and the third group no milk at all. The experiment lasted four months and 15,000 children took part. One finding was that children given milk showed an increase in weight during the four month period far in excess of that shown by the children who were not given milk.
7 A teacher of domestic science wished to develop a selectional procedure which would ensure that the most talented students would be accepted to do the course. For five years she selected incoming students by means of aptitude test and kept a record of their scores to compare with their marks in the final examination.
8 A study of stutterers reported that 8 per cent of the sample had experienced the onset of stuttering at the age of two.
9 An experiment set out to discover whether mothers of children whose fathers had been away in the army when the child was small were stricter disciplinarians than their husbands. A sample of such couples was selected and husbands and wives were rated for the severity of their discipline by an interviewer. It was found that the mothers were stricter and the experimenter concluded that the father's absence made the mothers more severe as a result of their having had sole responsibility for the children in infancy.
10 A primary school teacher wanted to know whether the experience of playing at shops, using toy money for making purchases, would transfer to formal arithmetic. Accordingly, he tested his children's ability at formal arithmetic, then gave them practice playing at shops for three weeks and finally compared their scores on a subsequent test of ability with their scores on the previous test.

II: *Problems*
1 How can one tell from the scattergram on p. 126 which of the tests is more difficult?

2 Which of the following measures are likely to be on an interval, which on an ordinal and which on a nominal scale?
   a position in the family
   b temperature in degrees
   c social class
   d bilingual or not
   e time taken to react to a stimulus in a word association task

3.1 Which measures of central tendency would be of interest to you:
   a For shoe sizes, if you were a manufacturer or buyer of shoes?
   b For examination results, if you could admit half the applicants to a course?
   c For the consumption of bread, if you were managing a canteen?
   d For the cost of a meal in France, if you were going there on holiday?
   e For contributions to a restoration fund, (i) if you wanted to know how much to give, (ii) if you wanted to know how many people to send requests to?
   f For schoolchildren's heights, if you wanted to send the taller ones to the back half of the hall for a school play?

3.2 Which measure of central tendency might be called the centre of gravity of a distribution?

4 In a study of stuttering, tape recordings of the speech of 12 children, some of whom were stutterers and some not, were played to the parents of 12 stuttering children and to the parents of 12 children with normal speech. The parents were asked to say which of the children on the recordings they thought were stutterers. Below is a record of the number of children each parent rated as stutterers, with husband's and wife's scores alongside one another.

Parents of stutterers		*Parents of non–stutterers*	
Father	Mother	Father	Mother
2	0	1	0
0	2	1	2
4	2	1	2
6	3	2	1
8	2	2	2
2	8	2	2
5	9	3	3
6	9	4	2
7	6	4	3
7	7	4	6
8	7	6	3
6	7	7	6

Which of the techniques for analysis summarized on p. 130, would you use:
  a to test whether the fathers of stutterers were more severe in their judgements than fathers of non-stutterers and mothers of stutterers more severe than mothers of non-stutterers?
  b to test whether fathers were more severe than mothers?
  c to test whether husbands and wives resembled each other in their degree of severity in judging the children?
5 Thirty-nine children were tested for their control of grammatical structures in two tests, one using prose and one using poetry as test material.
Their scores out of 10 for each test were as follows:

Child no.	1	2	3	4	5	6	7	8	9	10	11	12	13
Prose	10	10	10	10	10	10	10	10	10	10	9	9	9
Poetry	9	7	10	9	8	7	9	10	8	8	8	6	8

Child no.	14	15	16	17	18	19	20	21	22	23	24	25	26
Prose	9	9	9	9	9	9	8	8	8	8	8	8	8
Poetry	1	9	5	8	5	9	6	8	8	6	6	4	6

Child no.	27	28	29	30	31	32	33	34	35	36	37	38	39
Prose	8	7	7	7	7	6	5	5	4	2	2	2	2
Poetry	10	6	3	9	3	2	3	3	5	1	4	4	4

Draw a scattergram of these results and see what you can infer from it.

10 Acknowledgements

In Chapter 4, figures relating to previous language laboratory experience of students of Spanish come from a report of the Lindenwood Experiment, directed by Rand Morton, published by Lindenwood College, September, 1965.
The experiment on instruction in the use of pronouns was conducted by

M. Montgomery as a project for the Diploma in Applied Linguistics in 1970. One control group case scoring 6 was discarded for ease of presentation.

The figures on two different tests of logical connection come from a project for the Diploma in Applied Linguistics by G. Wells in 1967 entitled 'Logical connection: a psycholinguistic study'.

The birth weights of normal and speech retarded children were provided by Dr. T. T. S. Ingram of the Department of Child Life and Health, University of Edinburgh and were collected during the course of a study supported by the Scottish Social Research Council of the educational achievement of normal and speech retarded children.

The data on the age of onset of the first word among aphasic children came from *The Development and Disorders of Speech in Childhood* by M. E. Morley, Livingstone, 1957. Whereas in the book the ages were reported in three-monthly intervals, ages in terms of months, remaining within the intervals specified, were invented here for clarity of exposition.

The data introduced in the problem section in which understanding of syntactic structures was compared in prose and poetic contexts comes from a project performed by Sunanda Datta for the Diploma in Applied Linguistics, 1971.

The data on parents of stutterers and non-stutterers in problem 4 (p. 143) is from Bloodstein O., Jaeger W. and Tureen J., 'A study of the diagnosis of stuttering by parents of stutterers and non-stutterers', *Journal of Speech and Hearing Disorders* 17, 308–15 (1952).

5 RUTH CLARK
Procedures and Computations in the Analysis of Experiments

1 Introduction

In the previous chapter we discussed the planning and conduct of experiments, without getting too deeply involved in computation. When we discussed the preliminary evaluation of the four experiments, we concluded that in the case of each study the relevant data could be summarized in some appropriate way, to form the basis of a quantitative analysis. For experiments (b) and (c)—training in the use of pronouns and the understanding of logical connectives—two alternative methods of analysis were suggested. Before we can complete these analyses, we shall need to reduce each of the data summaries to one value which represents the outcome of the experiment. In the following chapter we shall see how these values can be used to reach decisions about our results.

(a) *Spanish-teaching experiment*

We need to know how to calculate expected values when the figures are less amenable than they were in the study of training in the use of pronouns. (For the concept of 'expected values' see p. 119.) Then we need to arrive at a composite figure for the differences between observed and expected values in the whole contingency table. These procedures are described in section 2 below.

(b) *Training in the use of pronouns*

For the median test, we need to know how to locate the median. Frequency tables and cumulative frequency tables are helpful for this purpose. Section 3.1 deals with frequency tables, and section 3.2 with cumulative frequency tables. When we have divided the sample into those above and those below the median, we need to arrive at a composite figure for the observed and expected values in the resulting contingency table, just as in the case of experiment (a).

Procedures and Computations in the Analysis of Experiments   147

For the analysis based on the sum of ranks, we shall need to rank the scores. Section 3.3 below explains how frequencies and cumulative frequencies are used in assigning ranks, and section 3.4 describes the summing of ranks. The sum of ranks has to be converted to a value labelled U before it can be used in the final analysis. Section 3.5 explains how this is done, and describes a technique for calculating U directly when the sample is small.

(c) *Understanding of logical connectives*
The first method suggested for treatment of this data is a comparison of the number of people doing better on one test and the number doing better on the other. These values are already in the appropriate form for final analysis.

The second method of treatment is based on sums of ranks of differences between scores on the two tests. The differences favouring one test are compared with the differences favouring the other. The differences are ranked in the same way as the scores are ranked in experiment (b). Section 3.4 describes the summing of ranks of differences.

(d) *Birth weight of normal and speech-retarded children*
The final analysis of the data from this experiment is based on the difference between the means of the two groups, which has already been calculated.

2 Analysing the contingency table

2.1 Calculating expected frequencies

In the last chapter it was suggested that the disproportion of cases in the various categories of a contingency table could be summarized in the values of the observed minus the expected frequencies. Figure 3b (p. 121) gave numbers above and below the median in instruction and control groups on the pronoun test. It was easy to see in that example that the expected values should be 15 in each box. Thinking about how we arrived at that figure should give us a clue as to how to deal with less obvious cases such as the contingency tables in Figure 1 (p. 118), which gives information about previous language laboratory experience of students of Spanish. The reasoning is that since half the children are in the control group, half the children above the median and half the children below the median should be in the control group if there is no tendency for this group to get lower scores.

Now let us look at a more complicated set of figures, invented to illustrate the technique:

	Arts	Science	Totals
Travelled	17	28	45
Untravelled	3(5)	12	15
Totals	20	40	60

Figure 1. *University students classified by faculty and travel experience*

We wish to test the hypothesis that arts students at a university go abroad more often than science students. The above figures were collected from a sample of 60 students who were asked if they went abroad the previous summer. We calculate that since 20 out of 60 or one-third of all students in the sample were arts students one-third of the untravelled should be arts students, i.e. one-third of 15, which is 5. We can formalize this in the following way:

$$\text{Expected frequency} = \frac{\text{column total} \times \text{row total}}{\text{overall total}} = \frac{20 \times 15}{60} = 5$$

The expected frequencies, which will not always be whole numbers, can then be entered in the table in brackets and checked to see if they add up to the right column and row totals. The reader will need to complete the table above by calculating the expected frequencies for the other boxes or looking them up on p. 220.

2.2 The chi squared test—calculating χ^2*

We said above that the difference between observed and expected frequencies would form the basis of an analysis. But compare the following contingency table with the one in Figure 1:

	Arts	Science	Totals
Travelled	92 (90)	178 (180)	270
Untravelled	28 (30)	62 (60)	90
Totals	120	240	360

Figure 2. *University students classified by faculty and travel experience (expected frequencies in brackets)*

* The value calculated from observed and expected frequencies in each instance is termed χ^2. The name of the distribution is chi squared, after the Greek letter pronounced 'kie' to rhyme with 'pie'.

The differences between observed and expected frequencies are the same for both these tables, but it is intuitively obvious that the differences of 2 in the second table mean less than those in the first. The way of adjusting for this is to express the differences as a proportion of the expected frequency. We want a value based on the sum of these proportions over all the boxes. It turns out that the squares of the differences have to be used to obtain a value whose distribution statisticians can specify.
Remember that:

χ^2 is the value calculated from observed minus expected frequencies
O stands for observed frequency
E stands for expected frequency

$$\chi^2 = \sum \frac{(O - E)^2}{E}$$

Σ denotes the sum across boxes.
χ^2 for Figure 1 is 1·6. The reader might like to verify this.

3 Frequencies, the median and ranking procedures

3.1 Frequency tables

Frequency tables are a useful aid in constructing diagrams, locating medians and calculating ranks. We construct such a table by writing out the scale in the leftmost column and taking each observation in turn entering it as a tally mark against the appropriate score. For example, consider the list of instruction and control group scores on the pronoun test which was discussed in the previous chapter. The thirty children in the instruction group achieved the following scores (out of 18): 8, 5, 10, 7, 6, 5, 8, 8, 6, 6, 8, 4, 3, 8, 5, 4, 6, 8, 7, 9, 7, 6, 6, 10, 6, 7, 9, 9, 6, 3. The thirty children in the control group achieved the following scores: 3, 4, 4, 5, 5, 4, 5, 2, 4, 3, 2, 5, 4, 4, 5, 10, 5, 10, 6, 6, 3, 4, 3, 14, 13, 6, 4, 5, 5, 5. In constructing a frequency table we would first make a mark against 8, then against 5, 10, etc. If we take the scores in turn we are less likely to overlook one than if we attempt to count up all the eights, all the fives, etc. It is convenient to make every fifth entry against a number an oblique line through the preceding four. This means that when we come to add up the frequencies for each score we can count in fives. This again makes for accuracy. The frequency tables for instruction and control group scores on the pronoun test (on which Figure 2 of chapter 4 is based) are as shown in Figure 3.

Finally, it is advisable to add the frequencies to make sure they add up to the right total. Diagrams can then be constructed on the pattern of Figure 2 or Figure 6 of chapter 4 by representing each tally, including the diagonal lines, as an X or a block.

	Instruction			Control		
Score		f	Score			f
18			18			
17			17			
16			16			
15			15			
14			14	I		1
13			13	I		1
12			12			
11			11			
10	II	2	10	II		2
9	III	3	9			
8	̶L̶H̶T̶ I	6	8			
7	IIII	4	7			
6	̶L̶H̶T̶ III	8	6	III		3
5	III	3	5	̶L̶H̶T̶ IIII	9
4	II	2	4	̶L̶H̶T̶ III	8
3	II	2	3	IIII		4
2			2	II		2
1			1			
0						
Total		30				30

Figure 3. *Frequency tables for instruction and control group scores in the training in the use of pronouns experiment* (see p. 118) (f = frequency)

3.2 Cumulative frequency distributions and the median

Cumulative frequency distributions are helpful for calculating the median and for assigning a rank position to each member of the sample. By the cumulative frequency of a score we mean the number of cases up to and including that score. For some purposes it may be more convenient to work down from the top of the scale but as a basis for the statistical tests we shall be using we need to work from the bottom upwards, i.e. we have to give the lowest rank to the lowest score. Remember that both the median and the rank positions have to be worked out for the sample as a whole so let us first combine the above frequency tables into a single table for all 60 children (see Figure 4). The cumulative frequencies have been entered in the rightmost column and will be explained below.

To find the cumulative frequency of a score x we simply add the frequencies of scores up to and including score x. Since we are calculating cumulative frequency beginning with the lowest score we will add 2 (the frequency of score 2) to 6, which is the frequency of score 3. This will give us 8 as the cumulative frequency working up the scale to score 3. To

Score		f	c.f.
18			
17			
16			
15			
14	I	1	60
13	I	1	59
12			
11			
10	IIII	4	58
9	III	3	54
8	ⅢⅡ I	6	51
7	IIII	4	45
6	ⅢⅡ ⅢⅡ I	11	41
5	ⅢⅡ ⅢⅡ II	12	30
4	ⅢⅡ ⅢⅡ	10	18
3	ⅢⅡ I	6	8
2	II	2	2
1			
0			
Total		60	

Figure 4. *Frequency table for scores of 60 children on pronoun test in the training in the use of pronouns experiment (f = frequency, c.f. = cumulative frequency)*

continue we add to this 8 a 10 which represents the frequency with which score 4 occurs. This gives us 18 as the cumulative frequency of score 4. 30 opposite score 5 is obtained by adding 18 and 12, 41 opposite score 6 by adding 10 and 11, etc. Naturally, by the time we get to the highest score we should have reached a cumulative frequency of 60 since we have 60 children in our sample. Looking at the column headed c.f. we can see immediately where the median will be. It will be between the 30th and 31st child, i.e. at 5·5. If the median falls within an interval, the division for the median test is made above that interval. This arbitrary procedure is followed so that the experimenter is not left with the choice of putting it above or below, since one arrangement of the figures may support his hypothesis better than the other, and the experimenter's bias cannot be allowed to influence the quantitative analysis of results.

3.3 Assigning a rank to each score
If no two children had obtained the same score we could simply give the child with the lowest score the rank of 1, the second lowest 2, the third 3,

and so on. However, in this set of data we have a number of tied observations so we shall have to share the appropriate rank positions among the children who have the same score. For instance, the two children obtaining score 2 will share rank positions 1 and 2. In fact we give each of them the average of these two ranks, i.e. 1·5. (It might appear to be simpler to give each of them a rank of 1 then all the scores of 3 a rank of 2 but this would mean that the sum of ranks assigned to a group of scores would not always be equivalent for a given sample size, since it would depend on the number and positions of tied scores. Statistical calculations involving ranking measures need to be able to depend on such an equivalence.) Similarly we give each child obtaining a score of 3 the average of the next six ranks (3, 4, 5, 6, 7 and 8) which is 5·5 (3 + 4 + 5 + 6 + 7 + 8 ÷ 6). Remember we have already used the first two ranks so we begin at 3.

There is an easier way to calculate ranks which is particularly useful for dealing with larger numbers. Instead of averaging numbers 3 to 8 for the score of 3 we can average 1 to 6 and add the result to the cumulative frequency in the row below. This gives us 3·5 + 2 = 5·5, which is identical to the result we got before. The advantage of this method is that we do not need to work out which ranks the people obtaining the score will share, we simply use the figure representing the frequency of the score, which is already in front of us, for calculating the average. These averages are very easy to calculate since for an odd frequency such as 3 (the frequency of the score of 9 above) we add to the previous cumulative frequency the middle number in the range 1 to 3, i.e. 2, since this is the average of 1 + 2 + 3. In fact we could divide 3 by 2 and add $\frac{1}{2}$ getting the same result. Similarly the average of 1 + 2 + 3 + 4 + 5 is the middle number of that range of numbers, i.e. 3 (5 ÷ 2 + $\frac{1}{2}$). This will be true for any odd number. In the case of a frequency which is even, the average to be added to the previous cumulative frequency will be half way between the two middle numbers in the range, e.g. for 4 it will be between 2 and 3, i.e. 2·5, which is again equal to 4 ÷ 2 + $\frac{1}{2}$. For 6 it will be between the middle two numbers in the range 1 to 6 (1 2 3 4 5 6) i.e. 3·5. (6 ÷ 2 + $\frac{1}{2}$). The general rule then is to divide the frequency by 2 and add $\frac{1}{2}$, then add the result to the c.f. in the row below. The table opposite includes a column of ranks.

3.4 Sums of ranks and sums of ranks of differences

We saw in the training in the use of pronouns experiment in chapter 4 that the sums of ranks for the scores of instruction and control group can serve as a basis of comparison between the groups. We shall see here how these sums of ranks are calculated and in the next chapter how they are used to test whether the instruction has had any effect.

We now have a rank for each score. The next step is to take one of the groups and add together the ranks of each of the 30 children's scores. Looking

Score	f	c.f.	Rank
18			
17			
16			
15			
14	1	60	60
13	1	59	59
12			
11			
10	4	58	56·5
9	3	54	53
8	6	51	48·5
7	4	45	43·5
6	11	41	36
5	12	30	24·5
4	10	18	13·5
3	6	8	5·5
2	2	2	1·5
1			
0			
Total	60		

Figure 5. *Table of frequency, cumulative frequency and ranks of scores of 60 children in the training in the use of pronouns experiment*

at Figure 3 again we see that there are two children in the instruction group with a score of 3. From Figure 5 we see that the rank of people obtaining this score is 5·5; 5·5 × 2 = 11. We perform this calculation for each score in the instruction group and add the totals to get R_1, the sum of ranks of the first group's scores. In Figure 6 the ranks are summed for all 30 children in the instruction group. R_2, the sum of ranks of the control group's scores, by a similar calculation comes to 693·5. We need to convert these sums of ranks to another value, known as U, before we can complete our analysis. The U score will be discussed in section 3.5 below.

Similarly, on p. 125 we saw that the sums of ranks of positive and negative differences could form the basis of a comparison between scores when we had related groups, as in the logical connectives study.[1] Working from the

[1] The use of this test for the logical connectives experiment presupposes not only that one can tell which of two scores from the same child is higher but also that one can rank the differences between pairs of scores in order of size. This is more stringent than the demand that the scores be on an ordinal scale.

Such a scale is intermediate between an ordinal and interval scale (p. 128). For further discussion of this point see Coombs (1950) and Siegel (1956).

Score	f	Rank	Total
10	2	56·5	113
9	3	53	159
8	6	48·5	291
7	4	43·5	174
6	8	36	288
5	3	24·5	73·5
4	2	13·5	27
3	2	5·5	11
Total	30		1136·5

Figure 6. *Calculation of sum of ranks of instruction group*

table of controlled production and selective completion scores (p. 124) we can construct frequency tables for positive and negative differences, then for all the differences combined. Remember that children getting the same score on both tests have to be excluded from the analysis. From the combined table we then construct a cumulative frequency distribution and use it to rank the differences.

Positive			Negative			All Differences			
Diff		f	Diff		f	Diff	f	c.f.	Rank
5	I	1	5	I	1	5	2	30	29·5
4	II	2	4			4	2	28	27·5
3	⁋⁋⁋⁋ I	6	3			3	6	26	23·5
2	⁋⁋⁋⁋ ⁋⁋⁋⁋	10	2	II	2	2	12	20	14·5
1	III	3	1	⁋⁋⁋⁋	5	1	8	8	4·5
Total		22	Total		8	Total	30		

Figure 7. *Frequency tables and ranks of differences for logical connective experiment* (*p.* 122)

The sum of ranks of positive differences here is 3 × 4·5 + 10 × 14·5 + 6 × 23·5 + 2 × 27·5 + 29·5 = 384. The sum of ranks of negative differences is 22·5 + 29 + 29·5 = 81. The figure we will need for our calculation is the smallest sum of ranks of differences of like sign which in this case is 81. This value is known as T. In the next chapter we shall see how T is used to evaluate the difference in difficulty between the tests.

3.5 The calculation of U

We looked in the last section at the sums of ranks as measures of the difference between sets of scores from two independent groups, such as instruction and control groups in the training in the use of pronouns experiment. There is another way in which we can quantify the relative positions of the members of two groups on a scale. Look at the following three sets of hypothetical results from experiments giving four children instruction and using four children as controls. Each instruction group child has been labelled I and each control group child C and the diagrams represent their scores in order of increasing size, regardless of the actual score.

Experiment 1:   C C C C I I I I
Experiment 2:   C I C I C I C I
Experiment 3:   C C C I I I C I

In the first experiment the instruction group clearly did better. No child in the control group did better than any child in the instruction group, i.e. there is no overlap between the scores of the two. In the second experiment the scores are completely interspersed. Clearly neither group's performance is superior. In the third experiment the situation is less clear-cut. There is a certain amount of overlap between the two groups. If we take each member of the control group and count how many people in the experimental group have a lower score, then sum these values for the control group we shall get a figure which reflects the degree to which the two groups' scores are interspersed. For instance in experiment 1 no control group score is preceded by an instruction group score so our total would be 0. In experiment 2 the first control group member would rate 0, since no I score precedes this, the second would rate 1, the third 2 and the fourth 3. The sum of these figures is 6. In the third experiment we get $0 + 0 + 0 + 3 = 3$. This total is known as U and we can see that it accords with what was said about the three experiments, namely that the result of experiment 3 represents a situation intermediate between 1 and 2.

A corresponding value, U', can be calculated by concentrating on the I scores rather than the C scores. This gives us for experiment 1: $4 + 4 + 4 + 4 = 16$, for experiment 2: $1 + 2 + 3 + 4 = 10$ and for experiment 3: $3 + 3 + 3 + 4 = 13$. Notice that if we add U and U' for each experiment we get the same total, namely 16. In fact $U = n_1 n_2 - U'$, where n_1 and n_2 are the sizes of the two groups.

Where our samples are very small it is simple to calculate the U value but with more complicated data the sums of ranks are easier to work out. Both values quantify the extent to which the scores in the two groups are interspersed, so we would expect them to be related to one another. In fact:

$$U = n_1n_2 + \frac{n_1(n_1 + 1)}{2} - R_1$$

$$\text{or } U' = n_1n_2 + \frac{n_2(n_2 + 1)}{2} - R_2$$

If we have found the sums of ranks we must use these formulae since it is the U value which we will need for evaluating the difference between the groups, as we shall see in the next chapter. Notice that, as these formulae imply, the test for comparing independent groups based on U can be used whether or not the two groups are equal in size. Let us substitute the values we have found for R_1 and R_2 in these formulae (see p. 153):

$$U = 30 \times 30 + \frac{30 \times 31}{2} - 1136 \cdot 5 = 228 \cdot 5$$

$$U' = 30 \times 30 + \frac{30 \times 31}{2} - 693 \cdot 5 = 671 \cdot 5$$

These results satisfy the formula relating U and U' quoted in the last paragraph, i.e.:

$$U = n_1n_2 - U'$$
$$228 \cdot 5 = 30 \times 30 - 671 \cdot 5$$

Thus if we calculate both sums of ranks we can check them by means of this formula. On the other hand we can just calculate one sum of ranks and find the corresponding U value from the earlier formula, then find U' by this latter formula. The value we will need is U or U' whichever is smaller, in this instance 228·5. When there are tied scores the sum of ranks should always be used for calculating U rather than the direct method given here as the latter will give misleading results.

4 Conclusion

Statistics such as χ^2, U and T vary in different samples. In the following chapter we shall discover how this variation can be specified, so that the probability of any specific value of χ^2, T or U if chance was the only factor influencing the outcome of the experiment can be determined. It is this probability figure on which our decision about the outcome of an experiment will be based.

5 Practical work

1 Construct separate cumulative frequency tables for instruction and control groups in the pronouns experiment (p. 118), and rank the scores within each group.

2 Construct a histogram of the selective completion scores in the logical connectives experiment (p. 122).
3 In a study of reading a group of 14 Ugandan students and a group of 20 Scottish schoolchildren were given a passage to read.[1] They were then tested both for general comprehension and for recall of the precise vocabulary used in the passage. The scores were as follows:

Ugandan Students n = 14

Subject no.	1	2	3	4	5	6	7	8	9	10	11	12	13	14
Comprehension:	10	2	7	7	5	4	10	10	6	9	7	6	5	6
Vocabulary:	9	6	4	7	7	9	9	9	1	9	8	3	1	9

Scottish Schoolchildren n = 20

Subject no.	1	2	3	4	5	6	7	8	9	10	11	12	13	14	15	16	17	18	19	20
Comprehension:	11	10	10	6	5	4	4	6	7	8	9	12	10	9	7	6	5	10	9	9
Vocabulary:	4	6	8	7	9	9	8	8	5	5	4	2	4	6	8	9	8	8	11	5

What are the medians of these four sets of scores? Plot them on a graph with median score on the vertical axis and type of test, comprehension or vocabulary, on the horizontal axis, joining the two Ugandan medians with an unbroken line and the two Scottish medians with a dotted line. What do we learn from the resulting graph?

[1] This experiment was done by M. Montgomery as part of the requirements for an M.Litt. degree, Department of Linguistics, University of Edinburgh, 1972.

6 RUTH CLARK
Statistical Inference

1 Introduction

Imagine a game in which two dice are tossed and the player calls a number. The stake is won if the numbers on the dice add up to the number called. What number would you call?

Clearly the number to call is the number that is most likely to come up. We can work out what that would be in the following way. The first dice can fall with any number from one to six uppermost. If one is uppermost any number from one to six can be uppermost on the other dice. The same applies if any number from two to six is uppermost on the first dice. We can list all the possible permutations as follows:

1st toss:	1	1	1	1	1	1	2	2	2	2	2	2	3	3	3	3	3	3
2nd toss:	1	2	3	4	5	6	1	2	3	4	5	6	1	2	3	4	5	6
Sum	2	3	4	5	6	7	3	4	5	6	7	8	4	5	6	7	8	9

1st toss:	4	4	4	4	4	4	5	5	5	5	5	5	6	6	6	6	6	6
2nd toss:	1	2	3	4	5	6	1	2	3	4	5	6	1	2	3	4	5	6
Sum	5	6	7	8	9	10	6	7	8	9	10	11	7	8	9	10	11	12

We can then make a table of frequency distribution for the sums of the figures showing on the two dice as shown opposite.

The number to call would clearly be seven, since out of thirty-six possible sequences of numbers on the two dice, six add up to seven. No other sum occurs as frequently. The probability of the numbers on the dice adding up to seven is 6:36 (six in thirty-six) or 1:6 (one in six) so if a person went on playing for a long time he could expect to win an average of one stake in six (unless the dice were loaded).

In the preliminary analysis of experimental findings in chapter 4 we kept

Sum	Frequency	Total
2	I	1
3	II	2
4	III	3
5	IIII	4
6	IIII	5
7	IIII I	6
8	IIII	5
9	IIII	4
10	III	3
11	II	2
12	I	1
Total		36

returning to the question of how to evaluate differences in frequency, sums of ranks, means, etc., between groups of observations. In fact, all statistical tests for making such comparisons depend on the same reasoning: we have to find out, as we just did for the dice, how likely a particular outcome is to occur by chance. In the case of the game with dice we were looking for the most likely outcome. In the case of an experiment it is when the observed outcome would have been unlikely to occur by chance that we can attribute it to a genuine experimental effect.

2 The binomial distribution—probability and significance

For the four experiments discussed in chapter 4 five different measures were put forward as suitable statistics on which to base comparisons between the groups. These were:

1 Differences between observed and expected frequencies—the Spanish-teaching experiment and the training in the use of pronouns experiment.
2 Sums of ranks of scores—the training in the use of pronouns experiment.
3 Number of subjects with higher scores in one test versus number with higher scores in the other—the understanding of logical connectives experiment.
4 Sum of ranks of differences in score on two tests—the understanding of logical connectives experiment.
5 Differences between means—the birth weight study.

The probability of these measures having a certain value needs to be calculated differently in each case but the general apparatus of statistical inference is the same for all these tests. We shall illustrate it with reference to the understanding of logical connectives experiment where the use of logical connectives in a controlled production test and a selective completion test were compared by means of the number of higher scores in one test and the number of higher scores in the other. Twenty-two children had higher scores in the controlled production test, eight in the selective completion test. Six children had equal scores on the two tests and are ignored for the purpose of analysis.

The question we have to ask is 'How likely is this outcome to occur if there is no real difference in difficulty between the tests?' If the tests are of equal difficulty, a child is as likely to do better in the first test as the second, just as when we toss a coin it will be equally likely to fall with the head up or with the tail up. For ease of presentation we will continue to use the coin analogy for the time being. We need to know how often in thirty tosses of an unbiased coin we would get the same face uppermost 22 times or more. If this event is very rare we can conclude that a proportion of 22 heads to 8 tails suggests a biased coin and that a proportion of 22 to 8 doing better on one test is due to a genuine difference in difficulty between the tests and not to chance variation, i.e. the tests are weighted to produce a given result more often than would be expected by chance in the same way as a coin is sometimes weighted for the same purpose.

We shall start with the simple case of two tosses, as we did with the dice. On the first toss the outcome could be a head or a tail. Either of these outcomes may be followed by a head or a tail on the second toss. This gives a total of four different permutations of heads and tails, each of them equally probable. They are represented diagrammatically in Figure 1a and listed in Figure 1b. Figure 1c summarizes the outcomes. Head-tail and tail-head are classed as one outcome, i.e. one head. Figure 1d is a histogram representing the probabilities of outcomes in random samples of independent tosses:

1st toss	2nd toss		Event	Frequency	Probability	Histogram
H	H	HH	2H	1	1:4 (0·25)	×
	T	HT				
			1H	2	2:4 (0·50)	× × ×
						2H 1H oH
T	H	TH				
	T	TT	oH	1	1:4 (0·25)	
				Total 4	(1·00)	
(a)		(b)		(c)		(d)

Figure 1. *Different ways of representing the possible permutations of two tosses of a coin (H = heads, T = tails)*

None of these outcomes is particularly rare and if we were seeking to establish bias in the coin we could conclude nothing on the basis of two tosses.

We can easily work out the possible outcomes of three tosses. The first two tosses will produce one of the four permutations listed above and each

Statistical Inference 161

of these four permutations can be followed by a head or a tail on the third toss. In Figure 2 we give the frequencies and probabilities of outcomes for three and four tosses. The reader can construct diagrams of permutations himself if he wishes.

	3 tosses			4 tosses	
Event	Frequency	Probability	Event	Frequency	Probability
3H	1	1:8 (0·125)	4H	1	1:16 (0·0625)
2H	3	3:8 (0·375)	3H	4	4:16 (0·2500)
1H	3	3:8 (0·375)	2H	6	6:16 (0·3750)
0H	1	1:8 (0·125)	1H	4	4:16 (0·2500)
	Total 8	(1·000)	0H	1	1:16 (0·0625)
				Total 16	(1·0000)

Figure 2. *The frequencies and probabilities of different outcomes when a coin is tossed three times and four times*

We see from Figure 2 that there is a probability of 1:8 of getting three heads in three tosses with an unbiased coin. If we suspected that a coin was biased in favour of heads, three heads on three tosses would be too likely an outcome by chance for us to infer bias. But clearly the point at which we decide an outcome is sufficiently unlikely to occur by chance to warrant such an inference is arbitrary. Perhaps four heads on four tosses which has a probability of 1:16, would qualify? In fact there are conventional probability levels adopted by statisticians, known as significance levels, and the highest of these is lower than 1:16. If the result has a probability of less than 1:20 of our result, or one more extreme, occurring by chance we can say it is significant at the 0·05 or 5 per cent level. If there is a probability of less than 1:100 of the result occurring by chance we may say it is significant at the 0·01 or 1 per cent level and if there is a probability of less than 1:1000 of it occurring by chance we may say it is significant at the 0·001 or 0·1 per cent level. If, then, in testing our coin, we threw four heads in four tosses, we could not infer bias. Before we could conclude that the coin was biased, we would need to get a result which was significant at one of these levels, the level having been chosen before testing began.[1]

The choice of significance level will depend on how critical the decisions are which will be based on the experimental findings. Adopting a 5 per cent significance level, for instance, is equivalent to accepting the possibility that in one case in twenty a result that is really due to chance will be attributed to

[1] An alternative to this procedure of adopting significance levels, an alternative which many statisticians find less arbitrary, is to quote the exact significance level of the result (i.e. the probability of the result obtained, or one more extreme, occurring by chance). This allows the reader to decide for himself how to react to the finding.

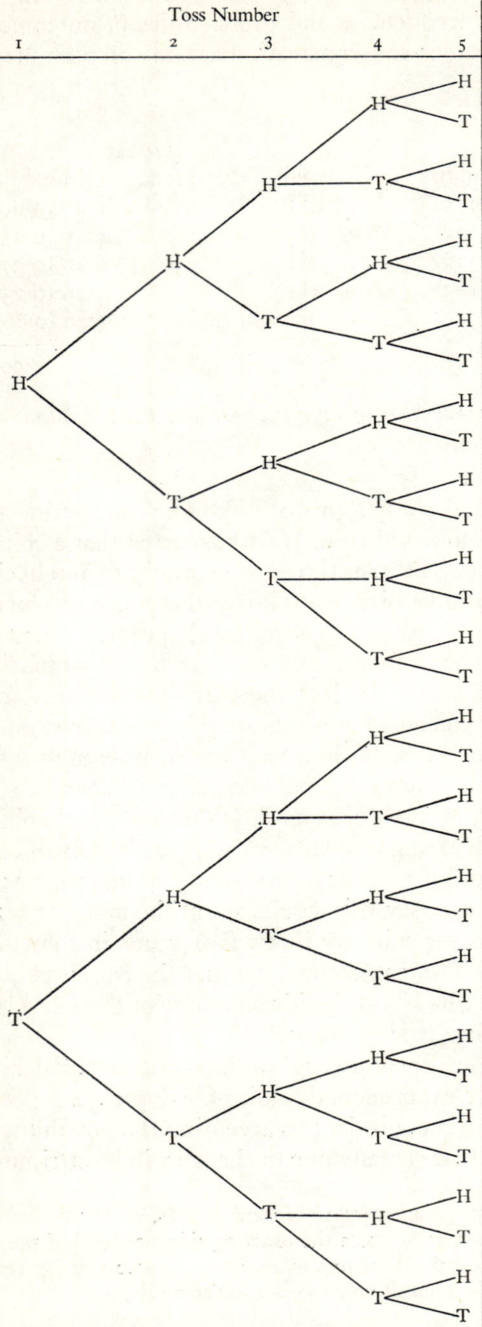

Toss Number 1	2	3	4	5	Outcome HT
H	H	H	H	H	5:0
H	H	H	H	T	4:1
H	H	H	T	H	4:1
H	H	H	T	T	3:2
H	H	T	H	H	4:1
H	H	T	H	T	3:2
H	H	T	T	H	3:2
H	H	T	T	T	2:3
H	T	H	H	H	4:1
H	T	H	H	T	3:2
H	T	H	T	H	3:2
H	T	H	T	T	2:3
H	T	T	H	H	3:2
H	T	T	H	T	2:3
H	T	T	T	H	2:3
H	T	T	T	T	1:4
T	H	H	H	H	4:1
T	H	H	H	T	3:2
T	H	H	T	H	3:2
T	H	H	T	T	2:3
T	H	T	H	H	3:2
T	H	T	H	T	2:3
T	H	T	T	H	2:3
T	H	T	T	T	1:4
T	T	H	H	H	3:2
T	T	H	H	T	2:3
T	T	H	T	H	2:3
T	T	H	T	T	1:4
T	T	T	H	H	2:3
T	T	T	H	T	1:4
T	T	T	T	H	1:4
T	T	T	T	T	0:5

Figure 3a: *permutations of heads and tails when a coin is tossed five times*

Event	Frequency	Probability
5H	1	1 : 32 (0·03125)
4H	5	5 : 32 (0·15625)
3H	10	10 : 32 (0·31250)
2H	10	10 : 32 (0·31250)
1H	5	5 : 32 (0·15625)
0H	1	1 : 32 (0·03125)
Total	32	(1·00000)

Figure 3b. *Frequencies and probabilities of outcomes when a coin is tossed five times.*

the independent variable. Significance levels should be chosen before the experiment is performed, since the stringency of the significance requirement should not be allowed to depend on the actual results of the experiment.

The use of the term significant should not mislead the reader into assuming that a result pronounced significant is necessarily meaningful in the general sense of the term. It may be a spurious effect due to a poorly controlled experiment, it may be trivial, or it may be obvious. Significant in the statistical sense merely means unlikely to have occurred by chance.

In order to test a coin for bias, then, we should need to toss it at least five times. Figures 3a and 3b give details of the permutations and outcomes for five tosses of a coin.

We see from this figure that five heads has a probability of less than 1:20 of occurring by chance. A result of five heads in five tosses would be sufficiently rare if the coin were not biased in favour of heads for us to dismiss the latter possibility at the 5 per cent level of significance. Notice that we cannot confirm directly the experimental hypothesis that the coin is biased. We can only adopt a counter hypothesis, known as the null hypothesis, namely that the coin is not biased, and then reject the latter if the result would have been unlikely to occur if that hypothesis were true.

Notice also that if we had set a higher significance level than 5 per cent a result of five heads would still not be sufficiently rare to justify rejecting the null hypothesis (symbolized H_0). This demonstrates the general principle that the more stringent the significance level the larger the sample of observations will need to be to demonstrate significance.

Furthermore, if our coin is weighted but not sufficiently to make it show heads on every toss we might get an outcome of four heads. The probability of getting four or more heads on five tosses of an unbiased coin is 0·1875 (i.e. 0·15625, which is the probability of getting exactly four heads, plus 0·03125, which is the probability of getting more than four heads). This demonstrates two points. Firstly, the smaller the sample the more extreme an outcome will have to be in order to be significant. Secondly, we must always ask, when assessing the significance of a result, what the probability is of getting a result as extreme as this or more so, rather than asking what the probability is of getting exactly this result. When we specify the significance level we are focusing on a certain percentage of extreme outcomes, whether 5, 1, or 0·1 per cent. If the outcome of the experiment falls within this small percentage of cases we will judge it to be significant. We are not concerned with the probability of precisely that outcome. The probability of any particular outcome will be quite small in most circumstances. What we are concerned with is finding whether our outcome falls within the extreme area of outcomes we have focused on in adopting our significance level, and to do this we need to determine what percentage of cases lies beyond our result. If this is smaller than the set significance level, our result falls within the area we have specified.

In general, Figures 1–3 illustrate the role of sample size in experimental design. The larger the sample the better it represents the true proportions of different values in the population, and the more unlikely it is that an extreme outcome will occur by chance. We are therefore better able to attribute an extreme outcome to the operation of the independent variable. The smaller the influence of our independent variable on events by comparison with other factors the larger the sample will need to be to demonstrate its effect.

There is one factor we have not yet taken into account in this discussion, namely, precisely what hypothesis are we testing? Are we testing the hypothesis that the coin is biased in favour of heads or merely that it is biased in one direction or other? The interpretation we put on a particular outcome must depend on the answer we give to this question. For instance, an outcome of five heads in five tosses may be treated as an instance of the coin falling with heads uppermost on every toss. This outcome has a probability of only 1:32 of occurring by chance if the coin is not weighted. On the other hand it may be treated as an instance of the coin falling with the same side uppermost on every toss. There are two outcomes that satisfy this condition, 5H and 0H. It therefore has a probability of 2:32 or 0·0625 (i.e. larger than 0·05) of occurring by chance. If our research hypothesis had anticipated a bias in favour of heads we could reject the null hypothesis at the 5 per cent level on the evidence of five heads in five tosses. However, if we had merely expected a bias without specifying its direction, we would need a larger sample of tosses. There will be further discussion of this point in the next section.

The following histograms representing the frequencies of different outcomes on five tosses of a coin illustrate the above points. It is important to realize that these are theoretical distributions representing probabilities and not actual observations. In Figure 4(a) the column representing 5H is shaded to illustrate that this event would be significant at the 5 per cent level ($p = 0.03125$ which is less than 0.05). In Figure 4(b) the area shaded

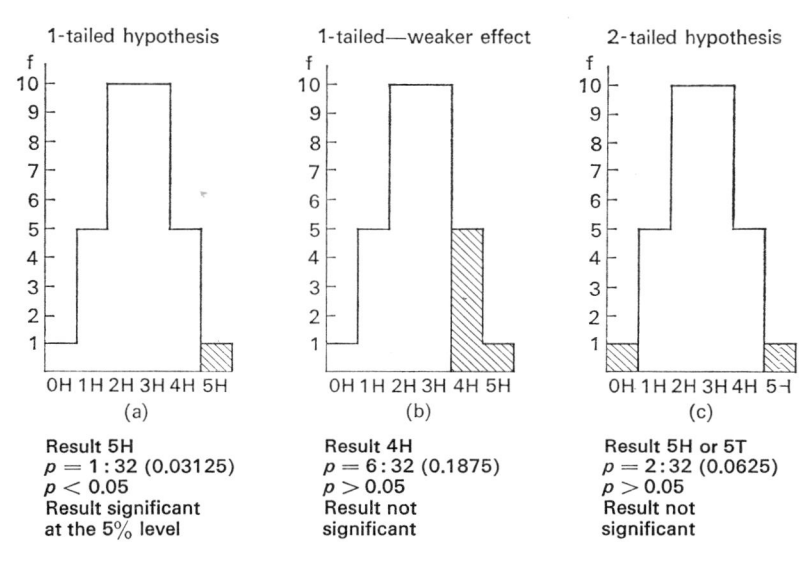

1-tailed hypothesis	1-tailed—weaker effect	2-tailed hypothesis
(a)	(b)	(c)
Result 5H	Result 4H	Result 5H or 5T
$p = 1:32$ (0.03125)	$p = 6:32$ (0.1875)	$p = 2:32$ (0.0625)
$p < 0.05$	$p > 0.05$	$p > 0.05$
Result significant at the 5% level	Result not significant	Result not significant

Figure 4. *Histograms representing probabilities of outcomes of five tosses (f = frequency, $<$ = less than, $>$ = greater than)*

represents outcomes in which heads are uppermost on four or more tosses. An outcome of 4H would not be significant at the 5 per cent level ($p = 0.1875$ which is more than 0.05). In Figure 4(c) the shaded areas represent the outcomes in which the same side was uppermost in all five tosses. An outcome of 5H or 0H would not be significant at the 5 per cent level unless the experimental hypothesis had anticipated the direction of bias ($p = 0.0625$, which is more than 0.05). Notice that the two-tailed probabilities are always twice the one-tailed ones.

A hypothesis in which direction of bias is stated is called one-tailed since we are concerned with outcomes at one end or tail of the distribution. A hypothesis in which direction of bias is not stated is called two-tailed since it has to take into account outcomes at both ends or tails of the distribution.[1] In the training in the use of pronouns experiment our hypothesis was one-tailed, since we expected the group which had received instruction to do

---

[1] Though we have presented the distinction between one- and two-tailed hypotheses as if it was straightforward, it is in fact a subject of controversy among statisticians. See Morrison and Henkel 1970.

better on the pronoun test. In the logical connectives experiment on the other hand, our hypothesis was two-tailed since we had no definite expectation that one test for the use of logical connectives would be easier than the other.

We have now introduced a number of basic statistical concepts—the null hypothesis, significance levels and one- and two-tailed predictions. However, we have not yet answered our initial question about the probability of the outcome of 22 pluses and 8 minuses from the connectives experiment having occurred by chance. We have reached five tosses of the coin and we need to continue to 30 tosses to get an answer. In principle we could go on working out the possible outcomes as we have been doing, but in practice this would be very inconvenient. For samples of 25 or fewer observations we can look up a table which gives the probabilities of all possible outcomes (see Appendix II, Table C). For samples larger than 25 we have to enter our sample size (30) and our smallest frequency (8) in a formula from which we can find the relevant probability figure. This formula will be introduced later. In fact the outcome of 22:8 has a two-tailed probability of 0·018 so it is significant at the 5 per cent level. That is if 30 pairs of scores on tests of equal difficulty were drawn at random from a population there would be less than one chance in twenty of 22 or more being higher on the same test.

Before leaving this section let us briefly consider a way of summarizing the same model which we could have used instead of the coin tossing example to represent choice between two alternatives. Suppose we have a large triangular area marked out in squares and we start at the top corner, moving diagonally downwards only. We can work out for each square how many possible ways there are of reaching it from the top corner. The result is known as Pascal's Triangle:

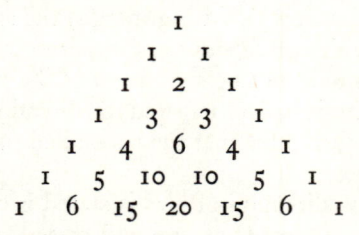

```
                    1
                  1   1
                1   2   1
              1   3   3   1
            1   4   6   4   1
          1   5   10  10  5   1
        1   6   15  20  15  6   1
```

Figure 5. *Pascal's triangle*

Reading horizontally, we have the frequencies of different outcomes for different numbers of tosses. Adding across the rows gives us the total number of permutations for each sample size of tosses. The reader may like to study the properties of the triangle and perhaps add more rows. Two further rows are given on p. 220.

The statistical test we have been looking at is called the sign test since it works with pluses and minuses. The theoretical distribution on which it is based is called the binomial distribution since it is concerned with two possible nominal categories as outcomes for each event, e.g. head/tail if the event is the tossing of a coin, male/female if it is the birth of a child, pass/fail if it is the result of an examination. The concepts introduced in this discussion—null hypothesis, one- and two-tailed predictions, levels of significance etc.—are central to all the statistical tests we shall be dealing with, and once the reader has understood these, he will have mastered the fundamental apparatus of statistical inference.

3 The normal distribution and standard scores

'Johnny's tall for his age' says one mother. 'My Billy's small for his age', says another. How do we interpret this information? In the first place we need to know each child's age. Let us suppose that Johnny is seven and Billy twelve. Secondly we would want to know the mean height for children of these two age groups before we could judge whether the mothers were right.

In the last chapter we defined the mean as the sum of the observations in the sample divided by the number of observations. We now need to introduce a few symbols so that we can express this definition in an accurate and concise way.

Σ means 'sum the following' (the Greek capital letter 'sigma')
x stands for the value of each of the observations in turn
n stands for the number of observations.

We can now define the mean as:

$$\frac{\Sigma x}{n} \text{ (read 'sigma x over n')}$$

since this is an instruction to add all the observations together and divide by the number of observations. If we give the mean itself a symbol ($\bar{x}$ stands for mean and is sometimes pronounced *x bar*) our formula will look like this:

$$\bar{x} = \frac{\Sigma x}{n} \text{ (read 'x bar equals sigma x over n')}$$

If we have the mean heights of seven-year-olds and twelve-year-olds we can check whether Johnny is in fact tall for his age and Billy small. Suppose Johnny is two inches taller than the mean for his age and Billy four and a half inches shorter than the mean for his age. This tells us something, but it does not tell us, for instance, whether Johnny would stand out from among his class mates or Billy find it difficult to get a school uniform to fit. As well as information about central tendency we need information about dispersion or variability within the groups to be able to place the boys with respect to their peers. The appropriate measure of dispersion for height is the standard deviation.

In chapter 4 we defined the standard deviation as the square root of the average of squared deviations from the mean. Thus to calculate it, we subtract the mean from each observation, square the resulting difference, sum the squared differences, divide by the number of observations and then take the square root of the result. We clearly need to be able to express this in a more concise way and we can do so with the symbols we have already. The standard deviation is:

$$\sqrt{\frac{\Sigma(x - \bar{x})^2}{n}}$$

This expression tells us to subtract from each observation (x) the mean of observations ($\bar{x}$), square these differences, sum (Σ) the squared differences divide by the number of observations (n) and take the square root of the result. With one more symbol (s stands for standard deviation) we can produce a formula:[1]

$$s = \sqrt{\frac{\Sigma(x - \bar{x})^2}{n}}$$

How will this help us with Johnny and Billy? Suppose the standard deviation of heights for seven-year-olds is three inches. Johnny is two inches above the mean so we can say he is two thirds (i.e. + 0·67) of a standard deviation above the mean in height. If the standard deviation of heights for twelve-year-olds is two inches, Billy who is four and a half inches below the mean will be more than two standard deviations below it (i.e. −2·25). To find each child's position with respect to his peers we have divided the difference between his height and the mean height by the standard deviation of heights in the relevant age group. Putting this in a formula we have:

$$\frac{x - \bar{x}}{s}$$

This value is called a standard score.

z stands for standard score.
Then:

$$z = \frac{x - \bar{x}}{s}$$

It is very convenient to be able to express quantities in standard scores as this means we can compare the positions of scores on two scales even when

[1] $s = \sqrt{\dfrac{\Sigma x^2}{n} - \bar{x}^2}$ is equivalent to the above and easier to compute.

the measures differ in variability, since we are expressing the positions as proportions of the standard deviation.

The standard score is really only informative if we can deduce from it what proportion of seven-year-olds are taller than Johnny with his standard score of $+0.67$. Many variables in nature, including physical characteristics such as height and weight, have in fact been found to be distributed for specific populations in a regular way such that the distance of a value from the mean in terms of standard deviations gives information about the proportion of observations which are larger than that value and the proportion that are smaller. This pattern of distribution of a variable is known as the normal distribution or Gaussian distribution (after Karl Gauss who first enunciated it). The normal curve representing the frequencies of such observations is symmetrical and bell-like in shape, its mean, median and mode are in the same place and over 99 per cent of observations fall within three standard deviations on each side of the mean. Figure 6 shows the percentages of cases falling within one, two and three standard deviations of the mean of a normal distribution. Notice that the ends of the curve do not touch the axis. This is because, unlike Figures 2 and 6 in chapter 4, this curve is an idealized representation of an infinite number of observations. This is why we can draw it as a curve instead of a number of adjacent columns. The distribution of a finite number of observations only approximates the normal distribution. It is important to realize also that not all distributions of data approximate the normal distribution; in fact very few do. We should not suppose that every set of observations we collect ought necessarily be of this form. More will be said about this in a later section.

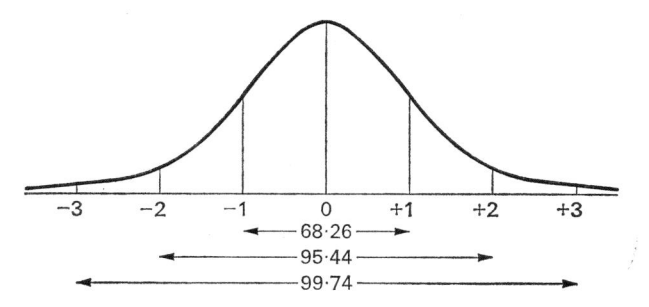

Figure 6. *Percentages of cases within one, two and three standard deviations of the mean of the normal curve*

We can relate a z score for a normally distributed variable to the proportion of cases between that value and the mean, or the proportion of cases of a lower or higher value. In a moment we will apply this to Johnny and Billy's heights but first, having looked at the percentage of cases lying within one, two and three standard deviations of the mean, let us look at the distance in standard deviations from the mean beyond which 5 per cent, 1 per cent and 0·1 per cent of cases lie. Figure 7 gives this information. Table A in Appendix II gives for any z score the probability of a score being as extreme or more so. We can check the information given in Figure 7 as a way of getting to understand the table. Firstly, let us take the z score of 1·65 given in Figure 7(a) as the score beyond which 5 per cent of cases lie. If we look up 1·6 in the column headed z on the left of Table A (on p. 200) then move across that row to the column headed 0·05 so that we have 1·65 we find the entry 0·0495 which is the nearest entry in the table to 0·05. This indicates that 0·05 or 5 per cent of cases lie beyond 1·65 standard deviations above the mean. The reader will find 0·0099 at the intersection of row 2·3 and column 0·03 and 0·001 at the intersection of row 3·1 and column 0·00.

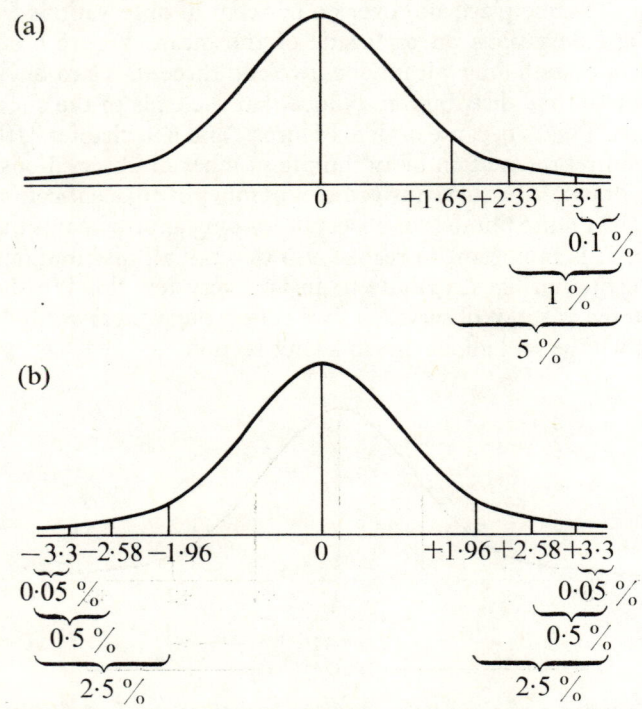

Figure 7. *Areas of the curve including the most extreme 5%, 1% and 0·1% of cases.* (a) *shows the observations concerned concentrated at one end.* (b) *shows the observations concerned distributed equally at both ends*

In Figure 7(b) we are concerned with the 5, 1, and 0·1 per cent of cases that lie at both extremes of the distribution, i.e. the two-tailed probabilities. As mentioned at the top, the table gives one-tailed probabilities for scores higher than z. For two-tailed 5 per cent probability levels 2½ per cent of the cases will be at one end of the distribution and 2½ per cent at the other. We therefore need to find in the table of one-tailed probabilities the z score beyond which 2½ per cent (0·025) of cases lie, because this z score will have a two-tailed probability of 5 per cent (0·05). We saw in the previous

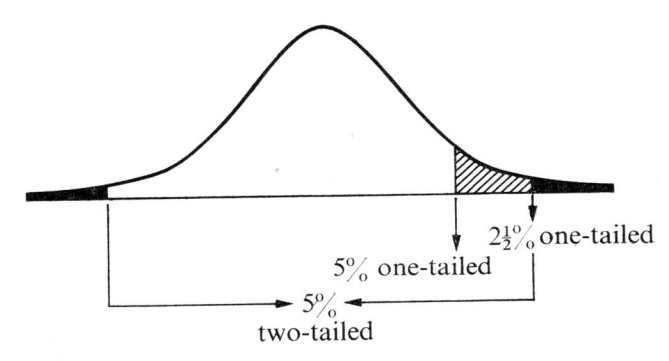

Figure 8. *Relationships between one- and two-tailed probabilities*

section that two-tailed probabilities are always twice one-tailed probabilities. Therefore, if we want to find a two-tailed value from a one-tailed table, we look for the value having half the required probability. The entry 0·025 is at the intersection of row 1·9 and column 0·06, therefore 5 per cent of cases lie beyond 1·96 standard deviations above and below the mean as Figure 7(b) indicates. Similarly, to find the number of standard deviations on either side of the mean beyond which 1 per cent (0·01) of cases lie we need to search for 0·005 in the one-tailed table. The nearest entry to this is at the intersection of row 2·5 and column 0·08. The one-tailed probability 0·0005, which is half the two-tailed probability 0·001, is in row 3·3.

Now let us return to the two boys. If we wished to find the probability of a boy selected at random being as tall or taller for his age than Johnny (a one-tailed hypothesis), i.e. having a z score of 0·67 or more we would look up 0·67 in Table A. In fact the probability is roughly 0·25. This means that one quarter of seven-year-olds are as tall as Johnny or taller according to our invented figure for the standard deviation. If we wished to know the probability of a seven-year-old being as different from the mean in height or more so than Johnny we would have to double the probability for 0·67 in the table, giving us 0·5. The reader may wish to calculate the probabilities of a twelve-year-old selected at random being as short or shorter than Billy and as deviant or more so in height (answers on p. 221).

4 The final steps in the analysis

In chapters 4 and 5 we discussed four studies and the type of analysis appropriate to each of them. In the course of that discussion five measures were proposed on which analysis could be based. These were: (1) difference between observed and expected frequencies in a contingency table, (2) U score related to sums of ranks of one group's scores, (3) number of children scoring more highly in one test versus number of children scoring more highly in the other, (4) T score sums of ranks of differences favouring one test, (5) differences between means.

The third measure has already been discussed in section 2 of this chapter where we found that we could use the binomial distribution to discover the probability of getting such a big apparent difference in difficulty between the tests if they were really equally difficult. In that section we mentioned that for samples of more than 25 observations a formula could be used to determine the probability of our outcome. The formula we use in fact converts our observation into a z score whose probability we can then look up in Table A (on p. 200). The reason this is possible is that for large samples the binomial distribution approximates the normal distribution.

In section 2 we saw that even when heads and tails were equally likely, the proportion of heads to tails would vary in different random samples of tosses. Using the theoretical distribution we could determine the probability of a sample having a number of heads equal to or larger than the number observed. Just as the proportion of heads to tails will vary in different random samples of tosses of a coin, even if the coin is not biased, so will the values of the other statistics we discussed in chapters 4 and 5 vary in different random samples. To take as an example statistic U, used to analyse the results of the pronouns test, the scores from the instruction group and the control group were arranged in order of size and the value of U was calculated. But if the two groups of subjects, I and II, drawn at random from a population were given exactly the same training before doing the pronouns test, a certain value of U would be obtained by putting the scores from group I and group II in order of rank. Two other groups of subjects drawn at random from the same population and given the same training would yield a different value of U when their scores were put in order of rank. Just as the theoretical distribution of the number of heads was specified by the binomial theorem, so can the theoretical distribution of U be specified by a formula so that the probability of obtaining various values of U by chance can be calculated. The observed value of U can then be evaluated in terms of the probability that it occurred by chance. We noted earlier that for large samples the binomial distribution approximated the normal distribution.

Similarly for large samples the distributions of the measures U and T and of differences between means all approximate the normal distribution. The four measures which approximate to the normal distribution, measures 2–5, will be discussed below. They will be presented in the order in which they were introduced in the earlier chapters. The difference between observed and expected frequencies will be taken up again at the end of the section.[1]

4.1 Mann-Whitney U test—for comparing independent groups by means of the sum of ranks

We saw in chapter 5 that we can calculate the U value directly from the data or calculate R, the sum of ranks of one group's scores, and find U from a formula which related the two. It is the U value that we need for finding the probability of our result having occurred by chance. For experiments in which the largest group is no larger than 20 we can look up tables which give the probabilities of various values of U. These tables are not given here since they would take up too much space. They can be found in Siegel (1956).

For samples where one group is larger than 20 we enter U in the following formula:

$$z = \frac{U - \frac{n_1 n_2}{2}}{\sqrt{\frac{n_1 n_2 (n_1 + n_2 + 1)}{12}}}$$

n_1 here is the size of one group and n_2 the size of the other. We can then look up the probability of the resulting z in Table A on p. 200. Alternatively we can simply note whether it is higher than the relevant critical value for z given in Figure 7 (p. 170). Notice that there is no need for the groups to be the same size for this test to be performed, though in our example, the pronouns experiment, both groups happened to be the same size, i.e. 30. What the above formula does is to find the difference between U and the mean of U for samples of this size, and divide that difference by the standard deviation of U, i.e. it is exactly like the formula for converting a value into a standard score given in section 3 above. All the formulae in this section for converting to z scores are of the same type, though it will not be possible to explain in every case how the means and standard deviations are derived.[2]

4.2 Sign test—for comparing related groups using number of positive and negative differences

The table of probabilities of x (the smaller of the two frequencies) for samples

---

[1] The probabilities of outcomes for all the examples introduced in the previous chapter (except the birth weight study) will be given at the end of the book so that the reader who wishes to work them out can check his results.

[2] If there are numerous tied scores the variability of U is affected and this will clearly affect the calculation of z. The effect will normally be negligible but see Siegel (1956) for details of a correction factor which may need to be used in certain circumstances.

of 25 or fewer pairs of scores will be found in Appendix II. The formula for converting x to a z score when the sample is larger than 25 is as follows:[1]

$$z = \frac{(x + 0.5) - \frac{n}{2}}{\sqrt{\frac{n}{4}}}$$

n being the total number of observations. In this case it should be fairly easy to see why the mean number of minuses should be $\frac{n}{2}$ by studying the diagrams in section 2. The reader might like to check the probability given for the outcome of 22:8 in section 2 (p. 166).

The 0·5 in the above formula is a correction factor. The normal distribution forms a smooth curve while the binomial distribution represents a number of distinct categories (see the histograms in section 2). The reduction of the difference between x and the mean by 0·5 gives a better approximation to the normal curve when a z score is being calculated.

4.3 Wilcoxon matched pairs signed ranks—for comparing related groups using the sum of ranks of differences

We saw in chapter 5 that the smallest sum of ranks of differences is labelled T. The probability of getting a T as small as or smaller than the one obtained if there is no difference between the tests is given by a table for samples containing up to 25 pairs of scores. The table can be found in Siegel (1956).

The formula for converting T into a z score for larger samples is:

$$z = \frac{T - \frac{n(n + 1)}{4}}{\sqrt{\frac{n(n + 1)(2n + 1)}{24}}}$$

n in this case is the number of differences that were ranked, i.e. it is equal to the number of pairs of scores after the subjects with equal scores have been discarded.

---

[1] This formula is a special case of a more general formula. In the situation we were concerned with the chance expectation was that the two events, + and —, would be equiprobable and this is always the case with the sign test. The binomial theorem can be used, however, when the two events are not assumed to be equiprobable. The formula for such situations can be found in Siegel (1956).

4.4 Test of difference between means—for independent samples where the variable is on an interval scale and normally distributed in the population

In the section on the normal distribution we were considering the distribution of values on a variable. What we have to think about here is slightly more abstract. Imagine we are drawing a pair of samples randomly from a population in which the variable is normally distributed. We calculate the mean of each sample and the difference between the means of the two samples. We make a note of this value, replace all the cases and draw a second pair of samples. We again calculate the difference between the means. We continue to draw pairs of samples in this way from the same population and calculate the difference between the means, replacing cases between each sampling. We will then have a number of values for the differences between means of pairs of samples drawn at random from the same population. We can then plot the distribution of the differences between means. For samples drawn from a normal population this distribution will itself be normal, provided the samples each contain 30 or more cases. The standard deviation of the distribution of differences between means is called the standard error of the difference, symbolized s.e. diff. It is smaller than the standard deviation of the population from which the samples come, but can be calculated from it.

In the birth weight study in chapter 4 we were comparing the mean birth weight of a group of normal children and that of a group of speech-retarded children. We wished to test the hypothesis that these samples came from populations with different mean birth weights, i.e. that speech-retarded children tend to differ in birth weight from normal children. To do this we adopt the null hypothesis that these samples come from the same population, find the probability, if the null hypothesis is true, of the difference between means being of that order (i.e. $2\frac{1}{2}$ oz.) and if this probability is sufficiently low we reject the null hypothesis. To find this probability we must of course divide $2\frac{1}{2}$ oz. by the standard error of the difference to get a z score and then look up its probability in Table A or compare it with the critical values in Figure 7 (p. 170). As mentioned above the standard error of the difference is related to the standard deviation of the population by a formula but usually we do not know the standard deviation of the population so we find s.e. diff. using the standard deviations of the samples as an estimate by means of the following formula:

$$\text{s.e. diff.} = \sqrt{\frac{s_1^2}{(n_1 - 1)} + \frac{s_2^2}{(n_2 - 1)}}$$

s_1 is the standard deviation of one sample and n_1 the size of that sample; s_2 is the standard deviation of the other sample and n_2 the size of that sample. Since the data in the birth weight study are grouped, the calculation is too involved to explain here and the answer will not be found at the end of the book (see Blalock 1960, p. 50ff.).

When the standard deviation of the population is calculated from less than 30 cases the z scores do not approximate the normal distribution sufficiently for the normal table of z scores to be used. So with fewer than 30 cases the t distribution has to be used. The reader is referred to Blalock (1960) for details.[1]

4.5 Chi squared and median tests for analysing contingency tables

We have left the chi squared test till the end, since it differs from the other four tests. Whereas the theoretical distributions of x, U, T and the difference between means approximate to the normal distribution, the chi squared distribution takes a different form, so the table of probabilities for z will never be used, even for large samples. However, this does not affect in any way the principles of the analysis, which still rests on determining the probability of a given χ^2 value having occurred if chance was the only factor influencing the results, and rejecting the null hypothesis if that probability is less than the particular significance level adopted.

In the previous chapter we showed how a composite χ^2 value is calculated for the contingency table as a whole. The value arrived at for the hypothetical data on student travel was 1·6. All we need do now is look up a table which gives critical values for χ^2 (Table B, p. 202). This table functions like Figure 7, i.e. instead of finding in the table the probability of getting a χ^2 of 1·6 or more by chance as we would in a z table, we find the values which χ^2 has to exceed to be significant at various levels, for instance 0·05 or 0·01. If 1·6 exceeds the value for the significance level that we have chosen our result is larger than we would have expected by chance and is significant at that level. The tables usually give two-tailed probabilities; we shall see why in a moment.

We have already seen in section 3 that to find a two-tailed value from the one-tailed z table we need to look for a value with half the probability, since a value having a two-tailed probability of x will have a one-tailed probability of ½x (see Figure 8). In the case of χ^2 if we want a one-tailed critical value from the two-tailed table we will need to look for the probability level which is double the one we have set. For 0·05 critical values with a one-tailed hypothesis we should look in the column headed 0·1 and for 0·01 critical values we should look in the column headed 0·02. For a significance level of 0·001 we would look in a column headed 0·002, but the values of χ^2 having that probability are not given in Table B.

---

[1] Note that the test of difference between means for related samples (called the test for difference between correlated means) is simply based on the rationale that if there is no difference between a group's scores on two measures then the average difference between the paired scores will be zero. See Hays (1963).

Statistical Inference

Calculating degrees of freedom

Table B has several rows of critical values. The row is chosen according to the size of contingency table. In the examples we have used we have always had two values on each axis of the contingency table (i.e. they have been 2 × 2 tables). But the χ^2 test can be used for larger tables[1] and the distribution of χ^2 is different for different sizes of contingency table. It is not the number of boxes that matters but the number of entries which are free to vary without affecting the row and column totals. Here is the contingency table discussed in chapter 5, with the expected values entered:

	Arts	Science	Totals
Travelled	17 (15)	28 (30)	45
Untravelled	3 (5)	12 (10)	15
Totals	20	40	60

Figure 9. *University students classified by faculty and travel experience, with expected values*

Expected values for this table are all predictable once the first value of 15 is established. Consider how many of the values are unpredictable, i.e. free to vary without affecting the totals, in tables of the following shapes:

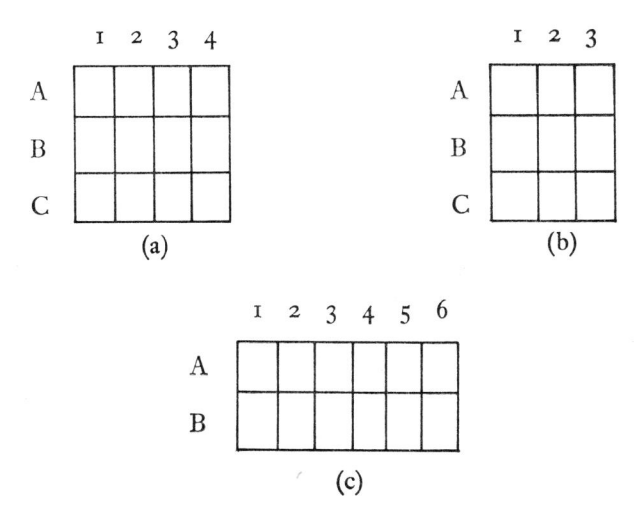

Figure 10. *Contingency tables of different shapes (totals columns are omitted)*

[1] Hence the median test applies to experiments with more than two groups. See Siegel (1956) for examples.

The answers can be arrived at either by chopping off the right-hand column and the bottom row and counting the remaining squares or by using a formula:

$$d.f. = (\text{number of columns} - 1)(\text{number of rows} - 1)$$

This quantity is called the degrees of freedom symbolized as d.f. or ν (the Greek letter *nu*). The d.f.'s for the above three tables are given on p. 221.

In Figure 9 we have a 2 × 2 table, hence one degree of freedom. We therefore look in the row marked 1 on the left-hand side. We had a one-tailed hypothesis, that arts students would go abroad more, so we look for the critical value at the 5 per cent level in the column headed 0·1. The critical value is 2·706 which is larger than 1·6 so we have to accept the null hypothesis that there is no difference between the students.

One-tailed and two-tailed hypotheses

Consider the following table of results. This study of student attitudes and enrolment status is part of the larger investigation of Spanish teaching from which we have already drawn the data on language laboratory experience and enrolment status which was discussed in chapter 4. There are

		Enthusiastic	Favourable	Open-minded	Somewhat negative	Apprehensive	Total
Still enrolled	Yes	19	14	12	4	0	49
	No	7	7	12	1	1	28

Figure 11. *Students on a language course classified by enrolment status and initial attitudes*

numerous ways in which we could rearrange the five columns and only two of the ways (the one presented and its mirror image) reflect the ordered relationship between the categories on a scale of increasing enthusiasm. Whichever order the columns were in the value of χ^2 would be the same. This illustrates the fact that the chi squared test is insensitive to any ordered relationship between categories and so is appropriate to nominal data only.

With contingency tables larger than 2 × 2 it becomes difficult to distinguish between different kinds of assymetry in the table, and therefore difficult to interpret a one-tailed hypothesis which would predict some consistent trend from category to category. For instance, in Figure 11 how would one decide whether the predominance of students still enrolled in the category 'somewhat negative' is sufficiently inconsistent with a hypothesis that enthusiasm is related to persistence on the course to counteract the figures in the first two columns which conform with expectation? It follows that one-tailed hypotheses are inapplicable with more than one degree of freedom. A two-tailed test is performed and the result has to be interpreted in terms of the boxes in the table which contribute most to the χ^2 value.

Correction for continuity in 2 × 2 tables

The following is a more convenient and more accurate formula for the 2 × 2 table incorporating a correction factor for continuity like the one mentioned in connection with the sign test on p. 174:

$$\chi^2 = \frac{n\left([AD-BC]-\frac{n}{2}\right)^2}{(A+B)(C+D)(A+C)(B+D)}$$

The following figure indicates what the letters A, B, C and D refer to; n is of course the size of the total sample:

A	B	A+B
C	D	C+D

A+C   B+D

Figure 12. *Contingency table labelled for use with formula incorporating correction factor*

Use of the chi squared test will not be meaningful if the total n is less than 20, if any expected frequency is smaller than 1 or if more than 20 per cent of expected frequencies are smaller than 5. Alternative tests exist for such cases (see Siegel 1956, pp. 46, 110, 178).

4.6 Summary

At this point it seems appropriate to repeat Figure 8 of chapter 4 classifying the tests of statistical inference introduced here in terms of type of sample and level of measurement. This time the names of the tests will be given as well as references to the studies which exemplify them in chapter 4.

5 Increasing the sensitivity of an experiment

Before passing on to the final section, in which some assumptions governing the use of these tests are reviewed, we will use the example of the difference between means test to re-emphasize a number of points which have already been made.

Type of experimental design

Level of measurement	Independent	Related	
	comparative	comparative	correlational
Nominal	chi squared *Spanish-teaching experiment*		
At least ordinal	median test Mann-Whitney U. *training in the use of pronouns*	sign test Wilcoxon matched pairs signed ranks *understanding of logical connectives*	(rank order correlation) *understanding of logical connectives*
Interval	difference between means (t test) *birth weight study*	(difference between correlated means)	

Figure 13. *Chart classifying tests introduced in chapters 4–6 (those merely mentioned rather than described are in brackets)*

5.1 Sample size
Here, once more, is the formula for the standard error of the difference:

$$\text{s.e. diff.} = \sqrt{\frac{s_1^2}{(n_1 - 1)} + \frac{s_2^2}{(n_2 - 1)}}$$

Remember that to find the z score we divide the difference between means by the standard error of the difference. Therefore the smaller the standard error of the difference the larger will the z score be for the same difference between means. One aim of experimental design, then, should be the reduction of the standard error of the difference. This will enable genuine effects which may be small to show up in the experiment. Since n_1 and n_2, the sample sizes, are in the denominators of the above equation it follows that increasing the sample size will increase the sensitivity of the experiment. Notice, however, that the standard error of the difference is related to the square root of the sample size so that to halve the standard error of the mean we would have to quadruple our sample size. It follows that increasing the sample size is not the most efficient way of controlling variability.

5.2 The control of variability
In section 5 of chapter 4 we pointed out that another way of increasing the sensitivity of an experiment is to reduce variability. This too is illustrated

in the above formula by the fact that the standard deviations of the samples, s_1 and s_2, are in the numerator and therefore the effect of a reduction in variability within the samples will be to reduce the standard error of the difference, which in turn will increase the z score for a given difference between means. This effect is represented in the following diagram:

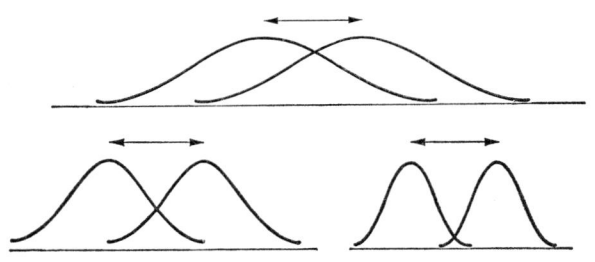

Figure 14. *Three identical differences between means of pairs of samples drawn from populations differing in variability*[1]

Another way of increasing sensitivity was to discount within-group variability altogether by using a matched or identical subject design and comparing paired scores between treatments without taking account of between-subject variability at all. (See sign test, p. 173 and footnote on difference between correlated means, p. 176.)

6 One-tailed and two-tailed hypotheses

A less extreme result will qualify as significant if we have adopted a one-tailed hypothesis than if we have adopted a two-tailed hypothesis, providing the result is in the predicted direction. This means that we may reject the null hypothesis under a one-tailed test on the basis of a smaller difference between groups than would be needed to reject it under a two-tailed hypothesis. It follows that we should have good reasons independent of the experiment in hand for adopting such a hypothesis, otherwise we run the risk of cheating by relaxing the stringency of our criteria unjustifiably. In particular, it is out of the question for a one-tailed hypothesis to be adopted after the experiment has been conducted, under the influence of the results. This may lead to results being classified as significant which would not have been had we held to our original hypothesis. We would be using information which we did not have at the outset of the experiment to support a one-tailed hypothesis which we were not prepared to commit ourselves to beforehand. We shall now explore the consequences of shifting hypotheses in quantitative terms.

[1] These diagrams are highly schematic. We would of course not get smooth curves by plotting results from samples.

The following diagrams show the one-tailed and two-tailed regions of rejection at the 5 per cent level on a diagram of the normal curve. This means that if a z score is large enough to fall within the shaded area the null hypothesis may be rejected. Consider what would happen if we had a one-tailed

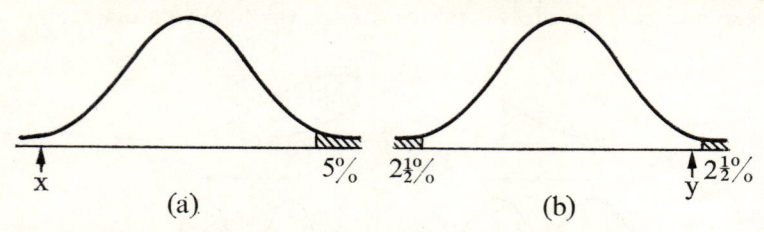

Figure 15. *One- and two-tailed regions of rejection and the effect of adopting a post-hoc hypothesis*

hypothesis that Group A would do better than Group B at a given task. We might find that in fact Group B do considerably better, so much so that if we had a two-tailed hypothesis the result would have been significant at the 5 per cent level (x in Figure 15a). Suppose we decide that we might as well have had a two-tailed hypothesis after all. If we do this we will really have been working with a $7\frac{1}{2}$ per cent significance level and not a 5 per cent level since any result falling within the top 5 per cent or the bottom $2\frac{1}{2}$ per cent will satisfy us. A similar argument applies to a finding under a two-tailed hypothesis which is not significant but which would have been significant if our hypothesis had been one-tailed (y in Figure 15b). The situation here is somewhat worse, since presumably a result in either the top or the bottom 5 per cent would satisfy us so we would in fact be working with a 10 per cent probability level.

7 Factors affecting the choice of tests

7.1 Level of measurement

We saw in the previous chapter that a nominal scale merely classifies cases into distinct categories, but for all its simplicity such a scale has certain formal requirements. The categories must be mutually exclusive, i.e. it must be impossible for a case to be entered in more than one category, and they must be exhaustive, i.e. it must be possible to place each case in a category. The only mathematical operation appropriate to nominal scales is counting frequencies. The chi squared test for independent samples is the only test we have considered for nominal data.

An ordinal scale specifies a relation of 'greater than' or 'less than' between the cases measured. The operation of ranking is admissible. An additional assumption made by some tests for ordinal data is that there is a continuous variable underlying the different scores, i.e. in principle we could measure any value on the variable, though in practice our method of measurement may restrict us to distinct values. We have met four tests applicable to ordinal scales which fulfil different purposes and make more or less use of the data. In fact the median test can be regarded as treating the data as if it were nominal. It is always permissible to treat data as if they were measured on a scale making fewer assumptions about the relationships between cases, but not the reverse. For instance, if we had information about the time taken by horses to complete a race we could make use of the times, which are on an interval scale, the positions the horses achieved, which are on an ordinal scale, or whether a horse achieved a position in the first three or not, which is a nominal scale.

An interval scale rests on measurements for which there is a common constant unit throughout. It is therefore permissible to perform the operations of addition, subtraction, multiplication and division on measurements which conform to an interval scale.

The status of test scores and other variables in psychological research with respect to these scales of measurement is controversial. For instance we cannot assume that the addition of one point to a person's score represents a constant increment of knowledge or capacity on the variable under investigation, however the extra point was attained, unless we are sure that the capacity to get item 20 right requires an equal amount of underlying skill as the capacity to get item 19 or any other item right. Test scores are nevertheless often treated as interval-based data.

Quite apart from the doubtful assumptions that test scores constitute interval scales, there is a case for saying that they do not always even constitute ordinal scales. One might argue that in cases where we do not fully understand the nature of the underlying capacity which governs the skill we are measuring we have no reason to suppose that it is a single capacity rather than a complex of separate capacities. However, adherence to such strict principles as these would be a serious handicap in the field of educational research. The fact that the test scores have produced for us a ranking of pupils gives us an order to work with and makes possible further investigation into the variables about which we need to know more.

One refinement of ordinal scales, to counter the argument that the items may not be contributing equally to the measurement of an underlying variable because they are not of equal difficulty, is to measure their difficulty level in terms of the number of testees who get them right, then use this measure as a basis for weighting the items. The scores can then be adjusted accordingly, but in cases where this has been done it has not usually resulted in any very radical difference in ranks.

7.2 Parametric tests

The assumptions about levels of measurement are not the only assumptions made by statistical tests. Many of the useful statistical techniques for interval data rest on further assumptions about the distribution of the variables in the populations from which the samples are drawn. The above discussion about the test for difference between means implied this. One assumption was that the variables were normally distributed in the populations. The two samples compared are also assumed to come from populations which have equal variances (see p. 195). Such tests are called parametric tests since they make assumptions about the values of various parameters, i.e. numerical characteristics of a distribution.

7.3 Power

The power of a test is its capacity to detect an experimental effect where one exists. We have seen in section 2 that this is related to the size of the sample, the type of hypothesis (whether one-tailed or two-tailed) and the significance level. It is also related to the level of measurement assumed by the test and how much use it therefore makes of the available data.

In general the more assumptions a test makes the more powerful it is. In cases where both parametric and non-parametric tests are applicable, parametric tests are more powerful than non-parametric tests (i.e. tests that do not depend on the normal distribution of the variable in the population and other such assumptions). However, non-parametric tests tend to require less computation and they can often deal with quantities of data which are too restricted for the use of parametric tests.

7.4 Normalization of scales

Sometimes tests of psychological characteristics are modified until they produce distributions which conform to the normal curve. Parametric statistics can then be used on the assumption that the normalization of the scores has produced equal interval scales. In other cases some conversion such as taking the log of a score is applied to the observations to render them normal. This procedure can be very convenient not only because it permits the use of parametric statistics but also because scores can then be expressed as z values and positions of people on different tests can be compared in terms of how many standard deviations they are away from the mean, without the difference in dispersion of scores complicating the comparison.

Sometimes the application of a procedure of adjusting tests until they produce scores which are normally distributed carries with it the implication that the trait or capacity under investigation is normally distributed in the population so that if a test can be produced which reflects this it will really be measuring the trait. Intelligence testing is sometimes looked at in this light. The statement that intelligence is normally distributed must be interpreted to mean that intelligence test scores are normally distributed. We do not really know a great deal about the distribution of intelligence as such.

If use is made of parametric tests in cases where the assumptions do not hold, mistaken inferences about significance do not necessarily result. Lack of equality of variability between the populations has more of a distorting effect than departure from normality. Results are most misleading where distributions are markedly skewed and where samples are small.

8 Conclusion

We saw clearly in our discussion of the binomial test that the use of a statistical test involves the adoption of a mathematical model. Where the relevant characteristics of the observational data match the mathematical model the model can be used to draw valid inferences about the observations. However, if the model is misapplied the results may be seriously misleading. For example:

If 1 herd eats 1 ton of oats in 1 week,
then 2 herds eat 2 tons of oats in 1 week,
and $\frac{1}{2}$ herd eats $\frac{1}{2}$ ton of oats in 1 week and $\frac{1}{4}$ ton in $\frac{1}{2}$ week.

It follows that:

If 1 man takes 1 day to dig 1 hole,
then 2 men take 2 days to dig 1 hole,
and $\frac{1}{2}$ man takes $\frac{1}{2}$ day to dig 1 hole and $\frac{1}{4}$ day to dig $\frac{1}{2}$ hole.

Very often a certain type of statistical manual which describes statistical procedures without making clear their rationale and function, rather like a bad foreign language phrase book, is referred to as a cook book. The metaphor is appropriate in so far as following the procedure laid down in a recipe will not produce edible results unless you have the right ingredients.

9 Practical work

1 We found that for 2 tosses of a coin there were 4 different possible permutations of heads and tails, for 3 tosses there were 8, for 4 tosses 16 and for 5 tosses 32. Can you construct a formula from which the number of permutations for a given number of tosses could be calculated?
2 Can you construct formulae which state the probabilities of getting (a) n heads in n tosses of a coin, (b) 1 head in n tosses of a coin, (c) 1 or 0 heads in n tosses of a coin?
3 What is the probability of cutting 7 hearts in a row from a pack of cards, if all the cards are replaced and the pack is shuffled between each cut?
4 In section 2 it was stated that 'adopting a 5 per cent probability level is equivalent to accepting the possibility of making a wrong inference in

5 per cent of instances'. Does this in fact mean that we will be mistaken in 5 per cent of instances?
5 Would the experiment with matched pigs whose results are depicted in Figure 11, p. 135, be significant at the 5 per cent level with a two-tailed hypothesis using the sign test? What would be a more appropriate test to use?
6 Calculate the expected frequencies for the results given in Figure 11 (p. 178) of this chapter. Can the χ^2 test be used? Calculate χ^2 for Figure 9 (p. 177) using the formula incorporating a correction factor.
7 In the section on the controlled experiment discussed in chapter 4 we outlined a study which compared the improvement of three groups of children over the course of a year, a group with retrained teachers, a group with improved materials, and a group with increased motivation (p. 114). In this chapter we have discussed one statistical test which could evaluate the results of this experiment. Which one is it?

10 Further reading (Chapters 4–6)

Amos, J. R., Brown, F. L. and Mink, O. G. 1965. *Statistical Concepts*. New York: Harper & Row. Very good programmed text presupposing no prior knowledge.

Anderson, B. 1966. *The Psychology Experiment*. Belmont: Wadsworth. Lively introduction to experimental design. Misleading on matching. Excellent section on how to write a research paper.

Blalock, H. M. 1960. *Social Statistics*. New York: McGraw-Hill. Thorough and sophisticated manual on statistics for the social sciences.

Cox, D. R. 1958. *Planning of Experiments*. New York: Wiley. Discussion of the principles of experimental design at an advanced level.

Hays, W. L. 1963. *Statistics for Psychologists*. New York: Holt, Rinehart and Winston. A demanding book. It is concerned with the mathematical theory underlying inferential methods and aims to give the reader a thorough understanding of the function of the basic statistical tests useful to psychologists.

Huff, D. 1954. *How to Lie with Statistics*. London: Victor Gollancz. An excellent and entertaining account of how statistics is commonly misused in popular writing.

Maxwell, A. E. 1970. *Basic Statistics in Behavioural Research*. Harmondsworth: Penguin. Useful short introduction.

Reichmann, W. J. 1964. *Use and Abuse of Statistics*. Harmondsworth: Penguin. Good readable introductory text, much wider in scope than Maxwell.

Siegel, S. 1956. *Nonparametric Statistics for the Behavioral Sciences*. New York: McGraw Hill. Readable source book for non-parametric tests.

Appendix I: Some Statistics used in Language Tests

1 Method for working item analysis E_{1-3}

Suppose we had a test of twenty items and gave it to 36 students, with the following results:

Script	Score	Script	Score	Script	Score
A	19	M	11	Y	14
B	16	N	10	Z	14
C	12	O	16	AA	13
D	5	P	3	BB	9
E	8	Q	15	CC	12
F	11	R	14	DD	12
G	13	S	10	EE	9
H	11	T	9	FF	8
I	10	U	17	GG	15
J	15	V	17	HH	7
K	18	W	15	II	10
L	12	X	10	JJ	12

First arrange all the scripts in order of merit. This is the equivalent of a frequency distribution.

The frequency distribution of these 36 scripts is:

Score	Frequency	Cumulative frequency
19	1	1
18	1	2
17	2	4
16	2	6
15	4	10
14	3	13
13	2	15
12	5	20
11	3	23
10	5	28

Score	Frequency	Cumulative frequency
9	3	31
8	2	33
7	1	34
6	–	
5	1	35
4	–	
3	1	36

Next, divide the scripts into three subgroups. When the number of scripts is exactly divisible by 3, the number in each subgroup is the same, here 12. If the total is not exactly divisible by 3, make sure that the upper and lower sub-groups are equal.

The cumulative frequency column shows that counting 12 down from the top includes two of the three scripts with a score of 14. So two scripts with a score of 14 go into the upper group, and one goes into the middle group. This is necessary and legitimate, provided the choice of scripts is random.

Usually one takes the first scripts one finds, for example scripts R and Y go into the top group, script Z into the middle group. Counting down further, we find that one of the scripts with a score of 10 goes into the middle group, and four go into the lower group.

The next step is to look at the pass/fail pattern for each item for each subgroup. If item 1 was answered correctly in all scripts of the upper group except J, the sum of correct answers for this item in the upper group would be 11. The sum of correct answers is established in this way for each item for each subgroup.

Add the subgroup sums to find the total of correct answers for the whole group. This is expressed as a percentage of the maximum possible number, which equals the number of scripts.

Item	Thirds			Total no. correct answers	% correct answers	= Facility value
	Upper group	Middle group	Lower group			
1	11	8	5	24	$\frac{24}{36} \times 100$	= 67
2	6	6	6	18	$\frac{18}{36} \times 100$	= 50
3	3	4	5	12	$\frac{12}{36} \times 100$	= 33

Facility values are presented as whole numbers, the first decimal is calculated only for deciding whether to round up. The observations are coarse; it would be spurious to try to lend them precision by including decimal places.

Only the upper and the lower subtotals are used to calculate E_{1-3}. For each item, subtract the number of passes in the lower group from the number of passes in the upper group. Then divide the actual difference by the maximum possible difference, which is the number of scripts in the subgroup, here 12:

Item	Upper subtotal		Lower subtotal		Difference	E_{1-3}
1	11	—	5	=	6	$\frac{6}{12} = 0 \cdot 50$
2	6	—	6	=	0	$\frac{0}{12} = 0$
3	3	—	5	=	−2	$\frac{-2}{12} = -0 \cdot 17$

The discrimination index is expressed to two decimal places, working the third to decide about rounding.

The method can be expressed as a formula:

$$\frac{u - l}{N}$$

where u = number of passes in upper group
l = number of passes in lower group
and N = number of scripts in the upper group (or lower group, which is the same)

For a more detailed description see Ingram, 1968.

2 Method for working rank order (Spearman) correlations

The rank order formula is:

$$\text{rho} = 1 - \frac{6 \Sigma d^2}{N(N^2 - 1)}$$

where d = the difference between the ranks given to each individual
d^2 = the square of this difference
Σ = the sum of
N = the number of people concerned.

Suppose 5 boys took a test of French consisting of 100 items and were ranked by their teacher for her estimate of their degree of command of French.

190   Testing and Experimental Methods

	Test score	Test rank	Teacher's ranking
Johnny	76	1	1
Bill	63	2	4
Sam	62	3	3
David	59	4	2
Jack	38	5	5

Note that ranking takes no account of the amount of difference there might be between people, only that differences in a given direction exist.

First, find the difference for the ranks given to each boy and then square the differences and sum.

	Test rank	Teacher's ranking	Difference d	d^2
Johnny	1	1	0	0
Bill	2	4	2	4
Sam	3	3	0	0
David	4	2	2	4
Jack	5	5	0	0
				$\Sigma d^2 = 8$

Now we have values that we can put into the formula.

$N = 5$; there are five boys involved
$\Sigma d^2 = 8$; which we have just worked out

So we get:

$$\text{rho} = 1 - \frac{6 \times 8}{5(25 - 1)} = 1 - \frac{48}{120} = 1 - 0.40 = 0.60$$

3 Formula and method for working product moment correlations

The formula for the product moment correlation can be written in a number of different, but equivalent ways. One of the most common is:

(1) $$r = \frac{\Sigma dxdy}{N \sigma_x \sigma_y}$$

where r = the product moment correlation coefficient
  dx = the deviation of a score in Test x from the mean
  dy = the deviation of a score in Test y from the mean
  $\Sigma dxdy$ = the sum of the products of the x and y deviations
  N = the number of people involved
  σ_x = the standard deviation for the x set of scores
  σ_y = the standard deviation for the y set of scores

Another way of writing the formula is:

Appendix I 191

(2) $$r = \frac{\Sigma dxdy}{N\sqrt{\frac{\Sigma dx^2}{N}}\sqrt{\frac{\Sigma dy^2}{N}}}$$

since $$\sigma = \sqrt{\frac{\Sigma dx^2}{N}}$$

Imagine that six people take two tests with the following results:

Person	TestX	Test Y
A	7	8
B	6	7
C	6	5
D	5	6
E	3	6
F	3	4
	Σ x 30	Σ y 36

We want to know the degree to which the two sets of scores correspond, i.e. the correlation. In order to be able to substitute values in the formula we need to know:
(i) the number of people involved: N
(ii) the sum of deviations squared for x: Σdx^2
and the sum of deviations squared for y: Σdy^2
(iii) the sum of the products of deviations for x and y: $\Sigma dxdy$

Here the means are:

$$\bar{x} = \frac{30}{6} = 5, \text{ and } \bar{y} = \frac{36}{6} = 6$$

So the deviations are as follows:

x	y	dx	dy
7	8	+2	+2
6	7	+1	+1
6	5	+1	−1
5	6	0	0
3	6	−2	0
3	4	−2	−2
		0	0

We do not need to know the sum of the deviations for the formula, but it is useful to have them as a check, because if the working has been correct, the deviations should add up to zero.

From the deviations we get:

(a) the sum of deviations squared

(b) the sum of the product of deviations

dx	dy	dx²	dy²
+2	+2	4	4
+1	+1	1	1
+1	−1	1	1
0	0	0	0
−2	0	4	0
−2	−2	4	4
		Σdx² 14	Σdy² 10

dx	dy	dxdy
+2	+2	+4
+1	+1	+1
+1	−1	−1
0	0	0
−2	0	0
−2	−2	+4
		Σdxdy 8

Before substituting these values in the formula, consider what would happen if the mean was not a whole number. The deviations would all have decimals, and the squaring of numbers with decimal places is laborious and likely to produce mistakes, particularly when there are large numbers of people involved. To make the computation easier in such cases, one adopts the fiction that the mean is zero, and works with the scores as they stand:

x	y	x²	y²	xy
7	8	49	64	56
6	7	36	49	42
6	5	36	25	30
5	6	25	36	30
3	6	9	36	18
3	4	9	16	12
		Σx² 164	Σy² 226	Σxy 188

This gives us the sums of squares and sum of products of the raw scores. To get values expressing deviations, we have to introduce a correction term, which brings in the mean in a single operation for each sum.

To get the corrected sum of squares: $\Sigma' x^2$ (sigma dash x squared) we subtract the sum of observations squared over the number of people from the sum of squares:

$$\Sigma' x^2 = \Sigma x^2 - \frac{(\Sigma x)^2}{N}$$

For the x scores we get the square of the sum of scores = 900:

$$(\Sigma x)^2 = 30^2 = 900$$

That over the number of people = 150:

$$\frac{(\Sigma x)^2}{N} = \frac{900}{6} = 150$$

So,
$$\Sigma'x^2 = \Sigma x^2 - \frac{(\Sigma x)^2}{N}$$
$$= 164 - 150$$
$$= 14$$

For the y scores we get the square of the sum of scores = 1296:
$$(\Sigma y)^2 = 36^2 = 1296$$

That over the number of people = 216:
$$\frac{(\Sigma y)^2}{N} = \frac{1296}{6} = 216$$

So,
$$\Sigma'y^2 = \Sigma y^2 - \frac{(\Sigma y)^2}{N}$$
$$= 226 - 216$$
$$= 10$$

The correction term for the sum of products is the product of the sum of x times the sum of y, over the number of people:
$$\frac{\Sigma x \, \Sigma y}{N}$$

Here $\frac{\Sigma x \Sigma y}{N} = \frac{30 \times 36}{6} = \frac{1080}{6} = 180$

So the corrected sum of products is:
$$\Sigma'xy = \Sigma xy - \frac{\Sigma x \Sigma y}{N} = 188 - 180 = 8$$

In the example $\Sigma'x^2 = \Sigma dx^2 = 14$
$\Sigma'y^2 = \Sigma dy^2 = 10$
$\Sigma'xy = \Sigma dxdy = 8$

In fact, the expressions are algebraically equivalent:
$$\Sigma'x^2 \approx \Sigma dx^2 \text{ and } \Sigma'xy \approx \Sigma dxdy$$

We can now rewrite the product moment formula further:

(2) $$r = \frac{\Sigma dxdy}{N\sqrt{\frac{\Sigma dx^2}{N}}\sqrt{\frac{\Sigma dy^2}{N}}}$$

(3) $$r = \frac{\Sigma'xy}{N\sqrt{\frac{\Sigma'x^2}{N} \frac{\Sigma'y^2}{N}}}$$

The N's cancel each other out and we are left with the final formula:

(4) $$r = \frac{\Sigma'xy}{\sqrt{\Sigma'x^2 \, \Sigma'y^2}}$$

Substituting the values in the example we get:

$$r = \frac{8}{\sqrt{14 \times 10}} = \frac{8}{\sqrt{140}} = \frac{8}{11 \cdot 832} = 0 \cdot 676$$

Extracting the square root can be done by the aid of log tables or by long hand, by the method of repeated approximations.

4 Formula and method for estimating equivalence reliability Kuder-Richardson (21)

Kuder-Richardson (21):

$$r = \frac{m}{m-1} \times \frac{s^2_t - (\Sigma p - \Sigma p^2)}{s^2_t}$$

Let us first re-label the terms in this equation:

$$r = (a) \times \frac{(b) - (c)}{(b)}$$

Then let us take an example to show what the symbols stand for. Imagine that 10 people take a test consisting of 6 items. The first term in the formula is (a):

$$(a) \; \frac{m}{m-1}$$

where m = the number of items. The number usually refers to the people involved. Here we are dealing with the number of items. To avoid confusion, the symbol m has been adopted.

Given the example, we can substitute values in the formula:

$$(a) \; \frac{m}{m-1} = \frac{6}{5}$$

The second term of the formula is (b):

(b) s^2_t = the variance of the test. (The subscript $_t$ means 'of this test')

The variance equals the standard deviation squared. The symbol for standard deviation is σ. But statisticians often use ordinary s, instead of Greek σ (sigma) when they are dealing with the standard deviation of a sample, rather than with the 'true' standard deviation of the population as a whole. So:

$$V = s^2$$

The formula for the standard deviation is:

$$s = \sqrt{\frac{\Sigma' x^2}{N-1}}$$

where $\sqrt{}$ = square root of
$\Sigma' x^2$ = corrected sum of squares
N = number of people involved.

Therefore the variance, or s^2, is obtained by the formula for the standard deviation, before the square root has been extracted:

$$s^2 = \frac{\Sigma' x^2}{N-1}$$

In other words, the variance is found by dividing the corrected sum of squares ($\Sigma' x^2$) by the number of observations minus 1 ($N - 1$). Imagine further that the scores of the 10 people on the 6 items are as follows:

Person	Score x	x^2
A	5	25
B	5	25
C	4	16
D	4	16
E	3	9
F	3	9
G	2	4
H	2	4
I	1	1
J	1	1
	Σ x 30	Σ x^2 110

The obvious way to get deviations squared is to subtract each score from the mean, and then square the deviations. But if the mean is not a whole number, each deviation will involve decimals, and such figures are laborious to square. The corrected sum of squares is a computational device which avoids this awkwardness. The scores themselves are squared, and then a correction formula is applied, which brings in the mean value in one single operation at the end. The corrected sum of squares is algebraically equivalent to the sum of deviations squared:

$$\Sigma' x^2 \approx \Sigma d^2$$

The corrected sum of squares consist of the sum of squares, minus the correction term. The correction term is the sum of observations squared, divided by the number of people:

$$\Sigma' x^2 = \Sigma x^2 - \frac{(\Sigma x)^2}{N}$$

Here, the square of the sum of observations = 900:

$$(\Sigma x)^2 = 30^2 = 900$$

and that divided by the number of people = 90:

$$\frac{(\Sigma x)^2}{N} = \frac{900}{10} = 90$$

So,

$$\Sigma' x^2 = \Sigma x^2 - \frac{(\Sigma x)^2}{N} = 110 - 90 = 20$$

Now we can calculate term (b):

$$\text{(b)} \quad s^2_t = \frac{\Sigma' x^2}{N-1} = \frac{20}{10-1} = \frac{20}{9} = 2.22$$

As a result, we have values for two of the terms in the formula:

$$r = \frac{6}{5} \times \frac{2.22 - (c)}{2.22}$$

The remaining term in the equation is (c):

$$\text{(c)} \quad \Sigma p - \Sigma p^2$$

where p = the proportion of passes for each item. A correct answer to an item is a pass, a wrong answer is a fail. If we say pass = 1, fail = 0, we can tabulate the passes and fails for each person for each item as shown opposite. Adding horizontally in the table we get the score for each person. Adding vertically we get the number of passes for each item. If the tabulation and adding has been correct, the sum of scores is the same as the sum of passes, here 30.

The tabulation gives us the number of passes, but we want the sum of the proportion of passes.

Person	Item	Score
	1 2 3 4 5 6	x
A	1 1 1 1 1 0	5
B	1 1 1 1 1 0	5
C	1 1 1 1 0 0	4
D	1 1 1 1 0 0	4
E	1 1 1 0 0 0	3
F	1 1 1 0 0 0	3
G	1 1 0 0 0 0	2
H	1 1 0 0 0 0	2
I	1 0 0 0 0 0	1
J	1 0 0 0 0 0	1
Passes	10 8 6 4 2 0	30

$$p = \frac{\text{number of passes}}{\text{number of people}}$$

So,

$$\Sigma p = \frac{10}{10} + \frac{8}{10} + \frac{6}{10} + \frac{4}{10} + \frac{2}{10} + \frac{0}{10} = \frac{30}{10} = 3$$

To get Σp^2, square these fractions and sum:

$$\left(\frac{10}{10}\right)^2 + \left(\frac{8}{10}\right)^2 + \left(\frac{6}{10}\right)^2 + \left(\frac{4}{10}\right)^2 + \left(\frac{2}{10}\right)^2 + \left(\frac{0}{10}\right)^2 =$$

$$\frac{100}{100} + \frac{64}{100} + \frac{36}{100} + \frac{16}{100} + \frac{4}{100} + \frac{0}{100} = \frac{220}{100} = 2 \cdot 20$$

Now we have values we can substitute in (c):

$$\text{(c) } \Sigma p - \Sigma p^2 = 3 - 2 \cdot 20 = 0 \cdot 8$$

And now we have values for all the terms in the equivalence formula:

$$r = \text{(a)} \times \frac{\text{(b)} - \text{(c)}}{\text{(b)}}$$

$$= \frac{6}{5} \times \frac{2 \cdot 22 - 0 \cdot 8}{2 \cdot 22} = \frac{6}{5} \times \frac{1 \cdot 42}{2 \cdot 22} = 0 \cdot 7676$$

With any realistic number of items and people this tabulation gets very laborious and consequently it is likely to yield mistakes. But one can get

198 Testing and Experimental Methods

term (c) from the facility values already obtained in the item analysis which has to be carried out anyway.

The item analysis of the example given would look like this:

Item	Thirds							Total	Facility value %
	Upper		Middle		Lower				
1	///	3	////	4	///	3		10	100
2	///	3	////	4	/	1		8	80
3	///	3	///	3		0		6	60
4	///	3	/	1		0		4	40
5	//	2		0		0		2	20
6		0		0		0		0	0

Since proportions are the same as percentages before one multiplies by 100, the facility values are readily converted into proportions by shifting the decimal point two places. Then the proportions are squared, and the sum of proportions and the sum of proportions squared is calculated:

Facility value %	Proportion p	Proportions squared p^2
100	1·00	1·00
80	0·80	0·64
60	0·60	0·36
40	0·40	0·16
20	0·20	0·04
0	0	0
	Σp 3·00	Σp^2 2·20

Thus, $\Sigma p - \Sigma p^2 = 3\cdot 00 - 2\cdot 20 = 0\cdot 80$, as before.

In practice the Kuder-Richardson (21) equivalence correlation formula is computed for terms (a) and (b) as shown, and term (c) is computed on the basis of the facility values obtained for each item in the item analysis, as shown in the last example.

5 Method for finding square roots by using logarithms

The square root of numbers can be found by converting them to logarithms, doing the operation on the logarithm and then converting back. It is necessary to have at least a four-figure log and antilog table. Logarithms are constructed in two parts, which are separated by a point.

To find the values of the part in front of the point, look at how many whole places the number has.

> If it has 3 whole places (e.g. 356 or 209·52 etc.) write 2.
> If it has 2 whole places (e.g. 48 or 65·9, etc.) write 1.
> If it has 1 whole place (e.g. 9 or 5·726, etc.) write 0.

If the number is larger than to 3 whole places, continue the series upwards. If the number is less than 1, difficulties set in. But in testing it is extremely rare to have to extract square roots of numbers less than 1. If this should happen, consult a school textbook or the nearest mathematician.

If we want to find the log of 356·8, the first part of it is 2. To find the value after the point, locate in the log table the row that corresponds to the first two digits of the number. So, for 356·8 find the 35th row. Then find the column that corresponds to the next digit, here the 6th. Follow that down to the 35th row, which gives the value 0·5514. Next, find the column on the extreme right side of the table which corresponds to the fourth digit, here the 8th, and follow that down to the 35th row. The corresponding value is added to the larger number: 0·5514 + 10 = 0·5524. Then join the two parts. The log of 356·8 = 2·5524.

The operation on logarithms which corresponds to extracting square roots is simply that of dividing by 2:

$$2·5524 \div 2 = 1·2762$$

Now we have to convert this back to ordinary numbers by the aid of the antilog table. We work with the part after the point. Find the row corresponding to the two first digits, here the 27th. Then locate the column corresponding to the next digit, here the 6th, and follow down to the 27th row; that gives 1888. Find the column on the extreme right-hand side of the table corresponding to the fourth digit, here the 2nd, and follow it down to the 27th row. The corresponding value is added to the larger number:

$$1888 + 1 = 1889.$$

The number in front of the point determines where to place the decimal.

> If the number is 2, place the decimal point after the third digit.
> If the number is 1, place the decimal point after the second digit.
> If the number is 0, place the decimal point after the first digit.

In our example we have 1 before the point. So the number corresponding to log 1·2762 is 18·89. The square root of 356·8 = 18·89. To make sure that nothing has gone wrong, check by squaring 18·89. Answer: 356·8321.

This is good enough for most testing purposes. For a more accurate answer, log tables to five, six or more figures would be needed. Alternatively, the answer could be worked by the method of successive approximations, to whatever degree of accuracy is required.

Appendix II: Statistical Tables

Table A. Table of probabilities associated with values as extreme as observed values of z in the normal distribution

The body of the table gives one-tailed probabilities under H_0 of z. The left-hand marginal column gives various values of z to one decimal place. The top row gives various values to the second decimal place. Thus, for example, the one-tailed p of $z \geq 0.11$ or $z \leq -0.11$ is $p = 0.4562$.

z	0.00	0.01	0.02	0.03	0.04	0.05	0.06	0.07	0.08	0.09
0.0	.5000	.4960	.4920	.4880	.4840	.4801	.4761	.4721	.4681	.4641
0.1	.4602	.4562	.4522	.4483	.4443	.4404	.4364	.4325	.4286	.4247
0.2	.4207	.4168	.4129	.4090	.4052	.4013	.3974	.3936	.3897	.3859
0.3	.3821	.3783	.3745	.3707	.3669	.3632	.3594	.3557	.3520	.3488
0.4	.3446	.3409	.3372	.3336	.3300	.3264	.3228	.3192	.3156	.3121
0.5	.3085	.3050	.3015	.2981	.2946	.2912	.2877	.2843	.2810	.2776
0.6	.2743	.2709	.2676	.2643	.2611	.2578	.2546	.2514	.2483	.2451
0.7	.2420	.2389	.2358	.2327	.2296	.2266	.2236	.2206	.2177	.2148
0.8	.2119	.2090	.2061	.2033	.2005	.1977	.1949	.1922	.1894	.1867
0.9	.1841	.1814	.1788	.1762	.1736	.1711	.1685	.1660	.1635	.1611
1.0	.1587	.1562	.1539	.1515	.1492	.1469	.1446	.1423	.1401	.1379
1.1	.1357	.1335	.1314	.1292	.1271	.1251	.1230	.1210	.1190	.1170
1.2	.1151	.1131	.1112	.1093	.1075	.1056	.1038	.1020	.1003	.0985
1.3	.0968	.0951	.0934	.0918	.0901	.0885	.0869	.0853	.0838	.0823
1.4	.0808	.0793	.0778	.0764	.0749	.0735	.0721	.0708	.0694	.0681
1.5	.0668	.0655	.0643	.0630	.0618	.0606	.0594	.0582	.0571	.0559
1.6	.0458	.0537	.0526	.0516	.0505	.0495	.0485	.0475	.0465	.0455
1.7	.0446	.0436	.0427	.0418	.0409	.0401	.0392	.0384	.0375	.0367
1.8	.0359	.0351	.0344	.0336	.0329	.0322	.0314	.0307	.0301	.0294
1.9	.0287	.0281	.0274	.0268	.0262	.0256	.0250	.0244	.0239	.0233
2.0	.0228	.2222	.0217	.0212	.0207	.0202	.0197	.0192	.0188	.0183
2.1	.0179	.0174	.0170	.0166	.0162	.0158	.0154	.0150	.0146	.0143
2.2	.0139	.0136	.0132	.0129	.0125	.0122	.0119	.0116	.0113	.0110
2.3	.0107	.0104	.0102	.0099	.0096	.0094	.0091	.0089	.0087	.0084
2.4	.0082	.0080	.0078	.0075	.0073	.0071	.0069	.0068	.0066	.0064

z	0.00	0.01	0.02	0.03	0.04	0.05	0.06	0.07	0.08	0.09
2.5	.0062	.0060	.0059	.0057	.0055	.0054	.0052	.0051	.0049	.0048
2.6	.0047	.0045	.0044	.0043	.0041	.0040	.0039	.0038	.0037	.0036
2.7	.0035	.0034	.0033	.0032	.0031	.0030	.0029	.0028	.0027	.0026
2.8	.0026	.0025	.0024	.0023	.0023	.0022	.0021	.0021	.0020	.0019
2.9	.0019	.0018	.0018	.0017	.0016	.0016	.0015	.0015	.0014	.0014
3.0	.0013	.0013	.0013	.0012	.0012	.0011	.0011	.0011	.0010	.0010
3.1	.0010	.0009	.0009	.0009	.0008	.0008	.0008	.0008	.0007	.0007
3.2	.0007									
3.3	.0005									
3.4	.0003									
3.5	.00023									
3.6	.00016									
3.7	.00011									
3.8	.00007									
3.9	.00005									
4.0	.00003									

Table A is reprinted from S. Siegel, *Nonparametric Statistics for the Behavioural Sciences* (1956), published by McGraw-Hill, New York, by permission of the authors and publishers.

Table B. Table of critical values of chi square

df	Two-tailed Probability under H_0 that $\chi^2 \geq$ chi square													
	.99	.98	.95	.90	.80	.70	.50	.30	.20	.10	.05	.02	.01	.001
1	0.00016	0.00063	0.0039	0.016	0.064	0.15	0.46	1.07	1.64	2.71	3.84	5.41	6.64	10.83
2	0.02	0.04	0.10	0.21	0.45	0.71	1.39	2.41	3.22	4.60	5.99	7.82	9.21	13.82
3	0.12	0.18	0.35	0.58	1.00	1.42	2.37	3.66	4.64	6.25	7.82	9.84	11.34	16.27
4	0.30	0.43	0.71	1.06	1.65	2.20	3.36	4.88	5.99	7.78	9.49	11.67	13.28	18.46
5	0.55	0.75	1.14	1.61	2.34	3.00	4.35	6.06	7.29	9.24	11.07	13.39	15.09	20.52
6	0.87	1.13	1.64	2.20	3.07	3.83	5.35	7.23	8.56	10.64	12.59	15.03	16.81	22.46
7	1.24	1.56	2.17	2.83	3.82	4.67	6.35	8.38	9.80	12.02	14.07	16.62	18.48	24.32
8	1.65	2.03	2.73	3.49	4.59	5.53	7.34	9.52	11.03	13.36	15.51	18.17	20.09	26.12
9	2.09	2.53	3.32	4.17	5.38	6.39	8.34	10.66	12.24	14.68	16.92	19.68	21.67	27.88
10	2.56	3.06	3.94	4.86	6.18	7.27	9.34	11.78	13.44	15.99	18.31	21.16	23.21	29.59
11	3.05	3.61	4.58	5.58	6.99	8.15	10.34	12.90	14.63	17.28	19.68	22.62	24.72	31.26
12	3.57	4.18	5.23	6.30	7.81	9.03	11.34	14.01	15.81	18.55	21.03	24.05	26.22	32.91
13	4.11	4.76	5.89	7.04	8.63	9.93	12.34	15.12	16.98	19.81	22.36	25.47	27.69	34.53
14	4.66	5.37	6.57	7.79	9.47	10.82	13.34	16.22	18.15	21.06	23.68	26.87	29.14	36.12
15	5.23	5.98	7.26	8.55	10.31	11.72	14.34	17.32	19.31	22.31	25.00	28.26	30.58	37.70
16	5.81	6.61	7.96	9.31	11.15	12.62	15.34	18.42	20.46	23.54	26.30	29.63	32.00	39.29
17	6.41	7.26	8.67	10.08	12.00	13.53	16.34	19.51	21.62	24.77	27.59	31.00	33.41	40.75
18	7.02	7.91	9.39	10.86	12.86	14.44	17.34	20.60	22.76	25.99	28.87	32.35	34.80	42.31
19	7.63	8.57	10.12	11.65	13.72	15.35	18.34	21.69	23.90	27.20	30.14	33.69	36.19	43.82
20	8.26	9.24	10.85	12.44	14.58	16.27	19.34	22.78	25.04	28.41	31.41	35.02	37.57	45.32
21	8.90	9.92	11.59	13.24	15.44	17.18	20.34	23.86	26.17	29.62	32.67	36.34	38.93	46.80
22	9.54	10.60	12.34	14.04	16.31	18.10	21.24	24.94	27.30	30.81	33.92	37.66	40.29	48.27
23	10.20	11.29	13.09	14.85	17.19	19.02	22.34	26.02	28.43	32.01	35.17	38.97	41.64	49.73
24	10.86	11.99	13.85	15.66	18.06	19.94	23.34	27.10	29.55	33.20	36.42	40.27	42.98	51.18
25	11.52	12.70	14.61	16.47	18.94	20.87	24.34	28.17	30.68	34.38	37.65	41.57	44.31	52.62
26	12.20	13.41	15.38	17.29	19.82	21.79	25.34	29.25	31.80	35.56	38.88	42.86	45.64	54.05
27	12.88	14.12	16.15	18.11	20.70	22.72	26.34	30.32	32.91	36.74	40.11	44.14	46.96	55.48
28	13.56	14.85	16.93	18.94	21.59	23.65	27.34	31.39	34.03	37.92	41.34	45.42	48.28	56.89
29	14.26	15.57	17.71	19.77	22.48	24.58	28.34	32.46	35.14	39.09	42.56	46.69	49.59	58.30
30	14.95	16.31	18.49	20.60	23.36	25.51	29.34	33.53	36.25	40.26	43.77	47.96	50.89	59.70

Table B is reprinted from Table IV of R. A. Fisher and F. Yates, *Statistical Tables for Biological, Agricultural and Medical Research* (1948 ed.), published by Oliver and Boyd Ltd, Edinburgh and London, by permission of the authors and publishers.

Appendix II

Table C. Table of probabilities associated with values as small as observed values of x in the binomial test

Given in the body of this table are one-tailed probabilities under H_0 for the binomial test when $P = Q = \frac{1}{2}$. To save space, decimal points are omitted in the p's.

N	0	1	2	3	4	5	6	7	8	9	10	11	12	13	14	15
5	031	188	500	812	969	†										
6	016	109	344	656	891	984	†									
7	008	062	227	500	773	938	992	†								
8	004	035	145	363	637	855	965	996	†							
9	002	020	090	254	500	746	910	980	998	†						
10	001	011	055	172	377	623	828	945	989	999	†					
11		006	033	110	274	500	726	887	967	994	†	†				
12		003	019	073	194	387	613	806	927	981	997	†	†			
13		002	011	046	133	291	500	709	867	954	989	998	†	†		
14		001	006	029	090	212	395	605	788	910	971	994	999	†	†	
15			004	018	059	151	304	500	696	849	941	982	996	†	†	†
16			002	011	038	105	227	402	598	773	895	962	989	998	†	†
17			001	006	025	072	166	315	500	685	834	928	975	994	999	†
18			001	004	015	048	119	240	407	593	760	881	952	985	996	999
19				002	010	032	084	180	324	500	676	820	916	968	990	994
20				001	006	021	058	132	252	412	588	748	868	942	979	998
21				001	004	013	039	095	192	332	500	668	808	905	961	987
22					002	008	026	067	143	262	416	584	738	857	933	974
23					001	005	017	047	105	202	339	500	661	798	895	953
24					001	003	011	032	076	154	271	419	581	792	846	924
25						002	007	022	054	115	212	345	500	655	788	885

Table C is reprinted from S. Siegel, *Nonparametric Statistics for Behavioural Sciences* (1956), published by McGraw-Hill, New York, by permission of the authors and publishers.

Answers to practical work

Chapter 2

1. Yes, since any attempt to improve examination methods is ultimately aimed at improving validity. But the arguments for introducing written examinations tend to stress their accountability; there is a permanent record of the student's performance, which allows the judgement of the examiner to be verified.
2. Yes. Many traditional testing methods have the advantage of being job samples, and therefore of possessing inherent validity, but this validity can be seriously reduced by the equally inherent variability of human judgement, which lowers reliability.
3. No. The format of objective tests is designed to increase reliability, and so to allow whatever validity they may have to be effective, but this does not relieve the test constructor of his duty to establish the degree of reliability and validity of his test.
4. Yes. Teacher ranking, if done carefully, is considered a very valuable form of assessment. When teacher judgement constitutes the criterion for a new test, ranking is far more useful than category estimates, that is, assigning students to a scale of marks, whether the marks are numerical, for example percentages, or represented by letters such as $A-$, $B+$, etc.
5. Yes. The standard deviation is the appropriate statistic for expressing the dispersion (see Appendix I for formulae and methods of working).
6. No. No amount of statistical sophistication can make up for careless data collecting or poor experimental design.
7. No. Neither tests nor examinations can be guaranteed to give accurate and truthful information. Unclear or irrelevant examination questions and ambiguous or irrelevant test items can yield very misleading information. Different methods have different advantages and disadvantages, but it is the actual questions plus the quality of the judgement which makes an examination good or bad, and it is the actual set of items which makes a test good or bad.
8. No. Eliminating marker variability eliminates one source of error, and

so helps to improve reliability. But there are other sources of error, for example individual students overperforming or underperforming on the day of the test. Improving reliability does not in itself improve validity, it merely allows the test to operate nearer whatever validity it may possess.
9 No. A more powerful statistic is preferable to a less powerful one, but only if there is reason to believe that the given statistic is appropriate to the experimental design and to the type of data involved.
10 No. A robust statistic is one which is not likely to provide distorted information, even if some of the conditions for its use are not met. For instance, Robson (1973) states that the T-test is a fairly robust measure.
11 Yes. A variation in the measurement values which comes from any other source is error, and reduces reliability.
12 Yes. This is a nuisance for testers, but it is sometimes to the advantage of the individual, who can with luck achieve a placement or a grading rather above his over-all level. It can of course have the opposite effect, but if an erratic performer is on the borderline he may have a chance, whereas a steady performer is unlikely to be over-rated.
13 No. If we want information about a skill which is difficult to test we take more trouble over assembling a test, and we are more cautious about interpreting the results. Testing something else is no answer, unless there is evidence of a very high correlation between the two skills.
14 No, in my opinion, though not everyone agrees. Theories can be wrong, content can be misleading. Item writers find themselves continually surprised by the way items work out. Until we can confidently predict the difficulty level and the discrimination power (or the dichotomizing power) of items, we have to go on establishing pragmatically the efficiency of items and the reliability and validity of tests.
15 Yes, provided the teacher is asked to judge one group at a time, knows the group well, and gives the judgement in terms of ranks, not in categories (See the answer to question 4 above).
16 Yes. Who knows what the criteria are for deciding whether someone is a good nurse or teacher or anything else?
17 No. Perfect correlation between two sets of scores is obtained when individuals occupy the same rank in both sets and, for equal interval correlations, the relative distance between them is the same.
18 Yes. Even with correlations as high as 0·80–0·90 there is still room for a sizeable number of mistakes.
19 No. If one is testing a complex skill, the subtests should probe different dimensions and so have a greater chance of sampling all the components of the skill. Subtests should correlate moderately with each other and highly with the total.
20 (a) Yes (b) Yes. One of the challenges of criterion-referenced testing lies

in identifying the relevant objectives and in specifying them clearly. Obviously, this has implications for the whole teaching operation.
21 No. In order to define the educational objectives we surely need the best theories and the best descriptions we can come up with.
22 No. In norm-referenced testing, items that are too easy or too difficult are not very efficient in discriminating between the individuals in a group. But in criterion-referenced testing we are not comparing individuals with individuals, we are finding out whether a person belongs to the group who can perform a given operation, or to the other group of people who cannot. The size of the two groups is irrelevant for judging whether an item is good or not. The problem of how to judge the effectiveness of an item in a criterion-referenced test remains.
23 Not true. On the contrary, the informal trying out of procedures is essential both for individual teachers to find out what suits them, and to enable us to add to the body of useful approaches and techniques, derived from experience, which is the basis of nearly all educational practice.
24 Yes. In the assessment part of an experiment, teachers' estimates are a very important component, but since one is comparing groups with groups rather than individuals with individuals, more formal tests are also required.
25 Apparently not. Most people find they have to construct their own special purpose tests to get sufficiently precise information. Obviously it is better if this is recognized well in advance, so that the special tests can be tried out and validated against established tests, or teachers' estimates, or both.

Chapter 3

Exercise A

1 the child . . . girl — the girl who behaves like a child
2 a rac . . . driver — a driver who takes part in races
3 two boil . . . eggs — two eggs that have been boiled
4 a use . . . car — a car that is of no use
5 a soldier . . . man — a man with the qualities of a soldier
6 some read . . . books — some books which are worth reading
7 a suit . . . house — a house that suits our requirements
8 some new floor cover . . . — some material to cover the floor
9 a leading histor . . . — an important history scholar
10 a house own . . . — a person who owns a house
11 a course in librarian . . . — a course for student librarians
12 a quick grow . . . tree — a tree that grows quickly

Answers to Practical Work

13	a well dress . . . lady	a lady who dresses well
14	a leaf . . . branch	a branch without leaves
15	a respons . . . student	a student who carries out his duties
16	a faith . . . friend	a friend we can trust
17	a long hair . . . youth	a youth with long hair
18	man . . . fibres	artificial fibres
19	a slow run . . . river	a river that runs slowly
20	some drink . . . water	some water for drinking
21	. . . done vegetables	vegetables that are not cooked enough
22	the . . . final match	the last match before the final
23	I cannot . . . verse my car	I cannot drive my car backwards
24	an . . . crowded street	a street with too many people in it
25	a . . . leading translation	a translation that is not quite accurate

Answers to Exercise A

1	-ish	8	-ing or -ings	15	-ible	22	semi- or pre-
2	-ing	9	-ian	16	-ful	23	re-
3	-ed	10	-er	17	-ed	24	over-
4	-less	11	-ship	18	-made	25	mis-
5	-ly or -like	12	-ing	19	-ning		
6	-able	13	-ed	20	-able		
7	-able	14	-less	21	under-		

Exercise B

1 Mary took her brother to school this morning and then went to school herself.
    a Mary and her brother go to the same school.
    b Mary's brother arrived at school later than Mary.
    c Mary arrived at her school after her brother arrived at his.
2 After the News at 6 the radio broadcasts a sports commentary every day except Sundays and National Holidays.
    a The News is not on at 6 on Sundays.
    b There are no sports commentaries on National Holidays.
    c On Sundays and National Holidays there are no radio broadcasts.
3 The old woman had her house painted.
    a The old woman painted her house.
    b The old woman got someone to paint her house.
    c The old woman had a painted house.
4 John should not have been rude to his teacher.
    a John was not rude to his teacher.
    b John should never be rude to his teacher.
    c John was rude to his teacher.

5 When the visitor entered the class the students stood up.
    a The visitor entered the class and then the students stood up.
    b The students stood up at the same time as the visitor entered the class.
    c The visitor did not enter the class until the students stood up.
6 The silver box in which I used to keep my gold watch and which I had put on the table near the radio has been stolen.
    a The watch has been stolen.
    b The radio has been stolen.
    c The silver box has been stolen.
7 Had Mr Smith come here yesterday afternoon he would have found Tom and Mary playing cards.
    a Mr Smith came but he did not find Tom and Mary playing cards.
    b Mr Smith did not come and Tom and Mary played cards.
    c Mr Smith did not come and Tom and Mary did not play cards.
8 Oh dear, I've forgotten my fountain pen. How am I going to fill in this form?
    a Don't worry, you can borrow of me.
    b Don't worry, you can borrow mine.
    c Don't worry, you can borrow of mine.
9 Do you mind lending me some money?
    a No, I don't, I'm only too glad to help you.
    b Yes, I don't, I'm only too glad to help you.
    c Yes, I do, I'm only too glad to help.
10 Does your brother live in Stirling still, Mary?
    a He lives in Stirling now.
    b Yes, he has lived in Stirling.
    c No, he lives in Edinburgh now.
11 Haven't you done that essay I set you?
    a Yes, I haven't.
    b No, I haven't.
    c No, I have.
12 Did the gardener water the vegetables after cutting the grass?
    a Yes, he's cut the grass.
    b Yes, he's watered the vegetables.
    c No, he cut the grass first.
13 Who was that boy who was with you this morning?
    a That boy was with me this morning.
    b Jack was with me this morning.
    c A boy was with me this morning.
14 What colour was that car which just passed?
    a It was a Ford Escort.
    b It was red.
    c Yes, it was a car.

15 Can you tell me how to get to the college on foot, please?
    a Take a bus from that stop over there.
    b The college is in Cramond—you can see it from here.
    c Follow that road for two miles and then turn right.

Answers to Exercise B

1 *c*	4 *c*	7 *b*	10 *c*	13 *b*
2 *b*	5 *a*	8 *b*	11 *b*	14 *b*
3 *b*	6 *c*	9 *a*	12 *b*	15 *c*

Exercise C

1 In what way can human beings form part of telecommunication systems?
    a as sources
    b as receivers
    c both of these
2 Name three kinds of communication system.
    a telephone, telegraph and radio
    b microphones, loudspeakers, headphones
    c sources, receivers, users
3 What has the development of telegraphy contributed to communication theory?
    a the concept of information capacity
    b the need to develop technical equipment
    c the possibility of transmitting 'intelligence'
4 When were the first practical achievements in distant communication by invisible means made?
    a in 1267
    b in the 16th century
    c in 1746
5 In what sense is the invention of the telephone of theoretical importance?
    a It brought in man as part of a communication system.
    b It introduced theoretical problems that had not been considered in the development of telegraphy.
    c Its economic importance necessitated further development of general communication theory.
6 Why has the development of frequency bands been the mainstay of electrical communication?
    a It has made it possible for different voices to use the telephone.
    b It has increased the information capacity of all telecommunication systems.
    c It has provided a theoretical explanation for all telecommunication work.

7 On two occasions the writer warns that human beings do not themselves form communication systems. Why does he do this?
 a to point out that one person cannot be a communication system by himself
 b to prevent people being thought of as machines
 c to avoid misuse of mathematical reasoning

8 "The material in this section must necessarily be rather technical and may be omitted at first reading." Which of the following comments on this statement is true?
 a Writers normally tell readers to skip.
 b The reader of *On Human Communication* expects technical material.
 c The material in this section contains no technical language.

Answers to Exercise C

1 c	3 a	5 a	7 c
2 a	4 c	6 b	8 b

Chapter 4

I: *Faulty designs*

1 The defect of this study lies in the lack of operational definitions of the two variables concerned. The study has an air of objectivity since the investigators have taken the trouble to assess a different sub-group on each variable, so that the relationship between the intelligence and popularity ratings will not be biased by their preconceptions. Nevertheless, the results will be difficult to interpret, since we have no idea what either of the investigators means by intelligence or by popularity, or what criteria they have adopted in judging them.

2 In this case we have operational definitions of the two variables, and the definitions are reliable, in the sense that it is easy for different people to apply them consistently. However, the assessment of the worth of a play in terms of the length of its run is of doubtful validity, although it is difficult to think of a more valid measure of worth which is also reliable. The results of such a study are likely to be influenced by factors other than the worth of young authors' plays. For instance, the theatre-going public might prefer plays by its own age-group. Also, the length of run may be influenced by the reputation of the playwright, which may in fact be determined by plays he has written late in life.

3 The clue to the bias in this problem is that only autistic children 'registered in clinics' are counted. There is a strong possibility that, rather

than the relative incidence of autism among the different social class groups, one is measuring the relative likelihood of different social class groups reporting the disorder to the medical profession.

4 The mistake here is in the wording of the question to the subjects. By asking them if they feel both, one is establishing a mental set for two pins, rather than one, and the subjects are therefore more likely to perceive, or say that they perceive, both. Subjects can be asked what they feel, and trials in which only one pin is applied can be interspersed among the others to break any set.

5 First of all there is an ambiguity in the statement. The research reported in *The Guardian* may have found that first children born to women over 35 have a higher average intelligence than any other group in the population or it may have found, on the other hand, that first children have a higher average intelligence than later born children and that children born to women over 35 have a higher intelligence than children born to younger mothers. Whatever the finding, this has the limitations of any natural experiment. Women who have children when they are over 35 are likely to differ in other respects from women who have all their children before that age. The children studied were not the offspring of a sample of mothers who had been divided by random or matching procedures into equivalent groups, each of which was instructed to have its children at specified ages. One cannot, therefore, conclude that there is any direct causal relationship between age and intelligence, and that it is therefore desirable to deliberately delay bearing children until after the age of 35. Similarly, one cannot attribute the higher intelligence of first children either to conditions of early pregnancy or environment merely on the basis of this experiment.

6 This experiment, which was actually performed, was vitiated by the fact that the teachers had control over the construction of the three groups. This meant that the children whom the teachers felt needed the milk were more likely to get it. As a result, the measurements were influenced, among other things, by the fact that more children from impoverished homes were in the milk-drinking groups, and the difference in weight of winter clothing and summer clothing was less for these children than for the other children. The children were weighed in their clothes and the weather got warmer over the four-month period of the experiment. Thus the gain in weight of both groups was underestimated because of the lighter clothing. But the gain was underestimated more in the non-milk-drinking group because the difference in the weight between their winter and summer clothing was greater. The milk-drinking group therefore appeared to have gained more relative to the other group than was in fact the case. As a result of poor matching of groups, the experiment was invalid, despite the very large size of sample.

7 The relationship between aptitude test and final examination is being measured here on a limited sample. These are the people who did well enough on the aptitude test in the first place to be admitted to the course. The people who failed the aptitude test might have done well in the final exam, but we have no information about them. Furthermore, bias enters as a result of the teacher knowing the aptitude test scores. It is very difficult not to give extra encouragement to students one has reason to believe are especially talented. Finally, the value of the aptitude test is being judged against the final exam, and we do not know how well that predicts future success in the profession.

8 Information about the percentage of cases of which something is true is of very little value unless we are told how large the sample was. As is shown in chapter 6, the likelihood of a disproportionate distribution between categories occurring by chance depends on the size of the sample. Also, problems of obtaining valid measures in retrospective studies would arise here, unless the study were longitudinal.

9 We have no control group of couples who had not been apart during the child's infancy. Therefore the result could be due to a tendency on the part of the interviewer to rate mothers' strictness more harshly than fathers'. There should have been a control group, and to avoid systematic bias, the interviewer should have been unacquainted with the purpose of the investigation, or ignorant as to which group the person being interviewed belonged to.

10 The children may have just improved over the course of three weeks and might have done so without any special efforts on the part of the teacher. He should have had a control group of children who were not playing shops with which to compare the experimental group.

II: *Problems*

1 If we drew a diagonal across the graph, joining points 6:6, 7:7, 8:8 etc. points above the diagonal would represent people who had attained a higher score on the controlled production test than on the selective completion; points below the diagonal would represent people who had attained higher scores on selective completion. Since more points fall above the diagonal than below, more people are scoring higher on controlled production, and selective completion is therefore more difficult.

2 *a* Position in family: ordinal
   b Temperature in degrees: interval
   c Social class: ordinal.
     You could attempt to construct an interval scale, using income and other quantitative measures, but it is doubtful whether it would reflect a genuine underlying continuity. See Blalock 1960 for discussion.

d Bilingual: nominal.
   You could attempt to measure degrees of bilingualism, and so construct an ordinal scale, but bilingual/not bilingual would be nominal.
e Time taken to react to a stimulus in a word-association task: interval.

3.1 *a* You would want to know which size sold most readily: the mode.
   b You would need to divide the sample into halves: the median.
   c The mean per person for any given day, if you wanted to supply enough bread to go round. If consumption fluctuated from day to day you would want to know the modal consumption to be sure to provide enough for the most likely contingency. You would have to make bread pudding with what was left over on the slack days.
   d If you were considering how much money to take with you, you would need to know the mean cost. If you wanted to know whether to eat in a particular restaurant, you might look for one charging the modal cost.
   e (i) Probably the mode, if you did not want to be conspicuous.
       (ii) The mean, because it is only from this that the total yield can be calculated.
   f The median, since you want to divide them into two equal groups.

3.2 It is the mean whose calculation involves using the actual quantitative score, and the mean is placed so that the cases balance around it. The mean, therefore, could be called the centre of gravity of a distribution.

4 We cannot assume that the measure 'number of children judged stutterers' is normally distributed, so we should use a test designed for ordinal data, which does not rest on such assumptions.
   a In these cases independent groups are being compared: fathers of stutterers with fathers of non-stutterers; mothers of stutterers with mothers of non-stutterers. An ordinal test for independent groups would be used like the one used to analyse the pronoun study.
   b Here we have related groups: each parent compared with his or her spouse. We want to know if one group is more severe, so it is a comparative test. It resembles the logical connectives study looked at from the point of view of whether the tests differ in difficulty.
   c Again, we have related groups. This time we are assessing the extent to which the scores of spouses are related to each other. This is therefore a correlational study. The appropriate analysis is the one we would use for the logical connectives study if we wished to see whether the same children did well on both tests.

5 *Scores of 39 children on poetry and prose tests of syntactic structures*

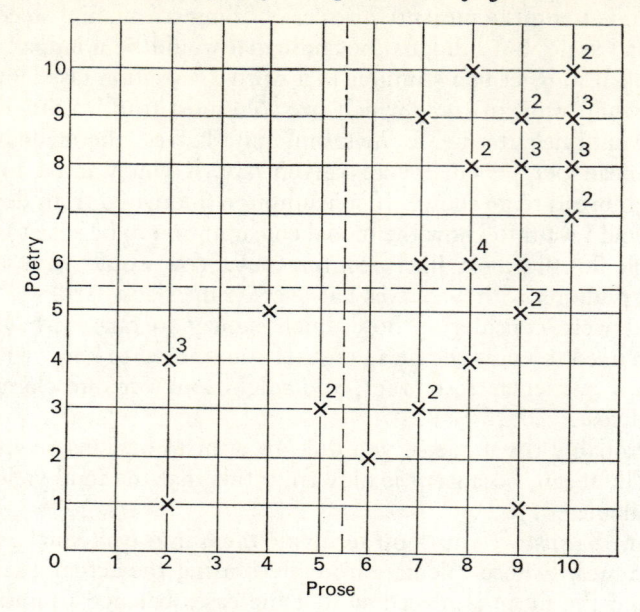

It is noticeable that the points form the shape of a reversed L. The top left-hand quadrant is empty. If we draw in dotted lines to represent half marks in a test, we see that no one who scored less than half marks on the prose scored more than half marks on the poetry. In other words, you had to be able to control syntactic structure in the prose test before you could cope with the poetry. However, while a good score on prose was a necessary condition for scoring well on poetry, it was not a sufficient one. A number of people who got more than half marks on the prose failed to do so on the poetry.

Chapter 5

1 *Cumulative frequency tables*

	Instruction				Control		
Score	f.	c.f.	Rank	Score	f.	c.f.	Rank
18				18			
17				17			
16				16			
15				15			
14				14	1	30	30
13				13	1	29	29
12				12			
11				11			
10	2	30	29·5	10	2	28	27·5
9	3	28	27	9			
8	6	25	22·5	8			
7	4	19	17·5	7			
6	8	15	11·5	6	3	26	25
5	3	7	6	5	9	23	19
4	2	4	3·5	4	8	14	10·5
3	2	2	1·5	3	4	6	4·5
2				2	2	2	1·5
1				1			
0				0			
Total	30			Total	30		

2a *Selective completion scores*

Score		Frequency
18	III	3
17	III	3
16	LHT	5
15	LHT	5
14	LHT I	6
13	IIII	4
12	II	2
11	LHT	5
10	II	2
9		
8		
7	I	1
6		
5		
4		
3		
2		
1		
0		
Total		36

2b *Histogram*

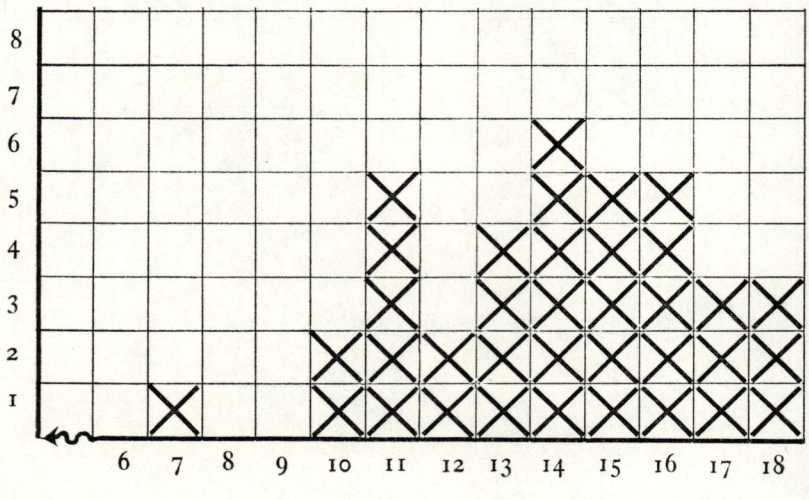

Answers to Practical Work

3 Scores of Ugandan students and Scottish schoolchildren compared for vocabulary and comprehension

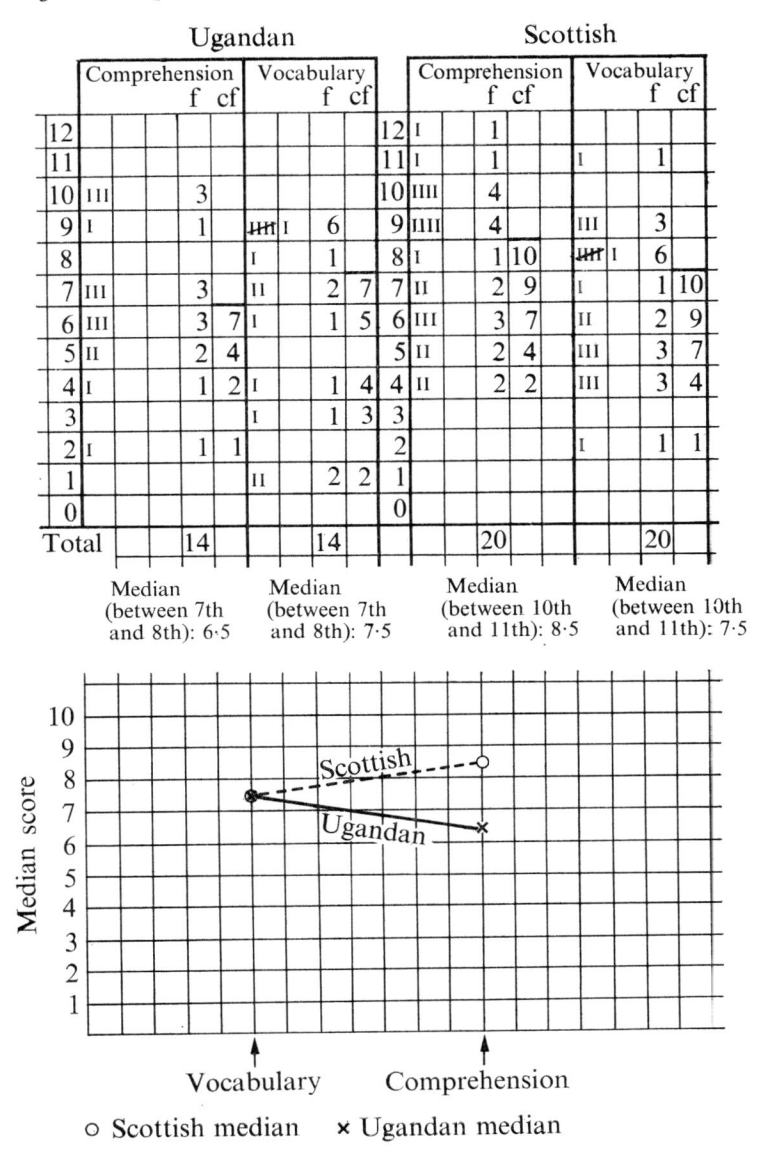

	Ugandan						Scottish					
	Comprehension			Vocabulary			Comprehension			Vocabulary		
	f	cf		f	cf		f	cf		f	cf	
12						12	I	1				
11						11	I	1		I	1	
10	III	3				10	IIII	4				
9	I	1	||||I	6		9	IIII	4		III	3	
8			I	1		8	I	1	10	||||I	6	
7	III	3	II	2	7	7	II	2	9	I	1	10
6	III	3	7	I	1	5	6	III	3	7	II	2	9
5	II	2	4				5	II	2	4	III	3	7
4	I	1	2	I	1	4	4	II	2	2	III	3	4
3				I	1	3	3						
2	I	1	1				2				I	1	1
1				II	2	2	1						
0							0						
Total		14			14			20			20	

Median (between 7th and 8th): 6·5   Median (between 7th and 8th): 7·5   Median (between 10th and 11th): 8·5   Median (between 10th and 11th): 7·5

○ Scottish median   × Ugandan median

The graph gives a clear illustration of the fact that the Scottish students do better as a group on the comprehension tests, whilst the Ugandan students do better as a group on the vocabulary.

Chapter 6

1 There are 4 permutations for 2 tosses = 2^2
            8   for 3   = 2^3
           16   for 4   = 2^4
           32   for 5   = 2^5

The formula, then, is 2^n where n is the number of tosses.

2 The permutations for 3 tosses are set out below to illustrate the solutions

$$\begin{array}{c} \text{HHH*} \\ \text{HHT} \\ \text{HTH} \\ \text{HTT**} \\ \text{THH} \\ \text{THT**} \\ \text{TTH**} \\ \text{TTT} \end{array}$$

a Only one of the permutations will be all heads, marked * in the tables and for n tosses there are 2^n permutations (see answer to question 1). The probability of n heads in n tosses is therefore one in 2^n, i.e.:

$$p = \frac{1}{2^n}$$

b The number of permutations containing one head will be the same as the number of tosses, since one head can occur on any of the tosses, marked ** in the tables. The number of permutations containing one head in n tosses is therefore n, and the total number of permutations for n tosses is 2^n. Therefore, the probability of one head in n tosses is n in 2^n, i.e.:

$$p = \frac{n}{2^n}$$

c The probability of 0 heads in n tosses will be the same as the probability of n heads, since there will be only one permutation of each type. We have seen that this probability is $1/2^n$. To get the probability of one or no heads in n tosses we have to add this to $n/2^n$ (see answer to *b*). This gives a probability of $n + 1$ in 2^n,

$$\text{i.e.:} \quad \frac{1}{2^n} + \frac{n}{2^n} = \frac{n+1}{2^n}$$

3 The probability of cutting a heart with the first cut is $\frac{1}{4}$, since there are 4 suits, with the same number of cards in each. The probability of cutting a heart with the second cut is also $\frac{1}{4}$ (provided we do not remove any cards). Since $\frac{1}{4}$ of the potential outcomes have a heart on the first cut, $\frac{1}{4}$ of that $\frac{1}{4}$ will have a heart on the second cut. To get the probability of a heart on the first two cuts, then, we multiply the probability on the first cut by the probability on the second cut. To get the probability of a heart on each of 7 cuts we have to multiply $\frac{1}{4} \times \frac{1}{4}$ seven times, i.e.:

$$\frac{1}{4} \times \frac{1}{4} \times \frac{1}{4} \times \frac{1}{4} \times \frac{1}{4} \times \frac{1}{4} \times \frac{1}{4} = \frac{1}{4^7}$$

4 We will not be mistaken in as many as 5 per cent of instances, since we will usually have had some good reason for postulating a departure from chance in the first place.

5 No. The probability of the B pig being bigger in all 5 pairs (by analogy with the probability of getting 5 heads in 5 tosses of a coin) is 1 in 32. If our hypothesis is two-tailed, we have specified that the 5 per cent of cases that we are interested in lie $2\frac{1}{2}$ per cent at either extreme. The probability of getting either the B pig bigger in each pair or the A pig bigger in each pair is therefore 1 in 32 plus 1 in 32, i.e. 1 in 16. 1 in 16 is more than 5 per cent, which is 1 in 20. Therefore our result would not be significant. Since we are dealing here with weight, which is a variable measured on an interval scale, we should use the test for differences between correlated means, which is the counterpart to the sign test, but suitable for interval data (See Figure 13, p. 180).

6 The chi squared test should not be used on data given in Figure 12 since two of the expected frequencies are smaller than 1 (See p. 179).

		Enthusiastic	Favourable	Open-minded	Somewhat negative	Apprehensive	Total
Still	Yes	19	14	12	4	0	49
enrolled	No	7	7	12	1	1	28
	Total	26	21	24	5	1	77

The expected frequency of people still enrolled and apprehensive is $49 \times 1/77$ which is 0·64 and the expected frequency of people no longer enrolled and apprehensive is $28 \times 1/77$ which is 0·36. We could increase expected frequencies by combining categories as is sometimes done. However, if we combined the categories 'somewhat negative' and 'apprehensive' we would still only have expected values in the final column of 3·82 and 2·18. 25 per cent of expected values would then be below 5. The use of chi squared would be misleading in these circumstances. Calculating of the value of χ^2 for Figure 9:

$$\chi^2 = \frac{n((AD - BC) - n/2)^2}{(A + B)(C + D)(A + C)(B + D)}$$

$$= \frac{60(204 - 84 - 30)^2}{(17 + 28)(3 + 12)(17 + 3)(28 + 12)}$$

$$= \frac{60 \times 90 \times 90}{45 \times 15 \times 20 \times 40} = 0.9$$

Notice that this is considerably smaller than the 1·6 arrived at by using the formula which did not incorporate the correction factor.

7 In the study concerned three independent groups were being compared. The measure of improvement would probably be on an ordinal scale. The tests for comparison between independent groups on an ordinal scale are the median and the Mann-Whitney U (see Figure 13). We know that the median test applies to experiments with more than two groups, so that is the only test we have met with that could be used to do an over-all analysis of the results of such an experiment, though the three groups could be compared in pairs by means of the Mann-Whitney U test.

Answers to questions in the text, Chapters 4-6.

Chapter 4, p. 133
For the group of 15 aphasics the mean deviation is 6·53 and the standard deviation 8·45.

Chapter 5, p. 148
Expected frequencies for Figure 1:

	Arts	Science	Totals
Travelled	17 (15)	28 (30)	45
Untravelled	3 (5)	12 (10)	15
Totals	20	40	60

Chapter 6, p. 166
Here are two more rows of Pascal's Triangle:

```
      1   7  21  35  35  21   7   1
    1   8  28  56  70  56  28   8   1
```

The figures are arrived at in each case by adding together two adjacent figures in the row above. If there are 7 ways of reaching the second square from the left in the eighth row and 21 ways of reaching the square next to it, there must be 28 ways of reaching the square between them on the line below, since it can be reached from either of these squares.

Chapter 6, p. 171
z = 2·25
p = 0·0122 1 tailed
p = 0·0244 2 tailed.

Billy is 2·25 standard deviations below the mean. The probability of a z score of 2·25 or more as given in Table A is 0·0122. This is the probability of a twelve-year-old being as short or shorter than Billy, since the table gives one tailed probabilities. The two-tailed probability (the probability of a boy being as deviant or more so) will be double this, i.e., 0·0244.

Chapter 6, p. 177
Degrees of freedom for contingency tables in Figure 10: (a) 6, (b) 4, (c) 5.

Results of statistical analysis of experiments (a) to (c) discussed in the text.
(a) *Spanish teaching experiment*
  $\chi^2 = 0.72$, d.f. $= 1$; not significant.
(b) *Training in the use of pronouns*
  Using the median test: $\chi^2 = 15.00$, d.f. $= 1$, $p = < 0.001$.
  Using the Mann-Whitney U test: $U = 228.5$, $z = 3.275$. This is greater than 3·1, the critical value for 0·001 level, one-tailed. See Figure 7, p. 170. Notice that the z table on p. 200 does not give exact probabilities for values of z as high as this.
(c) *Logical connectives experiment*
  The sign test has already been performed, see p. 166.
  Using the Wilcoxon test: $T = 81$, $z = 3.116$. This is greater than 2·58, the critical value for 0·01 level, two-tailed. See Figure 7, p. 170.
The analysis of experiment (d), the birthweight study, was not completed since the calculation from grouped data is too involved to explain here.

Glossary of Symbols

Statistical Symbols

A, B, C, D	symbols used to label boxes in a contingency table for use in the formula for a 2 × 2 table which incorporates a correction factor
c.f.	cumulative frequency
d	difference
d.f.	degrees of freedom. (See also ν below.)
E	expected frequency
E_{1-3}	difference between high and low groups in item analysis
f	frequency
H_0	null hypothesis
n (or N)	number of observations in the sample
O	observed frequency
p	(1) probability
	(2) proportion of passes for a test item
P	the probability of occurrence by chance of an instance of one of the categories on a two category nominal variable
Q	the probability of occurrence by chance of the other category
R	sum of ranks of one group in Mann Whitney U Test
r	product moment coefficient, also used to designate other correlations, including that of reliability
rho	rank order correlation
s	standard deviation. (When the standard deviation of the population rather than the sample is referred to the Greek letter σ is used, see below.)
s.e._diff	standard error of the difference
t	the difference between means for small samples is not normally distributed but follows the t distribution
T	smallest sum of ranks of differences for Wilcoxon Matched Pairs Test
U	value reflecting relative position of the scores of two independent groups which is related to R and is used in the Mann Whitney U Test
V	variance, i.e., square of standard deviation
x	(1) symbol standing for the varying value of a score
	(2) the frequency of the less frequent category on a nominal variable with two categories

x̄	(x bar) the mean. (When the population mean rather than the sample mean is referred to the Greek letter μ is used, see below)
z	number of standard deviations from the mean of a value on a normally distributed variable (also called a standard score)
<	less than
>	greater than
≈	relationship of equivalence
χ^2	(chi squared) the value reflecting the difference between observed and expected frequencies
μ	(mu) mean of the population. (See x̄ above)
ν	(nu) degrees of freedom. (See d.f. above)
σ	(sigma) standard deviation of the population. (See s above)
Σ	(sigma) the sum of, an instruction to sum all instances of the value specified to the right of Σ in the formula
Σ'	(sigma prime) corrected sum of squares

Testing Materials

EPTB	English Proficiency Test Battery
LAPP	Language Aptitude and Proficiency Project
TOEFL	Test of English as a Foreign Language

General

RP	Received Pronunciation

References

Amos, J. R., Brown, F. L. and Mink, O. G. 1965. *Statistical Concepts*. New York: Harper & Row.
Anderson, B. 1966. *The Psychology Experiment*. Belmont: Wadsworth.
Anderson, J. 1971. A technique for measuring reading comprehension and readability. *English Language Teaching* 25, 2, 178–82.
Beardsmore, H. B. 1974. Testing oral fluency. *IRAL* 12, 4, 317–26.
Blalock, H. M. 1960. *Social Statistics*. New York: McGraw-Hill.
Brière, E. J. 1969. Current trends in second language testing. *TESOL Quarterly* 3, 4, 333–40.
Buros, O. 1972. *The Seventh Mental Measurements Yearbook*. New Jersey: The Gryphon Press.
Carroll, John B. 1961. *Testing the English Proficiency of Foreign Students*. Washington D.C.: Center for Applied Linguistics.
CILT 1973. *Select Bibliography: Language Testing*. London: Centre for Information on Language Teaching.
Clark, John L. D. 1972. *Foreign Language Testing: Theory and Practice*. Philadelphia: Center for Curriculum Development.
Connolly, T. G. and Sluckin, W. 1971. *An Introduction to Statistics for the Social Sciences*. 3rd edition. London: Macmillan.
Coombs, C. H. 1950. Psychological scaling without a unit of measurement. *Psychol. Review* 57, 145–58.
Cox, D. R. 1958. *Planning of Experiments*. New York: Wiley.
Cronbach, L. J. 1961. *Essentials of Psychological Testing*. 2nd edition. New York: Harper & Row.
Darnell, D. K. 1970. Clozentropy: a procedure for testing English language proficiency of foreign students. *Speech Monographs* 37, 1, 36–46.
Davies, Alan (ed.). 1968. *Language Testing Symposium*. London: Oxford University Press.
Davies, Alan 1973a. Language proficiency testing and the syllabus. In M. C. O'Brien (ed.), *ATESOL Testing in Second Language Teaching: New Dimensions*. Dublin: Dublin University Press.

Davies, Alan 1973b. *Language Aptitude and Proficiency Project: Final Report.* Mimeo: Scottish Education Department, Edinburgh.
Fehse, K. D. and Praeger, W. 1973. *Bibliographie zum Testen.* Freiburg: Universitäts Verlag Becksmann.
Foss, B. (ed.). 1966. Introduction in *New Horizons in Psychology.* Harmondsworth: Penguin.
Guilford, J. P. 1942. *Fundamental Statistics in Psychology and Education.* New York: McGraw-Hill.
Harris, David P. 1969. Progress report on the testing of English as a second language. Report on the 6th meeting of the International Conference on Second Language Problems. London: Centre for Information on Language Teaching.
Hays, W. L. 1963. *Statistics for Psychologists.* New York: Holt, Rinehart, Winston.
Heaton, J. B. 1975. *Writing English Language Tests.* London: Longman.
Huff, D. 1954. *How to Lie with Statistics.* New York: McGraw-Hill.
Ingram, Elisabeth. 1969. Testing in the context of a language learning experiment. *Language Learning* 19, 147–61.
James, C. V. and Rouve, S. 1973. *Survey of Curricula and Performance in Modern Languages, 1971–72.* London: Centre for Information on Language Teaching.
Jones, R. L. and Spolsky, B. (eds.). 1975. *Testing Language Proficiency.* Washington D.C.: Center for Applied Linguistics.
Kuhn, T. S. 1962. *The Structure of Scientific Revolutions.* Chicago: University of Chicago Press.
Lado, R. 1961. *Language Testing.* New York: McGraw-Hill.
Levin, L. 1972. *Comparative Studies in Foreign Language Teaching.* Stockholm: Almquist & Wiksell.
Lindblad, T. 1969 *Implicit and explicit: an experiment in applied psycholinguistics, assessing different methods of teaching grammatical structures in English as a foreign language.* Göteborg Undervisnings Metod i Engelska, the GUME Project. Department of Educational Research, University of Gothenburg, Sweden.
Lindblad, T. and Levin, L. 1970. *Teaching Grammar.* The GUME Project. Department of Educational Research, University of Gothenburg, Sweden.
Maxwell, A. E. 1970. *Basic Statistics in Behavioural Research.* Harmondsworth: Penguin.
Moller, Alan. 1975. Validity in proficiency testing. *ELT Documents 75/3.* London: English Teaching Information Centre.
Montgomery, M. G. P. 1972. Reading strategies of native and non-native speakers. M.Litt. dissertation, Department of Linguistics, Edinburgh.
Morrison, D. E. and Henkel, R. E. (eds.). 1970. *The Significance Test Controversy: A Reader.* London: Aldine.

Murphy, M. J. 1969. *Designing Multiple-Choice Items for Testing English Language*. Lagos: African Universities Press and The British Council.

Oller, J. W. and Obrecht, D. H. 1969. The psycholinguistic principle of informational sequence. *IRAL* 7, 117–23.

Oller, J. W. 1973. Cloze tests of second language proficiency and what they measure. *Language Learning* 23, 1, 105–18.

Palmer, L. and Spolsky, B. (eds.). 1975. *Papers on Language Testing 1967–1974*. Washington D.C.: Center for Applied Linguistics.

Pilliner, A. E. G. 1973. Tests, norm-referenced and criterion-referenced. Mimeo: Godfrey Thomson Unit for Academic Assessment, University of Edinburgh.

Pimsleur, P., Sundland, D. M. and McIntyre, R. D. 1963. *Under-achievement in Foreign Language Learning: First Report*. U.S. Office of Education and Ohio State University.

Pimsleur, P. 1963. Predicting achievement in foreign language learning. *IJAL* 29, 2, 129–36.

Reichmann, W. J. 1964. *Use and Abuse of Statistics*. Harmondsworth: Penguin.

Robson, C. 1973. *Experiment, Design and Statistics in Psychology*. Harmondsworth: Penguin.

Rosenthal, R. and Jacobson, L. 1968. *Pygmalion in the Classroom: Teacher Expectation and Pupils' Intellectual Development*. New York: Holt, Rinehart, Winston.

Scherer, George A. C. and Wertheimer, M. 1964. *A Psycholinguistic Experiment in Foreign Language Teaching*. New York: McGraw-Hill.

Siegel, S. 1956. *Nonparametric Statistics for the Behavioural Sciences*. New York: McGraw-Hill.

Smith, P. D. and Berger, E. 1968. *An assessment of three foreign language teaching strategies utilizing three language laboratory systems*. Final report, U.S. Office of Education.

Smith, P. D. 1970. *A comparison of the cognitive and audiolingual approaches to foreign language instruction* (The Pennsylvania Project). Philadelphia: Center for Curriculum Development Inc.

Snedecor, George W. 1956. *Statistical Methods*. 5th edition. Ames, Iowa: The Iowa State Press.

Spolsky, B. 1968. Language testing: the problem of validation. *TESOL Quarterly* 2, 2, 88–94.

Valette, Rebecca. 1967. *Modern Language Testing: A Handbook*. New York: Harcourt Brace.

von Elek, T. and Oskarson, M. 1972. An experiment assessing the relative effectiveness of two methods of teaching English grammatical structure to adults. *IRAL* 10, 60–72.

Index of Names

Amos, J. R., 128, 186, 224
Anderson, B., 139, 186, 224
Anderson, J., 224

Beardsmore, H. B., 224
Berger, E., 6, 226
Blalock, H. M., 127, 128, 138, 176, 186, 224
Brière, E. J., 224
Brown, F. L., 128, 186, 224
Buros, O., 5, 224

Carroll, John B., 44, 45, 224
CILT, 5, 224
Clark, John L. D., 104, 224
Connolly, T. G., 25, 224
Coombs, C. H., 153, 224
Cox, D. R., 139, 186, 224
Cronbach, L. J., 5, 58, 60, 61, 104, 224

Darnell, D. K., 224
Davies, Alan, 5, 28, 33, 55, 104, 224

Ebbinghaus, H., 133

Fehse, K. D., 225
Foss, B., 2, 225

Gauss, Karl, 169
Guilford, J. P., 104, 225

Harris, David P., 28, 104, 225
Hays, W. L., 176, 186, 225
Heaton, J. B., 104, 225
Henkel, R. E., 165, 225
Huff, D., 186, 225

Ingram, Elisabeth, 33, 225

Jacobson, L., 226
James, C. V., 225
Jones, R. L., 225

Kuhn, T. S., 1, 225

Lado, R., 104, 225
Levin, L., 225
Lindblad, T., 35, 225

McCallien, Cath, 55
McIntyre, R. D., 226

Magnussen, D., 104
Maxwell, A. E., 186, 225
Mink, O. G., 128, 186, 224
Moller, Alan, 225
Montgomery, M. G. P., 225
Morrison, D. E., 165, 225
Murphy, M. J., 104, 225

Obrecht, D. H., 34, 225
Oller, J. W., 34, 225
Oskarson, M., 35, 226

Palmer, L., 225
Pilliner, A. E. G., 26, 225
Pimsleur, P., 6, 226
Praeger, W., 225

Reichmann, W. J., 186, 226
Robson, C., 104, 226
Rosenthal, R., 226
Rouve, S., 225

Scherer, George A. C., 33, 226
Siegel, S., 153, 173, 174, 177, 179, 186, 226

Sluckin, W., 25, 224
Smith, P. D., 6, 33, 226
Snedecor, George W., 22, 23, 226
Spolsky, B., 225, 226
Sundland, D. M., 226

Valette, Rebecca, 34, 104, 226
von Elek, T., 35, 226

Wertheimer, M., 33, 226

Subject Index

Achievement test, 4, 7, 8, 27, 28, 31, 44–9, 62–5, 69, 70, 74
Ad hoc test, 5, 51
Aptitude test, 4, 5, 45–9, 64, 65
Attainment test, 4
Averages, 4, 14, 119, 128–30

Binomial
 distribution, 159–67, 172, 174, 203
 table of probabilities, 203
 theorem, 174
Birth weight data, 126, 127, 131, 147, 175
Buffer items, 108

Cambridge Proficiency Examination, 46, 75
Central tendency
 —measures of, 14, 167
 mean, 4, 14, 128–30
 median, 14, 119, 128–30, 146, 150, 151
 mode, 119, 128–30
Chi squared (χ^2)
 contingency table, 117–21, 147, 148, 176–179
 degrees of freedom, 24, 177, 178
 expected and observed frequencies, 119–121, 147, 148
 formula, 149
 —with correction factor, 179
 table of critical values, 202
 test, 147–9, 156, 176–80, 202
Cloze test, 9, 82
Colorado Experiment, 33, 34
Comparison, 125
Concurrent validity, 5, 59–61
Construct validity, 5, 18, 21, 22, 29, 59, 62–64
Contaminating variables, 113

Content validity, 5, 7, 8, 18, 21, 22, 29, 59, 61–5
Contingency table, 117–21, 147, 148, 176–179
Control group, 115, 116, 118
Controlled experiment, 113, 114
Correction factor, 174, 179
Correlation, 8, 22–6, 60, 125, 189–94
 coefficient, 22, 24, 25
 —significance of, 23–6
 formulas, 189, 190, 191, 193, 194
 product moment, 22, 60, 190–4
 rank order, 22, 125, 180, 189, 190
Counterbalance, 136
Criterion
 measures, 19
 referenced test, 4, 8, 26–32, 35
Critical value, 173, 177
Cumulative frequency, 146, 150, 151, 153

Degrees of freedom, 24, 177, 178
Dependent variable, 115, 118, 123
Descriptive statistics, 2, 3, 10
Diagnostic test, 4, 5, 27, 45, 47, 48
Dictation, 20, 65, 66
Difference between means test, 176, 180
Difference between correlated means test, 176, 180
Discrete language skills, 9
Discrimination, 30, 31, 189
 index, 189
Dispersion
 —measures of, 131, 132, 167–70
 mean deviation, 132, 133
 range, 132
 standard deviation, 4, 133, 168–70, 195, 196
Double blind technique, 110–12

230 Testing and Experimental Methods

E_{1-3}, 189
English Proficiency Test Battery, 46
Equal interval scale, 13, 14, 128, 130, 180, 183
Equivalence reliability, 15–18
Essay, 11, 19, 20, 50, 52, 65, 71
Examinations
   and tests, 49–54
   traditional and new type, 52–7
Expected frequencies, 119–21, 147, 148
Experimental design, 107–16, 133–41, 180
   contaminating variable, 113
   control group, 115, 116, 118
   controlled experiment, 113, 114
   dependent variable, 115, 118, 123
   double blind technique, 110–12
   factorial, 114, 115, 138, 139
   gross comparison, 114, 115
   identical subject, 135–7, 140
   independent subjects, 140
   —variable, 115, 118, 123
   instruction group, 118
   matching, 134–8, 140
   placebo group, 116
   randomization of items, 140
   random sampling, 138
   related samples, 123, 140
   subject variable, 137, 140
   successive treatments, 140
   treatment group, 116
Experiment tests, 6, 9, 10
Experimental subjects, 110

Face validity, 9, 18, 60
Facility value, 30, 31, 188, 189
Factorial design, 114, 115, 138, 139
Frequency tables, 146, 149, 150

Gaussian curve, 8, 169
Gross comparison, 114, 115
Grouped data, 127

Halo effect, 111, 112
Hawthorne effect, 116
Histogram, 127
Hypothesis, 9
   null, 163, 164, 167
   one-tailed, two-tailed, 165–7, 170, 171, 178, 181, 182

Identical subject design, 135–7, 140

Immediate validity, 19, 21
Independent
   subjects, 140
   variable, 115, 118, 123
Inferential statistics, 2, 3, 10
Instruction group, 118
Integrative language skills, 9
Interaction, 115
Interval scale, 13, 14, 128, 130, 180, 183
Item analysis, 30, 31, 187–9, 198
   difficulty (facility value), 30, 31, 188, 189
   discrimination, 30, 31, 189
   —index, 189
Items, examples of, 76–100
   context, 82, 88, 94, 98
   extra-linguistic, 85, 89, 94, 99
   grammar, 80, 86, 91, 97
   lexis, 81, 87, 92, 98
   listening, 90–6
   phonology, 79, 86, 90, 96
   reading, 79–86
   speaking, 96–100
   writing, 86–90

Job sample reliability and validity, 19, 20

Kuder Richardson reliability, 17, 18, 194–8
   formula (K.R. 21), 194

Language Aptitude and Proficiency Project, 33
Language testing matrices, 66–74, 78, 79
Level of measurement, 130
Listening tests, 16
Longitudinal study, 111

McCallien Oral English Test for West Africa, 55, 76
Mann-Whitney U test, 173, 180
Mastery testing, 27, 31
Matched pair, 134
Matching, 134–8, 140
Mean, 4, 14, 128–30
   deviation, 132, 133
   difference between means, 176, 180
   —correlated means, 176, 180
Measures of
   central tendency, 14, 167
   —mean, 4, 14, 128–30
   —median, 14, 119, 128–30, 146, 150, 151
   —mode, 119, 128–30

dispersion, 131, 132, 167–70
—mean deviation, 132, 133
—range, 132
—standard deviation, 4, 133, 168–70, 195, 196
Median, 14, 119, 128–30, 146, 150, 151
test, 119, 121, 128, 146, 147, 150, 151, 177, 180, 183, 220
Mental set, 111
Michigan tests, 46

Natural experiment, 112, 113, 115
Nominal scale, 13, 117, 119, 129, 180, 182
Non-parametric statistics, 13, 184
Normal
curve, 4, 8, 169
distribution, 4, 5, 8, 167–71, 172
Normalization, 184
Norm-referenced tests, 4, 8, 26–32, 35
Null hypothesis, 163, 164, 167

Objective tests, 12, 50
Observed frequencies, 119–21, 147, 148
One-tailed hypothesis, 165–7, 170, 171, 178, 181, 182
Operational definitions, 108
Oral/written examinations, 11
Order effect, 136
Ordinal scale, 13, 14, 118, 119, 122, 123, 130, 180, 182, 183

Parallel forms reliability, 16–18
Parameters, 184
Parametric statistics, 14, 184, 185
Pascal's Triangle, 166, 220
Pennsylvania Experiment, 33, 34
Permutations, 158–63, 166
Placebo group, 116
Population, 5, 6, 107
Power of a test, 184
Pragmatic validity, 8, 18–20, 25, 27
Précis, 65, 66
Predictive validity, 5, 7–9, 59–64
Probability, 158–72, 218, 219
Product moment correlation, 22, 60, 190–4
Proficiency test, 4, 5, 7, 28, 29, 45–8, 60, 64, 69, 70, 75
Programmed instruction, 43, 44
Prospective study, 111

R, 153, 173

Randomization of items, 140
Random sampling, 138, 139
Range, 132
Ranking, 147, 151–3
summing of ranks, 147, 152, 153, 173
—of differences, 125, 128, 152–4
Rank order correlation, 22, 125, 180, 189, 190
formula, 189
Ratio scale, 13
Refusers, 107
Region of rejection, 182
Rejecting the null hypothesis, 163
Related samples, 123, 140
Related subject design, 133
Reliability, 2, 4, 7–11, 15–20, 22, 23, 51, 57, 58, 109
coefficient required, 23
effect of lengthening test, 58
equivalence, 15–18
job sample, 20
Kuder Richardson, 17, 18, 194–8
parallel forms, 16–18
Spearman-Brown correction formula, 58
split half, 17, 18
stability, 15, 16, 18
test-retest, 16–18
and validity, 7, 8, 11, 51, 57, 58, 109, 111
Retrospective, 111
Robust statistics, 14

Sampling, 2, 3, 137, 138, 164, 180
random sampling, 138
size of sample, 164, 180
Scales of measurement
(equal) interval, 13, 14, 128, 130, 180, 183
nominal, 13, 117, 119, 129, 180, 182
ordinal, 13, 14, 118, 119, 122, 123
ratio, 13
Scattergram, 125, 126
Significance, 10, 161–7, 219, 220
choice of test, 182–5
of correlation coefficient, 23–6
levels, 24, 25, 161, 163–5
tests
chi squared, 147–9, 156, 176–80, 201, 219
difference between correlated means, 176, 180, 219
difference between means, 128, 172, 175

Significance test (*cont.*)—
    Mann-Whitney U, 173, 180, 220
    median, 119, 121, 128, 146, 147, 150, 151, 177, 180, 183, 220
    sign, 166, 173, 174
    Wilcoxon matched pairs, 175, 180
Significant
  —at the 0·05 or 5 per cent level, 161
  —at the 0·01 or 1 per cent level, 161
  —at the 0·001 or 0·1 per cent level, 161
Sign test, 166, 173, 174
Skewed distribution, 129
Spanish teaching experiment, 117, 118, 130, 146, 221
Spearman-Brown correction formula, 58
Spelling test, 20, 66
Split half reliability, 17, 18
Square roots, 198, 199
Stability reliability, 15, 16, 18
Standard deviation, 4, 133, 168–70, 195, 196
    formulae, 168, 191, 195
Standard error of difference, 175, 180
Standardized test, 5, 6, 8, 10, 49–52
Standard scores, 8, 168–74, 176, 184
Subjects, 111
Subject variable, 137, 140
Successive treatments design, 140

T, 154, 156, 172, 174
    formula for converting to z, 174
t, 176
Test construction, 69–100
Test of English as a Foreign Language, 28, 46
Test-retest reliability, 16–18, 25
Tests
  achievement, 4, 7, 8, 27, 28, 31
  ad hoc, 5, 51
  aptitude, 4, 5, 45–9, 64, 65
  attainment, 4
  cloze, 9, 82
  comprehension, 16, 52
  criterion/norm referenced, 4, 8, 26–32, 35
  diagnostic, 4, 5, 27, 45, 47, 48
  dictation, 20, 65, 66
  discrete/integrative, 9
  essay, 11, 19, 20, 50, 52, 65, 71
  and examinations, 49–54
  experiment/test specific, 6, 9, 10

  grammar, 66
  items, 76–100
  mastery, 27, 31
  objective, 12, 50
  oral/written, 11
  parallel forms, 16–18
  précis, 65, 66
  proficiency, 4, 5, 7, 28, 29, 45–8, 60, 64, 69, 70, 75
  spelling, 20, 66
  standardized, 5, 6, 8, 10, 49–52
  traditional/new type, 52–7
  translation, 52
  vocabulary, 66
Theoretical distribution, 165
Training in the use of pronouns experiment, 118, 119, 130, 146, 149, 150, 221
Translation, 52
Treatment group, 116
Two-tailed hypothesis, 165–7, 170, 171, 178, 181, 182

U, 147, 153, 155, 156, 172, 173
    formula for converting to z, 173
Ultimate validity, 19
Understanding of logical connectives experiment, 122, 123, 130, 147, 153, 154, 221

Validity, 2–11, 15, 18–27, 51, 57–65, 109, 111
  coefficient required, 25, 26
  concurrent, 5, 59–61
  construct, 5, 18, 21, 22, 29, 59, 62–4
  content, 5, 59–61
  face, 9, 18, 60
  immediate, 19, 21
  job sample, 19, 20
  pragmatic, 8, 18–20, 25, 27
  predictive, 5, 7–9, 59–64
  and reliability, 7, 8, 11, 51, 57, 58, 109, 111
  ultimate, 19, 21
Variables, 108
  contaminating, 113
  dependent/independent, 115, 118, 123
  subject, 137, 140
Variability, 167
  reduction of, 15, 133–5, 180, 181
Variance, 17, 194, 195

West African Examinations Council (Davies's report to), 55–7
Wilcoxon matched pairs test, 174, 180
Work sample analysis, 71–4, 76
Written/oral examinations, 11

z score, 168–74, 176, 180, 184, 200, 201
   formula for converting T, 174
   —U, 173